Advance Praise For
Brightening My Corner

From an Otomi village in Mexico's Valley of Mezquital to wartime Vietnam, from newly-independent Kazakhstan to the steaming streets of Mumbai, in a lifetime as a global citizen, Ruth never stops trying to make connections across cultural divides or finding ways to make a difference. In an era where debates about race and identity are heated, Ruth's vivid memoir challenges us to think about justice, responsibility, family, culture, and belonging in more expansive ways.

Alison Li,
writer and historian

Ruth Lor Malloy's memoir takes us on a whirlwind trip to the more exotic corners of our world as she seeks a life of commitment and spiritual connection. Her account of a life devoted to the battle against racism couldn't be more timely today as we grapple with the challenges of Black Lives Matter and anti-Asian violence.

Louise Lore

Fortunate, we are, that Ruth Lor Malloy has chosen to share the story of her life with us. A life of integrity it has been, as shown by every choice along the way, and this account will surely serve as an inspiration to all.

Bette Logan,
author, *Life Lived Inside Out*

No book has made me tip in a spiritual direction quite this obviously or unexpectedly. It is a story of a life well-lived that struck me and stays with me as I teach, parent, relate and carry out my own adventures in a complicated world. Wisdom, honesty, discovery—I have found these gifts and more in this beautifully written memoir that gently, deftly, takes us through the many rooms and corners of life.

Aaron Haddad.
teacher and playwright.
author of *My Place Is Right Here:*
Hugh Burnett and the Fight for a Better Canada.

Ruth knows that greater learning comes from bringing differences together. It has been the story of her life. Ruth is an inspirational woman with a story that will inspire, challenge and it will make you better for reading it.

Heather McDonald,
health care leader

Ruth Lor Malloy has led an extraordinary life. Now readers can share her experiences from the Arctic to the tropics. Along the way, she wrote a full shelf of travel books and articles. But the real Ruth is defined through her help to those oppressed because of race, ethnicity, religion or gender-definition. I have known Ruth since our days in Almaty, Kazakhstan . . . and I feel blessed to know her even better through this engaging memoir.

Nancy Swing,
author, *Malice on the Mekong*
and the blog *Where in the World?* nancyswing.com

It is a fascinating tale of adventures spanning continents and decades, covering history as it was made, seen through the eyes of a curious, thoughtful Canadian. It also helps us understand the forces that shaped her outlook on life and her actions.

Sonali Verma,
journalist

*

Brightening My Corner

a Memoir of Dreams Fulfilled

by Ruth Lor Malloy

BARCLAY PRESS

Newberg, OR 97132

Brightening My Corner

a Memoir of Dreams Fulfilled

©2023 by Ruth Lor Malloy

Barclay Press, Inc.
Newberg, Oregon
www.barclaypress.com

Cover image: Ruth Lor Malloy Collection

Printed in the United States of America.

ISBN 978-1-59498-032-9

To the giver of all miracles
and to Mike, Linda, and Terry who helped me fulfill my dreams.

Table of Contents

Introduction

Ruth Lor was a puzzled little girl, growing up in a small Ontario town. Why did some of the other kids call her "chinky chinky"? Why did the immigrant cooks in her family's restaurant tease her because she couldn't speak Cantonese? What was she anyhow, Chinese or Canadian? How come she never had a date in high school? She was certainly pretty enough.

These puzzles made Ruth want to find out why people were prejudiced against each other and maybe do something about it. A lucky break started her on that path. She won a small car in a raffle and sold it to pay for tuition at the University of Toronto. There she met other Chinese-Canadians. She also met African, Indian, and European people too. She learned that there was more to the world than her little Ontario town. She became a social worker. She broke up fights between macho Portuguese and Sicilian factions at settlement-house dances. In Washington, D.C., she fought segregation by sitting in at "whites only" restaurants and swimming in "whites only" pools. She helped find homes for foster children. She wanted to do more, see more, experience more.

Next, she went to plant fruit trees to bolster the incomes of downtrodden Indigenous people in central Mexico. Then she painted houses for Inuit victims of tuberculosis in the Canadian Arctic and helped to distribute food to refugees in Taiwan. Journalism and photography paid her way around Asia. A tramp steamer sailed her home from Brazil.

It wasn't all just for adventure. She didn't lose sight of her goals. She arranged work camps where students from previously warring countries learned to work together. She helped set up conferences for junior diplomats from not-so-friendly nations. When they rose to senior positions in their own governments, might they help avoid a war? She couldn't save the whole world, but she could obey the old hymn that tells you to "brighten the corner where you are."

And there was still plenty of excitement: hitching a ride through the Khyber Pass, suspected of being a possible spy, scuba diving with poisonous sea snakes. When China reopened to foreigners after its Cultural Revolution, Ruth wrote the first English-language guidebook about that enormous country. Along the way, she was persuaded to dine on scorpions, snakes, and bees.

Her life changed forever one night in the glittering little city of Luang Prabang, the royal capital of Laos. That's where she said yes to Mike, her future husband, on the promise that he would give her at least one kiss a day for the rest of their lives.

The adventures continued. Ruth covered the war in Vietnam, crossed Himalayan passes on foot and horseback, and faced down an angry elephant in Africa. She worked in India to reduce prejudice against that country's caste of transgender *hijras*. She and her husband housed refugees in their Maryland home after the Vietnam War ended.

It was an up-and-down kind of life, rich one day and poor the next. In Mexico, her toilet was a barren hillside patrolled by hungry pigs. In Mumbai and Manila, there were maids and chauffeurs. In Bangkok, her shower was a dipper and a waist-high vat of cold water. Hong Kong provided a private yacht complete with captain. Her daughter learned horse dressage in white jodhpurs and shiny black boots.

There were other experiences of a different, bleaker kind: her son's tragic suicide; her daughter's brief, scary encounter with heroin; her husband's cancer and, for a while, his drinking problem; and the frosty relationship with her mother-in-law.

In her nineties, Ruth still works with refugees. Until it was interrupted by the COVID-19 pandemic, she maintained a blog where Torontonians could find out about the many ethnic festivals in their multicultural city. She still brightens her corner, wherever she is. She certainly brightens mine.

—Michael T. Malloy, 2021

Chapter 1:
Dresden, 1954

On October 29, 1954, a Chinese-Canadian woman became part of Black History Month in Canada, a predominantly white-raced country. No one, no newspaper, video, or law book ever mentioned why this was unusual. The two other principals were Black. "Chinese-Canadian" rated only a short phrase identifying my participation in an important test case. Although several decades later it would become a common question, I don't remember anyone asking then about discrimination against people of Chinese ancestry and why I had taken part.

My collection of newspaper articles about Dresden and links to the videos shot later by Canadian media are reminders of the date. We didn't have computers then. Every year during Black History Month, friends mention seeing me on television, in a book, or on a poster in the Toronto subway.

That day I didn't expect to become part of Black history. I was there because Wally Nelson had asked what Canadians were doing about racial discrimination, and Sid Blum had requested my participation because I had approached him with that very same question. Sid worked for a coalition of labor unions whose members fought for fair wages, working conditions, and human rights.

I had met Wally two months before at a workshop in Washington, D.C., on nonviolent methods to combat racial inequality.

Now that I seem to be the only survivor of the Dresden trials that I'm aware of, the only one who can tell that story firsthand, I feel obligated to share it. How did it happen, and what happened afterward? I can't tell you much about my other friends, but I can tell you how the incident encouraged a small-town girl to become an international journalist and an author of over a dozen books. At one time shortly before Dresden, people of Chinese ancestry were forbidden to become journalists in Canada. I hope this story will encourage others to follow their dreams in spite of such obstacles.

That day, I felt I was in a movie, pretending it was just like any ordinary day, one of three people sitting down together at a table in a little restaurant in a small Ontario town. At that time, I was a secretary for the Student Christian Movement at the University of Toronto, and a recent college graduate. My job was organizing meetings for students, but the trip that day had nothing directly to do with that.

Bromley Armstrong and Hugh Burnett were Black Canadians. Bromley and I were genuinely hungry. We had started out by car with Sid and hadn't even stopped for a drink since leaving Toronto five hours before. Lunch was an important part of the plot. We just wanted to get indisputable evidence that restaurants were breaking a newly minted law that forbade the refusal of services in public places because of skin color.

Hugh had joined us in Dresden. The restaurant was one of two in that little Ontario town that persisted in refusing to serve Black people. There was also a barber shop there that did the same. Several groups of activists over the years had also tried to do something about it and succeeded in publicizing the problem. Earlier that year, the government of Ontario had passed a law forbidding the practice.

Hugh had been born in the town and had served in the Canadian military. He didn't like having to go to another town to have a coffee. He also didn't like being shunned because of racial discrimination. He was a carpenter, and he had had to move to another town to make a living. Not enough people would hire him in Dresden.

After we sat down in a booth in Kay's Cafe, we looked around. Bromley recognized the three reporters Sid had tipped off and said they and Sid were already served at other tables. Sid was Jewish and would have added an unnecessary component to the plan if he had joined our table. The three of us waited about fifteen minutes, making small talk.

A waitress was standing nearby, trying to avoid looking at us. She had no legitimate reason to refuse to serve us. Jamaican-born Bromley was in his early twenties and wearing a suit coat and tie. I don't remember what Hugh was wearing, but he looked respectable. We waited and waited. It was obvious she didn't want to acknowledge us.

Finally, Bromley approached the woman and asked, "Can I get a cup of coffee?" She continued to ignore him. I started to breathe a little faster.

"Will you serve us?"

"No," she answered, a frown on her face, and he returned to our table.

Then Hugh got up and asked for the manager. Hugh was strong and tall with a pencil-thin mustache. Both men were my heroes because they were unwilling to tolerate injustices and were trying to do something about them.

"I'm too busy to see you, Hugh," said Morley McKay as he came out of the kitchen. McKay must have known what was happening. Hugh had been there before with other test groups.

McKay was a heavy white man, wearing an apron and a scowl. He was wielding a cleaver, one of those wide knives used for cutting big chunks of meat. He was trying to scare us as he made chopping motions with it—up and down, up and down. I wasn't afraid. Mr. McKay was a businessman, and I didn't think he would add assault to his troubles. I also expected our witnesses would step in to stop him if he tried. Besides, Bromley was a welder, and, like Hugh, he was in good physical shape.

Sid and the three reporters were white and were watching us carefully. When Hugh returned to our table, the photographer started taking pictures of us as McKay backed into the kitchen. McKay had refused us service. We thought we had a case.

The next day the front pages of Toronto newspapers reported the story. Newspapers were more important then than they are today. You can find us now in Wikipedia, Canadian law books, and in the video libraries of the National Film Board and the Canadian Broadcasting Corporation. Dresden residents might remember their parents talking about their town's infamy. We had proof that Morley McKay had broken a law and could be charged. We found out that the other restaurant and barber shop were closed. Still, we were pleased, and we drove home happy; however, it wasn't as easy as we had thought.

I helped Sid afterward in testing apartment building rentals in Toronto for landlords who refused to rent to people because of their skin color or ethnic origin. It was another satisfying project.

I had no idea then that I would find myself years later in the slums of Mumbai, India, helping a group of transgender people gain similiar respect; or in China, trying to open doors for foreigners to understand that much-misunderstood country. Each of us has a unique journey. I hope my story will help others to also fulfill their dreams of helping others.

Chapter 2:
Brockville, 1932-1951

Why was a Chinese-Canadian involved in Black history? If I hadn't been with Black companions, the waitress would have made me a hamburger with the works, for sure, no problem; but it's a long story.

I had been born in Brockville in 1932 and was brought up in that small Eastern Ontario town. As we traveled around the province, no restaurant had ever refused to serve us, but in other ways, I could understand the pain that people inflicted on those who didn't look the same as themselves. My skin was tinted darker than the majority, my hair was black, and my eyes had a different shape. I spoke English with the same accent as most everyone else, but my father and grandfather came from China. We were one of two Asian families in a predominately white town.

In grade school, I became aware that some people didn't like us. Some, but not all of them, called us insulting names on the street. It was the humiliating manner they said the rhyme that sent us home in tears to our mother: "Chinky, chinky Chinaman sitting on a fence, trying to make a dollar out of fifteen cents!"

My first reaction was denial. Why would a kid be trying to make a dollar out of fifteen cents? As I grew older, I wondered if there was anyone who wasn't trying to make a dollar out of fifteen cents. However, at that early age, I just didn't like people calling me a strange name in such a disparaging way. What did "chink" even mean?

One day at the local movie theater where we spent our allowance on Saturday afternoons, watching *The Lone Ranger* and Al Jolson movies, I sat down beside a stranger, a woman. She looked at me and immediately got up and stormed away hissing, "Chinese!" She took a seat on the other side of the theater, leaving me bewildered and devastated. Did I have body odor or bad breath?

High school was difficult. My sister Alice and I did well on the academic side, but no boy asked either of us for a date, not even for our senior prom. Was something wrong with us, I wondered, as I did arm and chest exercises, hoping to make my tiny breasts bigger? I tried to curl my naturally straight hair. The social slight hurt. We wanted to fit in with our friends as they planned their dresses and talked about their dates—like normal teenage girls.

Our mother's parents had come from China, too. Our mother was born and brought up mostly in Canada, in North Bay, Ontario. She had felt the sting of racism there and had learned to deal with it. Her reaction to the name-calling was to assure us that those nasty people were just ignorant: "They don't know what they are saying," she told us matter-of-factly. "Just ignore them."

But still, it hurt. At times, it made me feel unsure and filled with doubt. Maybe the people who called us "chinks" were right. Maybe we *were* weird. No, we weren't. *They* were weird. Why did God make us all so different? How could we make them stop calling us horrible names? I wasn't able to get a handle on those questions until after I left Brockville.

Our family had been fortunate. While many Chinese immigrants had been hired to build the trans-Canada railway, both sets of grandparents had arrived in Canada after it was built and before Canada passed the Chinese Exclusion Act in 1923. That law forbade more Chinese people and their families from migrating to Canada. Many Canadians were obviously afraid of us; newspapers referred to us as "the yellow peril," and many politicians said Chinese people were inferior.

I like to think that my grandparents were brave and adventurous, leaving the known security of their home village for a place where they didn't speak the language. Like other immigrants, they wanted a better life than China with its famines, civil wars, and foreign invasions could give them. My paternal grandfather went first to Cuba, which had just freed its slaves and needed cheap labor to work in its cane fields. When conditions there proved too difficult, he joined a fellow villager in Brockville.

Daddy was twelve years old when he arrived in Canada in 1910. At first, he helped in the steamy family laundry business. He told us how some white boys upset his wagon as he delivered loads of clean shirts and sheets to their customers. He laughed an embarrassed laugh as he said his father had to wash and iron them again. I doubt if he thought it was funny when it happened. It must have been really hard on him.

Our father and his relatives did relatively well in spite of the hostility because people wanted someone to wash their dirty sheets and clothes. Daddy said frequently that he worked sixteen hours a day, and he used to complain that we, his children, were lazy because we didn't. Later, he and his relatives had enough money to invest in a restaurant that could seat over eighty people, its tables covered in white linen and its walls decorated in an attempt at fashionable Art Deco style. It had ersatz Chinese dishes like chop suey and chow mein buns, and it was the only restaurant between Montreal and Toronto that served expensive dishes like live lobster, Winnipeg gold-eye, and raw oysters. They were able to make a living, save money, and send some back to their families in China.

While many Canadians objected to Chinese people moving into their country, a few Brockvillians did welcome us. Members of the local Presbyterian church volunteered to teach English to the immigrants. Like missionaries abroad, they were trying to get the heathen to join their church. Our father did.

Christians had befriended Mom's family, too. A traveling salesman who visited both Brockville and North Bay told my parents about each other. Our mother was interested in meeting this young Chinese man who was also a Christian. They met, liked each other, married, and started a family. We lived in an apartment above the restaurant.

I was their second child and grew up with mixed feelings about being Chinese. I spoke Chinese with my relatives until I was five, and then, like the children of many immigrants, I preferred to speak English, the language of my playmates and school. My childhood was full of conflicts.

When I was about seven, our father asked one of his nephews to teach us Cantonese. My sister and I refused our first and only lesson, and he gave up. I still remember, "Little, little kitten, jump, jump, jump." We were starting to rebel against Chinese culture. That he didn't insist on us learning Chinese made me think later that he was afraid of us girls. Later, I was sorry that I hadn't taken the opportunity to learn the language.

Our father kept trying to be authoritative. He wanted us to go with him to his hockey games, fishing, and duck hunting, but he never went to our school concerts or basketball games. He frequently lost out to our strong-willed mother, especially about piano lessons, which she insisted we take. He didn't know how to handle us, and I remember my sister Alice wanting to give him a hug once, but he pulled away from her attempt at affection. I don't remember ever getting a hug from him and learned not to expect one. Affectionate hugs were not part of Chinese culture.

I shot one duck. It was a hen, and I picked her up from the ground still alive. I had to give it to Daddy to end its suffering and never went hunting with him again.

But obviously, he cared about us, in addition to needing company. Every winter, Daddy ordered someone to make us a skating rink in the field behind our restaurant, so we could ice skate. In the summer, we had a cottage where we could swim and fish when we weren't working. After Mom started spending most of her time in the restaurant, we could eat pretty much what we wanted, including self-designed ice cream sundaes, hamburgers, juicy roast beef, and, occasionally, lobster.

Compared to some of our schoolmates, our lives were fortunate, but I had a love-hate relationship with being Chinese. We always had to work while our friends played. I didn't like waiting on tables because I felt that taking orders was demeaning and contributed to the stereotype of Chinese people as servants. I didn't mind working as the cashier or the hostess, leading people to their tables; that was different.

Once I had to chase some customers when a waiter noticed they had stolen our salt and pepper shakers. As I nervously approached their car, one of our friendly Brockville policemen just happened to come along and gently asked for the shakers. No guns. No pressure. Just a grin. The thieves responded to the authority of his uniform. He thanked them, and they drove off. I felt very lucky.

My biggest disappointment came when I was about fourteen. I wanted to take part in the local swimming races to see how I could do competitively. Mom had promised me the day off, but special visitors arrived unexpectedly. She changed her mind and wanted me to work that day, and I ended up angry and unconsolable. Our poor mother gave in. I didn't have to work, but I couldn't go to the competition either. I spent the rest of the day in bed, feeling sorry for myself. I wasn't meant to be a competitive swimmer.

But I survived adolescence and the negative attitudes of our town and, apparently, even thrived. Working in a restaurant taught us the value of service and sensitivity to the needs of other people. While some people made us feel like we were from another planet, the local Presbyterian church warmly welcomed us Chinese children. There were several dedicated people who genuinely cared for us and made us feel we belonged. We loved visiting Aunt Hat and Aunt Kate's little white house on the way home from school. It was fun when Mrs. Lawson read our fortunes from tea leaves after we drank tea with her. I taught Sunday School classes and played the piano every week for at least five years, pleased to have a role supporting the hymn singing.

I memorized the Presbyterian catechism with its questions and answers: "What is man's chief end? Man's chief end is to glorify God and to enjoy him forever." One minister told us we shouldn't read a newspaper on Sunday and, for a week or two, I obeyed. I found some peace kneeling beside my bed each night and praying for God's blessing.

Church was important. I attended its Mission Band before I was five and learned songs like "Brighten the Corner Where You Are" and regularly gave a donation to the "selfless" missionaries who were helping the "starving children in China." I idealized the missionaries and imagined their sacrifices. Somehow, that children's hymn and the Christian tradition of helping the poor stayed with me. But it wasn't just the church that started my drive to help Chinese people. In the movie theater, we saw newsreels of Chinese babies crying in the streets and Chinese refugees fleeing from Japanese bombs. I felt a connection with them. Japanese victories made me feel inferior. China needed my paltry few pennies.

We assisted our mother, Agnes Lor, as she worked with a few of Brockville's leaders, raising money for China War Relief, China's fight against the Japanese invaders. Some of those leaders were politicians and professionals. Their friendship gave our family a feeling that they accepted us. We were not outsiders to them.

Then, as a teenager, when people were staring at me as though I was some weird animal in a zoo, I realized I could do something about it. I stared back at them, a look of amused curiosity on my face. Within a minute, they would suddenly realize they were not invisible. They would look quickly away, and I knew I had some control over them. It was so funny.

I found out I had some worth outside of the school and restaurant. My uncle, Harry, was an amateur photographer and inspired me to spend my allowance on a camera. Then parents wanted to buy my pictures of their children performing in school events. I could make some money outside of the restaurant. I sold my first pictures, when I was about fifteen, to parents who wanted souvenirs of their children's high school performances. No one had cell phone cameras then because no one had cell phones. My uncle started my career in photography, a useful skill to have as a reporter.

As we became older, Mom continued to set an example for us. She helped raise money for other community projects like the town's new ice rink. She organized a professional women's group. She spent time chatting with her customers. Mom went on to be named the Brockville Citizen of the Year in 1984. It was indeed an honor.

Working together with other people made me feel useful and important. Playing on the school's basketball team encouraged self-confidence, and I remember our game against a team in neighboring Gananoque where our opponents admitted we frightened them because we were from bigger Brockville. I sang in the school choir, had lots of girl friends, and went to their birthday parties when I wasn't working in the restaurant. We counted the non-Chinese restaurant staff among our friends. They were like family. We learned to be punctual so the cashier and waitresses could leave on time when we replaced them on the evening shift. Mother made sure we were sensitive to their needs, too.

The war actually helped us. The Canadian government opened an officers training school in Brockville, and ours was one of two restaurants in town where the standards were high enough for its officers. We were busy most weekends. I learned how to tell a major from a colonel and loved it when I could order a colonel to follow me to an empty table.

Then I began to see that our family had prejudices, too. We certainly did not have any love for German or Japanese soldiers. In school, I spent the war years (1939-45) drawing pictures of Lancaster bombers and Spitfire fighters shooting down German planes when I was bored with memorizing multiplication tables. We knew our enemy was Hitler, the German dictator whose greed and obsession with being the leader of a "master race" led to the Second World War. I had heard of antisemitism, but one of our best friends in high school, Etta Binder, was Jewish, and I didn't understand why some people didn't like Jews. However, the Chinese word for China is "Middle Kingdom"—center of the world. Our mother tried to teach us pride in being Chinese and, at the dinner table, read us books like Lin Yutang's *A Moment in Peking* and Pearl S.Buck's *The Good Earth*. Mom hoped Lin Yutang would give us some pride in our heritage, but at that early age, we didn't care.

Our relatives and our father called Black people "hak gwei" or "black ghosts," people to be feared. It was an insult. It meant we thought that Chinese were superior.

After the war, tourists by the bus loads arrived in the summers, especially when television host Arthur Godfrey made our local scenery popular with a song that started with, "I left the one I love at one of the Thousand Islands." One noon hour, a Black couple came into the restaurant, the first Black people I had ever seen outside of movies and the porter on our train trip to Vancouver, B.C. Our father told me to seat them out of sight of the crowd waiting to get a table. He said other customers would leave the restaurant if they saw them, but we did serve them. I didn't see anyone leaving because of them.

I didn't know any Indigenous Canadians or Black people personally then. The Lone Ranger's pal, Tonto, was the only "Indian" we ever saw who wasn't attacking "heroic" white settlers or forts manned by white soldiers. The only Black people in movies then were slaves or villains. I took part thoughtlessly in a high school concert without questioning our teacher: like other choir members, I allowed my face to be painted black and thought it was fun. We sang African American spirituals and pretended to be plantation slaves. Fortunately, the school had no Black students then, but the performance added to the prevailing, mistaken image of Black people. Brockville had no Black residents. If we had had Black students, I'm sure they would have felt very uncomfortable, just as uncomfortable as I felt when people imitated Chinese accents from Charlie Chan movies.

The Chinese staff in our restaurant called my sisters and me an insulting name because we couldn't speak Chinese: "Yeen Cheen Nui" meant "Indian girls." These men were referring to Canada's Indigenous people. We lashed back that these relatives were ignorant and couldn't speak English properly, but we were too polite to say this to their faces. In reacting, I considered these Chinese men inferior. When I thought about it later, I realized we were prejudiced, too.

I remember joining a group of schoolmates aggressively shouting, "Catholic! Catholic!" at some children who went to the Catholic school. I was in grade school and had no idea why we were doing this except that our friends were doing it.

None of us, no one, was free of prejudice.

Looking back, I can think of many people like the church ladies, Uncle Henry, and Mom, who influenced my life. I also considered myself fortunate that I never liked smoking or drinking alcohol; I knew Mom and the ladies wouldn't have approved. I tried both, and they tasted awful. Illegal drugs were not popular then and, fortunately, I never had to struggle to give up smoking or drugs when these were no longer considered healthy. I saved a lot of money that way, too, money used later to spend on my dreams.

Then, in my senior year in high school, we had a vocational guidance session. I wanted to be a foreign correspondent, a journalist. I loved to write stories, and I loved to travel. The reporter who came to talk about his craft said that Chinese people were not allowed to be journalists because we weren't Canadian citizens. Because we had been born in Canada, I had never thought that we weren't Canadian citizens, and I didn't believe him.

I refused to abandon my dream of becoming a writer. I thought highly of Mr. Hunter, our English teacher; he had praised my writing assignments. He said that journalists had to have a wide range of knowledge. One didn't just go to journalism school to learn how to write. A journalist had to learn about the world. I already loved the trips we took outside of Brockville, and I wanted to see more. Mr. Hunter said I should go to college, and I never forgot his advice. He suggested his college, Victoria College at the University of Toronto. I had been to Toronto, the big city, a couple of times, and I had relatives there I loved to visit. That summer, 1948, I happened to win a car, a Chevrolet sedan, in a carnival lottery. We already had a car. Mom had taught us how to drive at sixteen, but I was much too young to own one. We sold it, bought Daddy a business suit, and shared the remainder with my siblings.

Mom wanted me to go to business college to learn shorthand, typing, and bookkeeping, so I could help type menus in the restaurant. She had worked as a secretary herself before her marriage. My elder sister, Alice, was training to be a nurse in Montreal, but Mom said I was too young to leave home. I compromised by staying in Brockville an extra year after high school graduation and learned skills that would become useful in my future. I argued that I had almost enough money from the car for college in Toronto. Then, Uncle Henry and Aunt Lil invited me to stay in their home in Toronto in return for a bit of babysitting while I went to school there. They only charged twenty-five dollars a month for food. I applied and was accepted at Victoria College. Tuition was less than $400 a year then, and I was able to get a bursary and a part-time job, too. That decided it.

Mom lost almost all hope that any of her children would be around to help her. College was my first step toward broadening my world. Though she kept fighting it, I was on the way to being her "world traveler" with a lifetime of travel photography and writing to show for it. Being a part of Black History Month didn't come until after college.

Chapter 3:
College in Toronto, 1951-1954

Before I graduated from college, I found at least one way to fight racial discrimination. Uncle Henry Lore was a doctor whose family came from a different Chinese village than ours. He had the same Chinese surname as we did, spelled with an additional "e" in English. The Canadian immigration officer, who processed his father on arrival in the country, probably made up the spelling from the way it sounded. Our father had given Uncle Henry a job in our restaurant while he was going to medical school.

We knew him well. He and Aunt Lil and their three boys and a girl lived in a tiny, two-story house near the corner of Bay and Dundas Street in Toronto, and I went to join this hospitable family for over three years. The neighborhood was still part of Chinatown then, before the city government tore part of it down to build Toronto's oyster-shaped city hall. I was able to save money and keep in shape by walking to school.

Some evenings before the Chinese New Year, I tried to sleep while cymbals clashed and Chinese drums thumped loudly next door. At first, I loved it. We never had Chinese drums or lion dances in Brockville, and these were teaching me more about Chinese culture. Fortunately, the drums stopped after the celebrations ended, and I could get a full night's sleep.

The house was around the corner from a bowling alley where young Chinese-Canadians met every weekend for fun and marriage prospects. I started spending Saturday afternoons at the bowling alley. There, I discovered I was not an ugly duckling. Guys did find me attractive, and I began to date. It was a welcome change.

Other young Chinese-Canadians were a joy to be with, largely because I didn't feel different when I was with them. As I got to know them better and benefited from the stimulation of college, I realized I *was* different from them. I wasn't interested in getting married; at least, not yet. Newlyweds talked of children, but I was just starting to enjoy my freedom and wondered: What was the point of having children, who would have children, *ad infinitum*? College was making me think of freeing myself from the confines of my own cultural community. I learned from friends about the likely domination by a Chinese mother-in-law and the pressure to produce at least one male child. Was there more to life than per-petuating one's species?

Uncle Henry's connections introduced me to many Chinese people. He was a chubby, cheerful man who suffered from gout. He treated patients in a tiny office in his house, organized a week-ly Chinese movie at a nearby cinema, and helped to create the Chinese-Canadian Association. Through him, I met many of Toronto's Chinese leaders and ate with his family in some of the best Cantonese restaurants. I also found myself pressured to teach English to newly arrived immigrants from China.

He told me that in the mid-1800s, Canada's leaders needed laborers to build a transcontinental railroad. They imported eager men from China, expecting them to disappear after they finished the job, but the Chinese workers wanted to stay because Canada offered opportunities to make a better living than back in China. Many Canadians objected to allowing them to remain and, even more, to have their families join them. They said the Chinese would change the "fundamental character of the Canadian people." At that point, Canada was largely white-skinned, British, and European. A 1902 Royal Commission on Chinese and Japanese Immigration had proclaimed that we were "unfit for full citizenship . . . so nearly allied to a servile class that they (Chinese people) are obnoxious to a free community and dangerous to the state."

It was bewildering to read that. How could my passive male relatives who worked all day—whose only entertainment was gambling—how could they be a danger to anyone? I never heard of any of them being charged with a crime. As for me, I knew my parents were respected in town, and I tried not to embarrass them. My only crime was dancing through the streets of Brockville with fellow high school students one Halloween evening while we held up traffic.

By the 1950s, Canadians began seeing Chinese people in roles other than laborers and laundrymen. I didn't hear the name "chink" anymore. At the bowling alley, I was pleasantly surprised to meet Chinese-Canadian women who were airplane pilots and aeronautical engineers. In neighborhood restaurants with Uncle Henry and his family, I met men of Chinese ancestry who had fought for Canada during both world wars. Many had become professionals like doctors, pharmacists, and civil engineers. Many of them had proved to be good citizens. In 1957, lawyer Douglas Jung would become the first elected Chinese-Canadian member of Canada's Parliament.

Uncle Henry said that, in 1947, we were finally granted citizenship and the right to vote in federal elections. The government also allowed Chinese wives and children to come to Canada but not grandparents. Uncle Henry needed help to persuade the Canadian government to expand its immigration policy to include grandparents.

Having Canadian citizenship meant that Chinese people could also be journalists. I was already writing short stories and articles about our history for *The New Citizen*, a Chinese-Canadian magazine. I studied the yearly figures in *The Canada Yearbook* and discovered that the actual percentage of Chinese people in Canada was going down. It didn't seem right that, as a group, we should be treated worse than other immigrants. I ended up a couple of years later on one of several Asian-Canadian delegations to Ottawa, petitioning the minister of immigration. We asked the government

31

to expand the immigration laws to include a wider definition of family members. I enjoyed working with other Chinese-Canadians on this project.

It was well after our sit-in at the Dresden restaurant that the Canadian government finally changed its immigration regulations regarding grandparents. I was elated when I heard the news. I felt that insignificant me, working with the Chinese-Canadian Association, had helped to change a government regulation. The government was no longer a big, impersonal entity. Asian-Canadians had some power; every Canadian had some clout. Petitioning our government was another way to fight discrimination.

While the government was trying to make that decision, I was having a glorious time in college. I studied comparative religion, philosophy, history, Spanish, sociology, and psychology. The psychology course was wonderful. It helped me understand my parents, and I learned to forgive them for not being perfect. I decided my children, if I ever had any, would be allowed to be whatever they wanted to be.

I loved the philosophy course taught by Professor Marcus Long. Was saving a life a good thing? What if the life you saved turned out to be someone like Adolph Hitler; would that have been a good thing? Is the world real, or is it just a dream? As I wrote in my scrapbook, Professor Long "succeeded in making me really think for the first time about the purpose of man, God, and the nature of the universe, and instilled in me a spirit of critical inquiry and constructive skepticism, which at one time led me to the brink of agnosticism."

The Student Christian Movement (SCM), a group that was questioning what I had learned in the Presbyterian church, kept me from becoming an agnostic. It became a big influence in my life. I compared the various accounts of the life of Jesus in different books of the Bible, which left me with a lot more questions. In my comparative religion classes, I studied other religions and was fascinated by Sufism, a branch of Islam.

My religious beliefs changed. Why should a minister pray on my behalf in words I didn't necessarily agree with? Why was I a member of the Presbyterian church? Was it only because my parents were members? Why didn't God answer all prayers?

The SCM made us think about our religion, question it, and, in turn, strengthen it. I loved Kahlil Gibran's book *The Prophet*, partly because it justified my being a carnivore. I also loved the prayer of Saint Francis of Assisi: "Lord, make me an instrument of thy peace." By the end of college, I came to believe that there was only one possible prayer—that humans be led to fit into God's plan. God was not a Santa Claus responding to petitions. God was a higher power or some undefinable greater being whose existence we couldn't yet understand. God had created the world or universe where, somehow, we were meant to grow spiritually to love one another. For me, Jesus was no longer just the "Son of God," as Christian churches defined him but one of the world's greatest teachers with a message of love and forgiveness.

And why would God create an imperfect world that needed saving? I decided we were meant to follow the vague leadings of this incomprehensible power, a "leap of faith into the hands of God," or a god—or whatever they were. My only prayer then was, "Thy will be done." I renounced my membership in the Presbyterian church.

The Student Christian Movement organized summer workcamps and introduced a couple of other worlds that were new to me. Members worked as aides in a mental hospital in Weyburn, Saskatchewan, and in factories, getting to know laborers and trade unionists. I listened to their discussions on mental illness and Weyburn's experiments with the hallucinatory drug LSD. Some of my friends at the Weyburn workcamp had tried LSD, and it changed their perception of the world and God. They wondered if mental illness and even religious feelings were physiological. The students who worked in factories struggled with economic inequalities; why were some people wealthier and more powerful than others?

The SCM's influence on me was immense. Prodded by a friend, Joan Harback, I went to many of its meetings. Its emphasis was on service to others. I supported its boycott against apartheid in South Africa, read Alan Paton's novel *Cry the Beloved Country,* and tried to argue with any white South African I met. At its meetings, I learned about China's new Communist government, which gave some hope of solving China's terrible poverty and fighting the Japanese invaders. I listened avidly to talks by missionaries like Dr. Katharine Hockin who had worked there for decades. She had just been expelled from China even though she supported the Communists, their disciplined army, and its land-to-the-peasants program. The situation was complex. The Korean War was on then, and China appeared to be the aggressor. Our father supported the Nationalist party, which opposed the Communists. Our mother, who had been raising money to help Chiang Kai-shek's Nationalists, was discovering that Mme. Chiang was spending our mother's donations on buying expensive shoes for herself.

The organization Friendly Relations with Overseas Students also opened a window on the world for me. FROS had an office in the heart of the university, and I frequently joined foreign students there with my bagged lunch. They were from all over the world, and I learned a lot from their lively discussions. I decided that the students who had been to Africa, for example, won the arguments about African politics. Most of the time, I just listened because I had never been to Africa and knew so little about it. I decided I had to go there someday.

One day, I naively complimented another close friend about the prominent tattoo on her arm. It was a pretty color. I was embarrassed at my lack of knowledge when she said the tattoo was not a decoration: the Nazis had marked all their Jewish prisoners with tattoos. The war had ended in time for her to escape being killed. She was a living example of the extremes of prejudice displayed by the Holocaust. I knew I had a lot to learn.

I went out with a turbaned Sikh who explained about his kirpan knife, bracelet, uncut hair, comb, and underwear. He said all Sikhs were obliged to carry or wear these symbols of their religion and history. This was interesting, but my mind was preoccupied writing articles for the Chinese-Canadian magazine. I didn't know then that I would have a very interesting Sikh father-in-law one day.

There was an Indian Hindu and a Nigerian, both perfumed when they arrived at our house separately for dates. They were shy and reserved and never asked for another date after I refused a kiss. I hung around with students from St. Lucia and Jamaica; Jake and Percy joked a lot and were the most fun. They later took part in our second Dresden test case.

A Japanese-Canadian introduced me to my first Japanese restaurant. Tom was charming. How could I have hated people like Tom? He told me about living in an internment camp in western Canada during the war, with all of his family's assets confiscated because Japanese people elsewhere were considered enemies. I thought a lot about that situation. It wasn't right. He was just as Canadian as I was.

Indian friends taught me to cook my first Indian food, a carrot halwa that I forced myself to like even though I burned it. Another Indian read my palm, and I learned a different way of fortune telling. I think he was one of the fortune tellers I consulted over the years who predicted that I would have two children, one of whom would give me two grandchildren. I didn't care about that then. I was more concerned about being free to travel.

A Taiwanese man named Louis courted me in an old car with a hole in its floor through which I could see the road move beneath us. He was fun, too, but I wasn't interested in getting married, and besides, he gave me the impression he just wanted my Canadian citizenship so he could stay in Canada. I could tell that his wealthy Canadian sponsor was trying to set us up as a couple just because I was Chinese. I didn't like that either. She assumed that the spouses of Chinese people had to be Chinese.

The university, and especially the Royal Ontario Museum, considered China important. I was pleasantly surprised. The ROM had a huge collection of artifacts gathered by a Canadian missionary years before. The university gave courses in Chinese religion and philosophy, so I took one from a former missionary to China, Dr. Lewis Walmsley.

I realized for the first time why my family made an annual visit to the family graves in Brockville's cemetery. There we shared a picnic with the dead and bowed three times at the tombstones. Our Christian mother had explained it was just a token of respect for our deceased relatives, but Dr. Walmsley said it was actually ancestor worship, and the bowing should be from the waist or even head to the ground and done by a son. We were bribing our relatives with liquor and food to influence our fortunes, he said. I remembered Daddy's story about a recently dead relative who appeared in a dream, wanting his body to be sent for burial in China. It was because he wanted his descendants to worship him, to keep him happy in the afterlife. I decided that part of my Chinese heritage was a lot of superstition.

We had also practiced a few other Chinese customs, like holding huge banquets and wearing new clothes on New Year's Day. Many other nationalities celebrate New Year's that way, too, but Dr. Walmsley explained that Chinese tradition was to insure that banquets and new clothes would continue throughout the coming year as a result. We already knew about the giving of *lai see* (lucky money) to children because relatives and visitors always gave us red packets of money at New Year's. I still practice that one with children during the New Year's season. I remember how our practical mother put my money into life insurance. It helped pay for my first journey after I graduated.

Dr. Walmsley also spoke of the ancient Chinese practise of never praising a child. This was to keep the gods from knowing about gifted children and consequently wanting them for themselves. That meant death for the child. True or not, the custom helped me accept our father's lack of encouragement in our upbringing. Our Canadian-born mother, on the other hand, bragged about us frequently to customers in our restaurant. We siblings found it annoying to discover our secrets were no longer secret.

The ROM's collection gave me a wider view of Chinese things, that of wealthy emperors living in splendid palaces. I knew that my family had come from a tiny village because Daddy had once said that he rode a water buffalo. We were from lowly peasant stock, but

China wasn't just villages. From the ROM and my Chinese classes, I learned more about the Great Wall, the emperors, the dominant philosophy of Confucianism, and the republican revolutionist Dr. Sun Yat-sen. Dr. Walmsley also talked about an ancient philosophy called Mohism, which said that the highest form of human communication was silence. What a novel idea! I was to learn more of the value of silent meditation from other religions later.

The ROM made me realize that it was important for everybody to study the history and achievements of their own cultures, as well as those of others. Museums became very important to me.

Through my new friends and school in Toronto, my eyes were opening to the world, and I wanted to see more. Every group, every country, not just Chinese people, considered themselves the center of the world. I wasn't ready for marriage and a family then. I knew what I wanted to do. In a letter to my mother, I wrote: "If my purpose in life is to take down one stone from the wall that separates races and nationalities, I shall be most happy to do it. For if I take down one stone, and someone else takes down another, someday, there will be no more wall."

When I graduated in 1954 and was ready to announce my future in the University of Toronto yearbook, I put "travel and writing" as my goals. Of course I wanted a husband someday but not right away. Mom came to my graduation.

Chapter 4:
Summer in Washington, D.C., 1954

Before our trip to Dresden, I learned about an annual Washington, D.C., workshop about nonviolent methods to combat racial inequality organized by the Congress of Racial Equality and the Fellowship of Reconciliation. I had never heard of these groups, but the notice had been posted outside the SCM office, and it sounded as though it had some answers to what could be done about racial discrimination. I applied and was accepted with a scholarship covering my expenses. I had just graduated from college and was eager to start seeing the world. Mom had saved some of my lucky Chinese New Year *lai see* money, so I used that to travel.

Going to the United States was nothing new. We could see New York state from the back window of our Brockville apartment, only three miles (almost five kilometers) away by boat across the St. Lawrence River. We frequently went shopping in Ogdensburg or Watertown, New York, because the prices were better. We didn't need a passport, just a border crossing card or a driver's license.

I took a couple of buses from Toronto to the U.S. capital, changing at Buffalo and New York City. In Washington, D.C., our group lived together for a month in a large house in a middle-class residential neighborhood. Our teacher was Wally Nelson, an amazing Black man so dedicated to nonviolence that he kept his income low in order to avoid paying taxes that would support military solutions to conflicts. He had learned to live on very little, growing his own food. He had been jailed several times for not paying taxes, once for over three years, but he was a gentle person with a lovely sense of humor. Only once did he lose his temper at our workshop, and then he apologized. I had never met anyone like him, and I admired his courage and consistency.

The day I arrived, I went with a new Black friend, Irene, to a lunch counter in a nearby drug store in D.C. It was just a "let's get something to eat" moment because we were the first of our group to arrive. The waitress, who was also Black, apologized as she said she could serve me but not my friend. Of course I had read about this kind of discrimination before. These insults made what had happened to me in Brockville so insignificant in comparison, but it was the first time it had happened to a friend and me wanting to eat together. Irene was embarrassed. The slight made me upset, and I felt sorry for the waitress. We left without either of us getting fed. I should have known what to expect.

Our group of eight Black, Jewish, and one Chinese participant was the first of Wally's classes in several years with no arrests. We went together to see what would happen if we tried to go swimming in a previously segregated public pool. No one called the police, though there had been riots at other pools earlier that year when Black people tried to use them. Refusal of service was still going on in D.C., but things were changing.

The whole class went to another soda fountain. It seems that it was now integrated, too, and no one called the police. I think Wally would have been delighted if our multiracial group had been arrested because of the publicity and the lessons for us. I was apprehensive, but Wally and the other members didn't seem afraid, and their support melted my own fears. Upon reflection later, I was glad the police hadn't put us in jail. My law-abiding parents would have been mortified.

Wally's lectures included the technique of picketing businesses that would not serve everybody. Hopefully, carrying signs outside a store would discourage possible patrons from going inside to shop. Hopefully, the publicity would pressure management into making changes that would allow friends of different races to eat together. Years before, Wally himself had gone on hunger strikes and Freedom Rides, defiantly riding in the front rather than the back of public buses.

Wally also taught us how important it was to convince governments to enact laws against racial discrimination. While the passing of laws was important, it was not enough. Laws had to be tested with news media coverage. Wally also talked about the need for feature films with sympathetic Black protagonists. I didn't know of any. We spoke at Black churches and told them what we were doing. We distributed leaflets to our neighbors to inform them of what our multiracial group was up to.

Wally's wife, Juanita, was a former journalist who had interviewed him for a story while he was in prison. She was so impressed with what he was doing that she married him after his release. He thought it was funny that she insisted on building an outhouse for their home because it was environmentally friendly, a new concept for her. He, on the other hand, was used to outhouses because he had been raised poor. He was happy to please her.

Our workshop took place in the summer of 1954. The following year, police in Montgomery, Alabama, arrested a Black woman named Rosa Parks for refusing to move to the back of the public bus she was riding, as required by the law in that state. Her arrest led to boycotts and riots. Rosa Parks's action was a milestone in the long fight for civil rights in the U.S. Although he didn't become as famous, I knew Wally had helped, too.

One day, before we finished the workshop, Wally asked what was happening in Canada regarding race relations. At that point, I didn't know, so I decided to find out when I returned to Toronto and looked for a job. I didn't know what I wanted to do then except to get some money for more travel.

Back in Toronto, I talked with Alvan Gamble of the Canadian Mental Health Association, an organization I chose because I was still interested in learning about people with mental disorders. Alvan didn't have a job available, but he directed me to Sid Blum of the Joint Labour Committee on Human Rights. Sid invited me to help test the Fair Accommodations and Practices Act. Maybe he wanted a woman in the group, or maybe he was desperate for a volunteer, or he might have wanted to show that Chinese people were also concerned about racial discrimination, but that wasn't true. I didn't represent any organization. I took part because I wanted to tell Wally, our esteemed teacher and my new father figure, that we were doing something positive about the problem in Canada. Without hesitating, I volunteered with Sid's group. The SCM needed someone to work as a secretary for only four months, organizing student meetings. I took the job, moved in with SCM staffers, and started saving money.

Finding and prosecuting Morley McKay, of the Dresden restaurant guilty of breaking the anti-discrimination law as laid out in the Fair Accommodations Practices Act, did not stop racial prejudice: however, at least in Ontario, friends of all colors had a law to keep anyone from refusing to serve them in a restaurant. It seemed to give McKay an excuse to accept Black patrons. This Act led to the passing of the Ontario Human Rights Code.

One day years later, Bromley and I were back in Dresden filming *Journey to Justice* for the National Film Board, the Canadian government's documentary film production company, when an elderly Black man on the street recognized us and gave hugs to both Bromley and me. He said he had never even been able to buy an ice cream cone in town before our efforts. I felt very good about my part in the process.

Aaron Haddad wrote a play about Hugh: *My Place is Right Here: Hugh Burnett and the Fight for a Better Canada*. It was performed at least four times in 2019. In 2000, Bromley published a memoir: *Bromley, Tireless Champion for Just Causes: Memoir of Bromley L. Armstrong*. In 2013, York University in Toronto bestowed an honorary doctorate on him. In 2010, a plaque was installed near the city hall in Dresden that honored Hugh and his National Unity Association. Bromley and I were thrilled to see it, but unfortunately, Hugh died before it was in place.

It was a privilege to have had a small part in the Dresden case, and I realize that it could have happened without me. Additionally, we did have some fun with it. At the time, Sid suggested that we take a first-class train coach to Chatham for the trial so that Morley McKay would have to pay more for costs when he lost his court case, but our first case was dismissed because McKay's lawyer questioned the legality of the Act itself. A second test with my Caribbean friends, Jake and Percy, proved that the law was indeed valid. A group of us celebrated at a party afterward at Sid and his wife Mary's house with our lawyers and supporters. Sid especially loved to dance, even though he had a bad leg. I think we danced the hora as we enjoyed the sweet high of victory.

Perhaps we should have given some kind thoughts to people like the misguided Morley McKay, too. Why did he feel such hatred toward Black people? As for my family, none of them seemed to care. Daddy told Mom that he was afraid I would marry someone Black, but marriage to anyone was not on my radar.

Chapter 5:
Life Changers:
Mexico and Brazil, 1954-1955

Before I graduated from college in 1954, I saw a notice in the Student Christian Movement office. I applied and was accepted as a steward at the Second Assembly of the World Council of Churches in Evanston, Illinois. The WCC covered living expenses at the huge meeting, and it took place after the nonviolent workshop in Washington, D.C., and before Dresden. It was a travel and learning experience. The writing was to come later.

For two weeks, we volunteers from fifteen countries delivered mail, collated press releases, and served as ushers—whatever work needed to be done at a big conference with thousands of delegates from forty-eight countries. More than 160 Protestant and Orthodox churches were represented. As usual, I enjoyed being with a group of young people working on a project. I also listened in on discussions and learned office skills that proved useful in later life.

At this time, I was still searching for another spiritual group to join, and the assembly gave me a chance to see many in action. In spite of their common message of love for humanity and forgiveness, many Christian groups had been squabbling for centuries.

The division of Germany into east and west had recently taken place, and delegates discussed what this meant for the churches there. I still felt comfortable in a Christian environment and was especially thrilled to be with the whole assembly as each participant prayed the Lord's Prayer in his or her own language. In spite of my rejection of it, elements from my Christian upbringing were still part of me. The conference provided an opportunity for another international experience, and I was sorry when it was over.

At the conference, I learned that the WCC was looking for volunteers for a workcamp in Brazil the following summer. That appealed to me more than the theology and the politics covered by the assembly. The Brazil project offered a chance to go to South America, with all expenses paid for one month, while helping to build a conference center for a church near São Paulo. I only had to pay for transportation.

Perhaps it was what I was meant to do because I expected to have enough money saved for a one-way plane ticket to Brazil by that time. I looked at a world map. Maybe something would happen afterward, so Africa would be my next stop. Africa looked relatively close to South America. I should have looked at an airline map because flights to Africa all went through Paris then.

My one-way ticket was a "leap of faith into the hands of God," a phrase I liked from existentialism, which I had tried to study in college. Although I didn't know where I would go after Brazil, I was eager to finally get away, learn about the world, and be able to argue about issues authoritatively. I looked for something else to fill the time before Brazil.

I first learned about American Friends Service Committee (AFSC) workcamps from the glossy *Seventeen* magazine while I was in high school. AFSC was the service arm of the Religious Society of Friends, the Quakers. I read that a young, untrained American volunteer had assisted in the birth of a baby in a Mexican village when there was no doctor, midwife, or nurse available. She was there, trying to help make the world a better place. If a teenager could do that, I could do that, too.

Previously, I hadn't thought about going to Mexico, but my job with the SCM would be over in December. It was too close to home, and I had seen movies set there. It wasn't exotic enough, so it was not on my wishlist, but the idea refused to go away, and maybe it was meant to be. AFSC had several workcamps in Mexico, and Mexico was on the way to Brazil. I applied to its office in Philadelphia about a camp that fit my schedule. Shortly afterward, an AFSC staffer wrote back, offering me a scholarship to cover expenses in Mexico and asked if I could I join immediately. I didn't hesitate.

Sandy Runciman, the editor of the Brockville newspaper, *The Recorder and Times*, was a regular customer in our restaurant. Its office was next door. I think Mom must have told him about my plans to go to Mexico, and he offered to pay five dollars per article for every story with photographs that I sent him for publication. I was very pleased at his offer. Five dollars wasn't much, but it was something, enough to encourage my dreams of being a journalist. Sandy tried to inspire other fledgling writers, too, he said.

I already knew the basics of photography from Uncle Harry, our mother's brother who lived in northern Ontario. Like Mom, he had been born in Canada. He lived with us in Brockville while being treated for a lost eye, the result of what might have been a carelessly tossed carrot from a passing truck. Or was it a deliberate attack because he was Chinese? We would never know.

Uncle Harry never complained about his eye; he never seemed to feel sorry for himself even though he was a self-taught sign painter and needed both eyes for his work. He played games with us children, peeled grapes for us to eat, and took my sister, Alice, and me on a cruise up the Saguenay River in the province of Quebec. He was closer to us than our own father and more fun, although he never gave us hugs, either. We adored him.

My travel plans were working out. It must be what God wanted me to do. Mom promised to save the clippings from the newspaper. I was grateful she had told Sandy about the trip and was glad that she was resigned to my leaving. By then, the SCM had convinced me that working as a waitress was not demeaning, and

I appreciated the opportunities the restaurant had given me, but I felt I had other things to do with my life. While it wasn't the main reason I chose to go to Mexico, the topic of how to solve racial prejudice surfaced there, too.

By chance, Mom mentioned the trip to one of our regular American customers. Moved by thoughts of the poor Mexicans I hoped to help, the woman offered to pay for my bus ticket from Brockville to Laredo, Texas, on condition I spend the night with her and her family in Tennessee on the way. And so, I set out in early 1955; staying with them worked out fine and foreshadowed other such opportunities that might come later. I enjoyed my last comfortable bed at her home in Chattanooga. I don't remember much of that leg of the trip except for one change of bus where a bus company employee had to rescue me from an inebriated man in a bus station.

In Laredo, Texas, on the Mexican border, I met up with two of the other volunteers, Doris and Phyllis, at Hatch's Motel. It was exciting to meet them because my destination was finally in view. Fortunately, Doris had studied Spanish longer than I had. She taught us how to pronounce our destination town, "Iks-me-keel-pan," with the emphasis on "keel." Mexican border officials spent an hour studying our visas. Maybe it was a ploy for us to pay a bribe, said Doris, but they finally let us enter the country with no explanation why they had kept us waiting. The bus trip from the border to our new home took another twenty-eight hours, but I had no complaints: everything was new and exciting.

In Texas, we had picked up sandwiches to eat on the way because AFSC had warned us not to eat anything in Mexico unless it was cooked, peeled, or soaked in disinfectant. We had to be careful, or we would be laid low with diarrhea. Such was my first lesson on eating in developing countries, a lesson that has kept me mostly healthy during my travels around the world.

On our bus trip south, we rode through deserts dotted with prickly cactus. Scrawny cattle wore bells around their necks to scare away rattlesnakes and seemed to eat whatever they could find in a terrain where there wasn't much grass. I saw one group of huge vultures circling in the sky above us. The towns had tiny, bright blue, white, or pink bungalows, and horse-drawn surreys as well as modern trucks and cars.

My seatmate was a delightful sixth grader named Jose, who jabbered away in Spanish and English. My year of Spanish lessons helped me understand him a bit, and I could read some signs. I didn't know enough to converse at his speed, but he became my teacher as he talked about the birds while Phyllis and Doris sat in another part of the bus.

After the desert, we rode through mountains, their welcome greenery painted with misty clouds. We were still in the mountains when we arrived in Ixmiquilpan, which seemed to be in an oasis in the desert.

Stuart and Chuteau Chapin, an American couple, were the leaders of our camp. They greeted us enthusiastically and, after a much appreciated rest, told us about the house and project. Our group of twenty or so volunteers were mainly Americans, but it also included one Finn, one Mexican, one British woman, and me. The camp was run on Quaker principles.

The United States had conscription, and AFSC was officially in charge of the alternative service of the conscientious objectors in our camp, pacifists like Wally Nelson with whom I had worked in Washington, D.C.

Our house was then known as La Casa de los Amigos (Friends House). Chuteau showed us around. The one-story building was near the *zocolo*, the main square. It was light cream with simple brown, wooden shutters and looked like most other houses in town. No sign outside announced who we foreigners were.

The men and women slept in separate dormitories. Cobblestone paths through the garden led to two large outhouses with two-seater toilets, actually two holes in a wooden plank over a pit. I had no problem with outhouses. I had been to cottages and summer camps in Ontario that used them. The shower was out of doors, its water heated by the sun. We would spend our weekends together in relative comfort in this large sprawling building in town, our

49

privacy protected by a high stone wall. On weekdays, we would work in smaller groups in different villages.

The Otomi, the indigenous group we were there to help, had needed assistance for centuries. The powerful Aztecs ruled them until Hernán Cortés and his Spanish army defeated the Aztecs in the early 1500s. The smallpox virus that his men unintentionally carried from Spain helped Cortés make the conquest.

Fortunately, modern science has eliminated rampant smallpox today. Many of us now know about the challenges of COVID-19, which helps us understand how the Aztecs and other tribes felt as a strange disease killed so many of them. The Otomi were right to isolate themselves, fleeing to land no one else wanted—the desert and surrounding hills of the Mezquital Valley, about 100 miles (161 kilometers) north of Mexico City. There they survived; census takers counted 90,000 Otomi in 1950.

Shortly before our arrival, the Mexican government completed the Pan-American highway from Laredo to Mexico City. It forced the Otomis out of their isolation as the government realized these people weren't paying taxes, and they weren't voting. Many Otomis didn't even speak Spanish, only Otomi, and they couldn't read or write their own language. How could they compete in the market? When contractors used them to work on the highways, they considered the Otomis too lazy to be useful. Their "laziness," however, was actually caused by malnutrition; they weren't eating adequate food.

The Mexican government created the Patrimonio Indígena del Valle de Mezquital (Valley of Mezquital Indigenous Heritage) to promote Otomi culture, economy, and education. AFSC was working with the Patrimonio.

The Chapins assigned Doris and me to work with volunteers, Tony and Chonita, in the tiny village of Xochitlan. Chuteau pronounced it "Soo-chit-lan." We arrived that first morning at our weekday home in the back of a pickup. It was about a half-hour drive along the paved highway and then down a very bumpy, dusty road. We shook off the sand that covered us as we jumped off the truck, eager to finally get to work. For a second, as our driver left us with our water and food in the plaza to return to Ixmiquilpan, I felt a bit of panic. Our only contact with civilization was leaving us, and we had no telephone. Our companions, Tony and Chonita, didn't seem bothered. Their smiles assured us that we would be okay.

Tony and Chonita led us to our casa at one side of the village square. It had two tiny rooms. Our "toilet" was the secluded hill behind our cottage where semi-wild pigs ran freely and cleaned up after us. I must have gotten used to it and the lack of electricity because I don't remember that part well. It's amazing how the young can adapt when they have to. I was in my early twenties.

The unpaved plaza was surrounded by a simple, white church, a school, and the government water tank. Below the church in a valley was the sandy water hole. Tony explained that before the government started trucking in clean, drinkable water daily, the villagers and the animals relied on its stagnating water for all their needs. Twice a year, rains usually filled up the water hole. When it dried out, the children sometimes came to school drunk because there was nothing else to drink except *pulque,* the sweet, fermented liquid from the maguey cactus. As a result, the children frequently fell asleep in class.

Tony told us that there was never enough water in the tank by the end of the day. Sometimes the water truck bounced so much on the stony roads that much of it splashed out of its uncovered top. We were not to use Xochitlan's trucked water supply. There was barely enough for the village.

"No worry. We have enough bottled water and food for five days," said Tony. "Just be careful, and don't use too much."

Because it wasn't "natural," as in "not from the sky," the villagers at first refused to use the cleaner, safer water, Tony said. They reconsidered after some of the village men caught and killed a robber trying to steal from the church. The man died near the water hole, and the villagers decided the death was a sign that they shouldn't use the traditional supply. It was contaminated by the blood of the robber.

We settled in. Tony asked us if he could enjoy his only luxury. He wanted to wash his feet with a few drops of the precious fluid before going to bed. We agreed. The rest of us decided to just brush off the dust every evening. He warned us to be sure to shake our shoes in the morning in case a scorpion decided to crawl into one during the night. A scorpion bite could kill or cause serious pain. Fortunately, that didn't happen.

Quakers believe in "that of God in everyone." They try to show respect for everybody and don't go into a problem situation and tell others what they should do. The first thing they ask is, "What do you want done? How can we help you do it?" And they listen to the answers. I liked that approach. The key word was "respect."

Xochitlan had a population of about 2,000. Its main crop was agave, which is also known as maguey—from which the alcoholic drink tequila is made. They also used maguey fiber for manufacturing rope, baskets, and mats. We rarely saw women without a spindle, their fingers constantly twisting the fiber as they walked. Spinning, cooking, and child care were women's work here. We had to accept that if we were to be of any assistance.

The Otomis wanted their church repaired. They agreed to supply one *finero* to help each *amigo*. A finero is a farmer who gives one day a week of his time to work for the community on projects like paving the roads or building a school. It was like a tax, only paid in labor, a system the Spanish introduced. The Otomis had little cash to pay taxes, but they had time, lots of it.

Repairing walls was men's work. Tony, and sometimes other male volunteers, spent their days fixing the walls of the church. Work proceeded very slowly. Sometimes the finero didn't show up, and Tony had no one to work with, so nothing was done.

We shared our cottage from time to time with a government seamstress / social worker / census taker named Chelo. A cheerful woman with a mass of curly, black hair, she spoke Spanish and some Otomi. She was *sympatica*, pleasant, and easy to get along with. We loved her.

Tony and Chonita were an item. She was shy, her face marked from smallpox. She was our major interpreter. Tony was a doer. He came from a midwestern farm family in the U.S. and was handy. He had a lot of basic skills like carpentry, and knew about cement and masonry. Doris had a Philadelphia accent; for example, she said "war-der" for "water." I loved to hear her speak. With her college major in Latin American studies, she taught us a lot of local history and culture. We were a compatible group.

At first, we women accompanied the Patrimonio's nurses to visit families. Xochitlan was a widespread community of tiny family farming plots and huts surrounding the central square. We had to hike along sandy and stony paths, up and down hills, and past long lines of maguey to get anywhere. Two miles (3.2 kilometers) north of our little house, we could see trucks and cars moving on the Pan-American highway, high above our valley. It was amazing to see the modern world so near and yet so far away.

The families lived in one-room huts made of wooden planks or stone. They were surrounded by fences of spindly bushes or stone or long, narrow cacti. The latter were like logs in Canadian pioneer houses but vertical and standing tall and alive. The Otomi used long, wide leaves for their roofs.

The government nurses visited occasionally and gave smallpox shots. They also dusted the people and houses with DDT; unfortunately, we didn't know anything about DDT's damage to wildlife, bees, birds, and even humans. That insecticide was the most effective one available then. Rachael Carson didn't publish her damning exposé in her famous book, *Silent Spring*, until 1962.

Most village deaths were from bronchial pneumonia, the nurses told us. Three or four a week occurred, mainly in winter with its cold nights. That's when the family and its animals huddled together for warmth close to an open fire and its smoke. They slept on the ground on mats. Infants and toddlers were burned if they fell into the fires. No one had a stove. Still, the Otomi seemed happy, apparently accepting whatever fate brought them.

The Otomi believed that their deaths, the vomiting, and their headaches were the result of evil spirits, damage to their church, and the inadequate performance of religious rituals. They also suffered from tuberculosis, which they believed was cured by blowing smoke from burning chilis into the face of the victim. Drinking a mixture of soap and urine was supposed to alleviate the pain of childbirth.

We wanted to show them we appreciated their customs, but we couldn't do that by telling them what to do. They had to make their own decisions. The Patrimonio had designed a simple waist-high stone stove that the women could use safely, out of reach of small children. It was Chelo who convinced one of the village leaders to let us build one for his family. They watched closely as we mixed cement and picked up nearby rocks. Tony showed us how to sculpt the rocks to fit.

The stove had one large central depression for the main cooking and smaller holes for other pots. It had a sideboard where the women could stand instead of kneel while grinding corn. A hole in the roof let out the smoke.

When our first stove was finished and in use, other Otomi women saw it and asked for one, too. Soon we were in the stove business. The women and children worked with us, carrying rocks from nearby hills and fields. Following Tony and the Patrimonio's instructions, we all learned basic masonry. We must have built at least two a week. I like to think that our stoves saved a few babies and toddlers from serious burns and women from bad backs. It was good to be doing something useful.

In return, the hospitable women shared what little food they had with us. Their tortillas were tasty and usually just off the fire, so they were fresh and warm. Sharing their food gave them an opportunity to do something for us in return. Although we ate as little as possible, we didn't refuse.

We also contributed to the school lunch program. Almost every morning at the school, I helped grind corn with a metal hand grinder to make tortillas. The Patrimonio's cook filled the pancakes with healthy black beans for the children. For some, this was the only nutritious meal they ate each day. For the government, it was a bribe so families would send their children to learn to read, add, and subtract. These were skills they needed to compete in the modern market.

The Otomi children didn't seem to mind working. The girls looked like they enjoyed carrying their younger siblings around on a hip. Many hauled water and knew how to spin, but girls as well as boys attended school. They were all shy with us at first, but gradually the girls came to our cottage to visit or just to look at our belongings. We had a bench to sit on, and we slept on cots in sleeping bags. They were especially curious about our socks since these didn't exist in their culture. No one had socks; some didn't even have shoes. Most wore Otomi-style clothes, obviously passed down from sibling to sibling. The girls wore long cotton skirts and loose white blouses decorated around the neck with red embroidery. I bought one and wore it for years back home in Canada.

We encouraged the children to play and taught them singing games. The school had only a skipping rope and a ball, and there were no toys in their homes. We didn't keep score. It was the game itself that was fun, not whether anyone won or lost. It was my first experience with non-competitive games, a Quaker tradition. Everybody won; nobody lost.

After about ten weeks, Tony and his workmates managed to finish a couple feet of wall on the church. We all cheered. I considered the guys in our camp as brothers and admired their dedication to the work. Some people consider conscientious objectors cowards, but they were not cowards. They worked hard in difficult circumstances and made friends, not enemies.

Toward the end of my stay, we introduced figs as a possible crop. I helped to plant some of the seedlings, but I left Xochitlan before the first crop appeared.

We assisted where we could. Whenever we were traveling in our truck and had room, we picked up everyone possible along with their goats and ropes. Most of the people in our valley were too poor to have a donkey or burro to carry their produce to market, and some had to walk at least ten hours on market day, there and back.

One day, Chelo, bless her, suggested we drive three children and their uncle to visit the children's mother, who had been hospitalized for three months in a nearby town with a broken leg. Why no one had taken the woman to the closer hospital in Ixmiquilpan was a mystery. Maybe her fracture was too complicated for that hospital to fix. I thought Chelo was wonderful because no one else had thought of finding out what had happened to the mother.

We scrubbed the children for the visit. Chelo made pants for the younger ones because they didn't have any, nor did they have shoes. The ten-year-old wore his torn hat, dirty white suit, and sandals. He would have been clean, too, if he had had something to wear while we washed his clothes.

We entered the hospital together, but the receptionist stopped us. "Do you have the doctor's permission?" We didn't. "Then you'll have to wait," he said.

We waited for five hours while other people went into the hospital. I was getting angry and impatient, but the boys were well behaved. They just sat there quietly. The receptionist could have let the children see their mother, and finally, he allowed them to go in, one by one.

The mother could speak no Spanish; people in the hospital spoke no Otomi. She was lonely and frightened. Her doctor reluctantly agreed to let us take her to the hospital in Ixmiquilpan, and we put her in the back of our truck on a stretcher. The Ixmiquilpan doctor discovered her leg was still broken. She had been three months in a hospital without treatment. We never found out why or what happened to her while she was there. We could think of no other reason for the neglect except for racial discrimination. No wonder the Otomis were afraid of hospitals and other Mexicans. We were glad to be able to help.

They were such sweet people, kind and generous in spite of, or perhaps because of, their poverty. And they appeared happy, frequently smiling and accepting us as friends, although we were so different. We had fun dancing at their festivals, their fiestas. At times, I wondered why we were trying to change them.

In Ximiquilpan, we visited the market for our food. It was full of locally hand-made clothes, pottery, and baskets. The Otomi section of the market offered lower prices. I learned the fun of haggling, not paying the first price the vendors asked. Vendors always quoted a higher price than they knew the buyer was willing to pay because they knew people would try to haggle. This was the practice in Mexico, and I found out later it was the same in markets all over the world.

Doris pointed out how haggling was not fair to illiterate peasants who didn't know basic arithmetic. So, if we bought something from an Otomi vendor, we paid the asking price. I was glad their children were in school, so they could learn skills to help.

On weekends, we went sightseeing in neighboring towns. We saw very fancy churches with gold statues of Madre Maria and finely carved wooden saints. Compared to Canada, the parishioners were not wealthy, but obviously, they felt it important to decorate their churches lavishly in an attempt to appease their gods; I wondered why they couldn't spend money helping the poor, instead.

One weekend, many of us squeezed into our two pickups with sleeping bags and air mattresses and camped. We slept on the beach in Vera Cruz and swam in the lovely warm waters of the Gulf of Mexico. We climbed three-thousand-year-old pyramids and visited the city of Guanajuato to see one-hundred-year-old naturally mummified bodies of adults and children in a tunnel under the cemetery. A sign above them announced, "Once they were like us, and someday we will be like them." It was a gruesome reminder of our mortality. It was good that we were seeing different sides of the country. Mexico was more than our poverty-stricken valley.

The Quakers certainly didn't accept the religion of the Otomi people, but they appreciated their simple faith and their quest for a relationship with a higher power. I was very pleased that we were working to fix a Catholic church. Our village church in Xochitlan was a mixture of the old indigenous religion and Spanish Catholicism, a fusion of their old beliefs with the religion of the conquerors. A cross crowned its dome, but among the statues of the holy family, human skulls decorated its altars. The priest from

Ixmiquilpan arrived on Sunday to celebrate mass, and the ritual included bowing to the north, south, east, and west.

We were especially delighted when one of our Roman Catholic volunteers returned from Sunday mass to report that the priest in Ixmiquilpan had admonished his flock that day saying "Look at the Amigos. They treat the Indigenous people with respect. You should, too." The presence of a foreign religion did not threaten this priest. In fact, he supported us and our work with the Otomi. Wow! Maybe Quakerism was the religion I was looking for.

I was also pleased with our Sunday meditation, which we didn't have to join if we didn't want to. It was primarily a quiet time during which anyone could give a few words of insight. It was ideal for our interfaith group. I liked our never-ending search for spiritual direction and how we sought consensus rather than a majority vote when making decisions. After each person spoke at our business meetings, we would have some silence to absorb their position and not react to it. No one was overruled.

Although I don't think Quakerism is for everybody, I began to feel at home with Quaker practices. I believe that everybody should search for what is meaningful for themselves. We each have a unique path to follow.

After a little over four months, the dust from our weekly trips to the village gave me such a sore throat that I had to go to Mexico City to see a doctor. I was ready for a break. I stayed at the Casa de los Amigos in the capital where everyone was very hospitable. A young couple invited me to their wedding, and I saw my first Mexican dance theater with its flamboyant Aztec costumes and giant headdresses. A handsome young Quaker took me sightseeing on the back of his motorcycle, but I already had tickets onward to Brazil, so I didn't linger.

I really liked belonging to the workcamp community. We shared almost everything, talked, and listened to each other. Since I left the Presbyterians, I had not found any spiritual group to join and, in the strangeness of a new city, it felt good to be with people who thought like I did. In addition, no one in the workcamp group made me feel different because I was Chinese. I realized that Mexico wasn't just a land of *siestas* and *mariachi* bands. The Mexican government was trying to improve the living conditions of its people, and nongovernmental organizations (NGOs) like ours and ordinary people like me could help.

On the train south to the border, as we passed people in their distinctive ethnic dress, I kept thinking that people like the Otomis were the ones who would inherit the earth because they knew how to make a living from it. Warmongers would probably destroy it.

After a stop to visit a Quaker group in El Salvador and in Bolivia, I flew to Sao Paulo in Brazil, with an overnight stop in La Paz. There I looked for a Canadian missionary whose name someone had given me. Mary Beard's only address turned out to be a post office box. I found her just by asking someone on the street for a Canadian, and Mary invited me to spend the night at her place. It was my first experience with altitude; La Paz ranges between 10,650 and 13,250 feet (3,250 and 4,100 meters above sea level). Climbing up the hills was a struggle.

The Brazilian workcamp experience was not as profound as the one I had in Mexico. It had participants, mainly from Latin America, but also from Europe. It was fun. We built a one-room conference center together, spending hours on making a thatched roof while laughing and singing. If I ever find myself marooned on a desert island, I think I could make a hut out of stone with a decent roof to keep dry, as well as a stone stove. I was picking up more essential life skills.

Switching from Spanish to Portuguese was relatively easy. Spanish-speakers considered the Portuguese language as badly-spoken Spanish. After the one-month workcamp, a couple of Brazilians invited me to stay with them in Rio de Janeiro. One was a lady who had an apartment on Copacabana Beach. It was thrilling to find myself on that famous beach, but it was winter and too cold to swim. The other invitation came from the daughter of an Armenian Orthodox priest who invited me to stay as long as I wanted in their home.

I spent much time praying that God would lead me onto my next step. I had little money left. One day, I had a vision of a strange elderly man in a robe telling me to "write your book." I had the presence of mind to ask him to say it again, and he repeated, "Write your book." He seemed to be vaguely Middle Eastern and from a different dimension. I could see him clearly, but somehow I knew he wasn't really in my world, and I was too bewildered to study him. It was the only vision I have ever received so far in my life, if indeed it was a vision. I had no thoughts of writing a book at the time.

Lots of people have visions. Maybe I was in a dream state or a temporary psychosis. Maybe he was a messenger from God. I was awake, and I hadn't been taking any drugs at all.

When my Armenian friend asked how much longer I would be staying, I knew it was time to move on. I cabled Mom. If she wanted me home, please send money. Fortunately, she did, and I took a freighter north to Tampa, Florida. In those days, freighters were small compared to today's gigantic container ships. It was the cheapest fare I could find, and I was the only passenger. I ate in the same dining room as the officers and was seasick for most of the way. From Tampa, I rode public buses back to Brockville. My sisters teased me mercilessly about my lack of foresight and the one-way ticket, but for me, it was a spiritual test. I wanted to follow the leadings of the Spirit. My mother's response meant I was destined to return to Canada. I was relieved that she wanted me home.

Back that first night in our apartment in Brockville, I sat, drinking a glass of milk, exhausted from the long trip, which had taken about a week, including a stop in Bahia to pick up some freight. After a series of tiresome buses from Tampa to Brockville, I found myself trying to get rid of the vibrations from the long rides. My brother's friend, Mikey Lynch, was about ten then, and he was sitting across from me at our kitchen table. Mikey, an especially mischievous kid, was bouncing a rubber ball on the table. I asked him politely to stop, but he kept on bouncing. The noise was annoying and added to my fatigue. I asked him again, and he refused to stop. Then I threatened him with the milk.

When he tested my threat with another infuriating bounce, I threw the milk in his face. He looked bewildered, and he stopped.

Then he laughed. It was obvious I hadn't learned much from my nonviolent friends. After I threw the milk at Mikey, I felt elated. I had won that conflict, or so I thought then.

Years later, when we met again as adults, Mikey said how surprised he had been at the time. He assured me he wouldn't charge me with assault and said he forgave me. He had become a lawyer and a Crown attorney, and knew the law by then. He could have charged me. At the time, I didn't think it was serious enough to apologize. I knew I had to work on my temper.

Fifty-two years later, I went back to Xochitlan with my husband and daughter. What a change! The road and streets were paved, and there was electricity. A very deep well under the old water tank was supplying the village with clean water. Education had become important. The village had three schools, and students were wearing uniforms, shoes, and socks. We found a boy wearing a T-shirt with "Otomi" in large letters on the front. He was obviously proud of his heritage. As we walked around the village, we asked people if they had stone stoves. A couple of homes still had them in use "because gas is too expensive," and they also had refrigerators.

We found a lot of fig trees, irrigated by wastewater from Mexico City. In our early days, there had been no fruit trees at all. Now trucks were full of figs for sale in the Ixmiquilpan market, and I was thrilled because the figs could have been from our trees. I felt like any proud mother.

The old water hole was now a soccer field. So much water was now available in the area from digging deep wells that three huge water parks had been built near Xochitlan with the largest swimming pools I've ever seen. No one we spoke with was old enough to remember Los Amigos. It didn't matter; I saw the changes. It was a very satisfying feeling.

We learned that the Otomis were no longer afraid to leave their valley. Many had migrated to Florida, sending money back to their families. Later, I even met an Otomi worker from Ixmiquilpan at a vineyard near Niagara Falls. Without migrant workers such as the Mexicans, we would not be able to grow much food in North America. For them, it was another step upward to equality, but they still had a long way to go. When COVID-19 hit us in 2020, migrant workers were among the most vulnerable to the disease. They lived in crowded quarters, and they could not change employers. Some were in the country without papers and others were afraid they would lose their jobs and immigration status if they complained. Many caught COVID-19, and they needed help, but I was not in a position to do anything except petition the government.

I benefited a lot spiritually from those months in Latin America. Back in Toronto, I started going to Quaker meetings for worship and appreciated their quiet waiting on God. Their focus on silence helped relax me. Their contacts around the world figured in many of my later travels as I searched for other ways to be useful. In addition, my articles in the Brockville newspaper were the beginning of a professional travel-writing career. Mom had saved all the clippings.

Today, I am ashamed to say that Canada still does not have clean drinking water in a couple dozen Indigenous communities. Mexico in 1955 was way ahead of us.

Chapter 6:
Toronto and Canadian Arctic, 1957

Back in Toronto, I looked for a job to pay Mom back. Years later, I felt guilty when brother Joe said the restaurant was going through financial difficulties at the time, but I doubt my getting involved would have helped. The trip home cost less than $200.

Sandy Runciman paid his promised five dollars per article for my five or six stories about the workcamp. Mom showed them to her customers. I felt proud, seeing my stories and pictures in print. I was very modest then. I didn't take any pictures of myself in Mexico because I didn't think I was important enough, so I don't have pictures of myself there.

I started to save for another trip, hopefully to China. I had no idea my next journey would be in a completely different direction. Jobs were easy to get then, and I answered an advertisement in a Toronto newspaper for a social worker with a knowledge of Portuguese. It was for organizing a program teaching English to immigrants, and I wanted to work directly with people. As for Portuguese, well, why not? I had picked up a few words of the language in Brazil. During my college days, Uncle Henry had persuaded me to teach basic English to some Chinese immigrants. That gave me some experience but no actual teacher training.

St. Christopher House must have been desperate. I didn't need to use the one phrase of Portuguese I had practiced for the interview, and I got the job easily. It was exactly what I wanted to do. The students were recently arrived Portuguese from the Azores and Madeira. We also had Italian students, many from Sicily. Almost all of the students were men.

Arranging classes taught by a dozen English-speaking volunteers, mainly women, was not overly difficult. It wasn't always easy because teachers might get sick, and I had to find substitutes at the last minute. I was also in charge of the Wednesday evening after-class social dances, which required finding someone to play the music. We wanted to make it fun, and usually it was; unfortunately, we had more students than women teachers, so I found myself breaking up fights between the Portuguese and the Italians over the few dancing partners. My years of experience ordering people around as a hostess in the restaurant turned out to be good training. The guys were used to authority. All I needed was a simple, "What seems to be the problem?" or, "If you are going to fight, please do it outside." I don't think they ever had a real fight, either indoors or outdoors. We never had to call the police, and, aside from that, we all had a good time. I learned to dance the tarantella.

The position also required me to supervise the settlement house's senior program. About ten seniors met a couple afternoons a week. I made sure we had ping pong balls and paddles and cards for bridge. I learned to play cribbage and got to know our clients well. I went to the funeral of one of my favorites, an elderly man who said people at St. Christopher's were his only friends. He didn't have contact with his own family, so I didn't expect to see any of them at the service, but a handful of his relatives showed up and eulogized him. He inspired one of my few poems; it was about the neglect of the elderly. It started with, "I hear you laughing." I knew he would think it funny that his relatives had gone through the motions of talking about what a wonderful person he was.

My home was a tiny bedroom at St. Christopher's. It was all I needed, and it didn't cost much. Eating with the staff and any other regulars who happened to be around was always amusing and interesting. They were a very diverse group of gay, Black, and white people. Alas, the job was only for a year.

Then I worked at a YWCA with "pre-delinquent girls." We managed to get a group to meet together weekly for a couple projects that included organizing a neighborhood party with their friends. Unfortunately, our "no smoking, no drinking" rules, which our young group agreed to, meant that none of their friends came. We had to learn to make compromises with the culture of the group we were trying to help. That job only lasted one season.

The Student Christian Movement and its concern about factory workers was still on my list of things to experience. That meant a month operating an industrial-grade sewing machine in a garment factory on King Street in Toronto. I knew how to use my mother's sewing machine, so I had no problem keeping up. Sewing was one of the few jobs that immigrant women with little or no English could do, and I wanted to get to know some of them. We were a mix of Asians and Europeans. I found out how badly they were paid and made some factory friends; one of them even invited me to her home for dinner. I felt accepted.

I still felt driven to learn about everything through direct, personal experience. I lived in a variety of places after St. Christopher House, including almost a year with Lewis and Marie Perinbam. I needed a cheap place to stay and preferred to live with people of different ethnic backgrounds. Torontonians generally were very boring then, and some of them even called themselves WASPs (white, Anglo-Saxon Protestants). But Lewis was head of the World University Service of Canada at the time, and he later became director of several international development organizations. He was born in Malaya (now Malaysia), of Indian ancestry, and was educated in Scotland. Marie was a scholar of mixed racial background from Jamaica. She was beautiful, elegant, and a fantastic cook. I was lucky to be invited to an occasional Indian meal. I still remember a lecture on Asia that Lewis gave about the cultural diversity of that continent, how every country there had several unique minorities. Their conversations were always stimulating, but then they bought a house without a spare room to rent. I needed another place to live, and Lewis introduced me to Danièle Marx.

Danièle was a Jewish student from France, who had been a refugee because of the Nazis. She was happy to share my bedroom with communal bath and tiny kitchen near the university. She taught me how to choose perfectly ripened cheeses and shared her distaste for what she considered was the arrogant behavior of French tourists traveling abroad.

At the time, she was being courted by a charming Frenchman, Michel Gervais, who was studying in Michigan. They later married, and Danièle went on to become a journalist in France. She wrote a book later called *La ligne de démarcation* about her childhood hiding from the Nazis, having to use a fake name and identity. It must have been difficult living in fear and pretending to be someone else. We are still good friends, and they have a bed for me whenever I manage to get to Paris.

About this time, I experienced the kind of love known as *eros*. I learned how it felt to walk on clouds, to be breathless upon hearing his voice, and to fall to the ground when he decided to choose someone else over me. I was fortunate because he turned out to be an alcoholic. Choosing a partner primarily based on attraction is not always wise.

Attending Quaker meetings became a regular practice. I felt at home with its silent meetings for worship every Sunday, and I especially felt welcomed by a friendly couple, Leroy and Pearl Jones. Leroy's roots had been in Gambia in Africa; his ancestors had been slaves, and he was working as a personnel officer for the Ontario government. Pearl had come from a family of "fighting Irish," although her gentle demeanor gave no indication of it. They had met as neighbors in Toronto, and they made me feel right at home.

The office of the Canadian Friends Service Committee, the Canadian arm of the group that sponsored the Mexican camp, offered me a job. I loved it. In its small, three-person office, I did some basic bookkeeping, reports on its programs, and answered mail. I worked with some exceptional Quaker bosses—Fred Haslam and Cecil Evans. Like the Chapins in our Mexican workcamp, they were sensitive, caring people. They always listened carefully to what people had to say, and they could be very funny.

Concerned about Indigenous peoples in Canada because of my Mexican experience, I wrote a report encouraging Quakers across Canada to see if there was anything we could do to help. Not many mainstream Canadians cared in those days. Some of the churches were operating residential schools where the children would learn how to be like other Canadians. We didn't know then that the schools were trying to destroy Indigenous cultures by punishing children who spoke their native language. They wanted to "take the native culture out of the child" while they taught them English and skills they needed to "survive outside" their communities. This colonial attitude was very strong. We didn't know then that some of the children were sexually abused and some had died and were buried in unmarked graves near the schools.

Canadian Quakers didn't have the resources to do anything like workcamps on Indigenous reserves. There were only about 700 Quakers scattered across the country at that time, but somehow, a workcamp with Indigenous people was in my future.

It was the McCarthy era in the U.S., and Canadians were also caught up in the fear of Communism. I still wanted to go to China and heard about a free YMCA trip. An RCMP officer came to my little bedroom to talk about my application. His interview ended with, "We didn't think you were a Communist." I laughed after he left. I didn't know enough about Communism to make a decision like that. Unfortunately, I wasn't chosen for the group.

I did not have the money to go to China for several more years. Visas were not easy to obtain, yet somehow, China became the country I knew I had to visit someday. I had a lot of questions, many of them to do with my own identity.

Connections are so important. I happened to be talking with an Irish-Canadian named Andy Thompson about a possible job with immigrants. He was working in the multicultural affairs section of a federal government office, was interested in my Mexican experience, and put me in touch with one of his friends. The Department of Northern Affairs was hoping to send a group of young people from southern Canada to Frobisher Bay (now called Iqaluit) in the Arctic's Baffin Island for the summer. Soon, I was helping to organize a workcamp as a volunteer, delighted to use my Mexican experience for another interesting and useful adventure.

Frobisher Bay was a U.S. Air Force refueling station for the DEW line, the Distant Early Warning system. The station had been designed to alert the U.S. of an imminent Soviet air attack arriving by way of the North Pole. This was during the Cold War, and, so far, there had been no actual invasion. It was not really within the Arctic Circle, but it was in treeless tundra, considered Arctic, and home to Inuit in Canada.

The Canadian government was having a hard time recruiting Canadians from the south to work in the Arctic. For thousands of years, the Inuit people who lived there had been nomads, making a living hunting and fishing. The government needed people with skills like engineering, construction, mining, and tourism. It was hoping to encourage us southerners to make careers there, and it was trying to move the Inuit to settlements. It needed workers to develop its north and establish Canadian sovereignty there.

The government was discovering that the Inuit had the highest rate of tuberculosis in the world. Newcomers like whalers had accidentally introduced the bacteria that caused the disease, just like the Spanish who had brought the smallpox virus to Mexico. The Inuit had no immunity to TB. During our pre-trip briefing in Ottawa, Northern Affairs officers told us that 15 percent of the Inuit population were infected. Crowded living conditions, poor nutrition, and the very severe winter climate helped spread it. The government had to do something about that, too. The only place TB could be treated was in sanitariums in southern Canada. A hospital in the Arctic was not opened for another five years.

And how could Inuit who had recovered make a living? They couldn't continue their strenuous nomadic lifestyle with one lung. Government officials decided there should be a rehabilitation center where the survivors could learn new money-making skills like operating a laundromat or a bake shop or organizing hunting trips for tourists. They thought about encouraging old skills like stone and ivory carving that were beginning to have a market in southern Canada. The center was to be based near Frobisher, and they needed help because there was both a labor shortage and a tight time limit. Work could only be done in the two or three months of summer.

I invited the Canadian Council of Churches (CCC) to cosponsor the project with the government's Department of Northern Affairs (DNA). We recruited twelve eager young people through CCC's member churches and the Student Christian Movement. I helped with the selection and included myself as one of the leaders. The government would pay for our flights north and back, plus our room, board, and expenses for eight weeks. We were cheaper than hiring professional laborers. We considered ourselves fortunate.

Luckily for me, an editor of a Toronto newspaper, *The Globe and Mail*, heard that I was going. Since few people from southern Canada went to the Arctic in those days, even in the summer, they asked me for a series of articles with photos about our unusual experience. My writing career was back on track. James Lee, a friend, lent me a movie camera I could use, too. It wasn't China, but that didn't matter. It was an opportunity to learn about another culture and to help people in need. Very shortly, we were to become aware of another example of racial discrimination.

Each summer, medical people sailed to the north on a ship called the *C.D. Howe* to test people for tuberculosis. Because it was extremely contagious, those Inuit found to be infected were kept on the ship, which then continued on its way to other northern settlements and eventually back south. Sick people could not even say goodbye to their families. Although no government official would use the word, the sick were, in effect, kidnapped. We novices to the Arctic didn't know then that many Inuit people did not see their families again. If the patients died, they were buried in southern Canada, some in unmarked graves.

In the summer of 1957, a dozen of us university students and graduates flew to Frobisher Bay. Our home was in a little village called Apex, three miles (five kilometers) by road from the air base. It had started as a Hudson Bay trading post in 1943, and by the time of our arrival, Apex had at least forty almost identical prefabricated "512" houses—named that because of their square footage. Apex also had a couple of big buildings and about a dozen canvas tents. On our first evening, we were surprised to find ourselves in one of the big buildings where a hundred Inuit were dancing Irish reels with grand chains and do-si-dos. Two women squeezed happy music out of tiny accordions. I suspected that whalers had introduced these dances a hundred years ago.

We joined the dances and had fun. Many women stood watching us. They were wearing white summer parkas, traditionally designed with tail pieces and big hoods for carrying babies. I expected furs, but they were wearing clothes made of Hudson Bay blanket cloth or light cotton and sweaters. Little children chased each other dangerously close to the heels of the dancers. We were surprised to see a handsome, young Inuk man wearing a western-style business suit. His name was Simonee, and he had represented Canada's Inuit at the coronation of Queen Elizabeth II in England a couple of years before.

That first evening immediately destroyed my image of isolated nomads and erased any thoughts of sick Inuits. The dances continued for ninety minutes without stopping. It appeared to be a competition to see who would give up first. They had more energy than we did. When we finally found our beds, the sun was still shining. It never set while we were there, and we had to get used to sleeping in daylight and hearing children play long after midnight.

We were put to work the next day. The resident Northern Service Officer assigned one of our women to scrub cupboards, change beds, and take temperatures in the nursing station. Another volunteer was asked to organize and serve food in the canteen. Two of our men worked with half a dozen Inuit, fixing the roads and later building a new wharf. They reported that their fellow workers were just as curious about us as we were about them.

Between jobs, our guys tried to learn Inuktitut. Somehow, they managed to discuss such things as how much money our Frank had when he was married. We discovered that they gave us all nicknames. Mine was something like "Square Head" because of the shape of my hair style. We learned Inuit sign language: raised eyebrows meant "yes" and a wrinkled-up nose meant "no."

Some of us women worked with four Inuit men, painting the exterior of new prefabricated houses that would be used for the rehabilitation center. I learned that mosquitoes had color preferences. They landed on our wet, turquoise-colored paint and stayed stuck there; they avoided khaki and black. At times, the work was hard, but we got used to it and actually enjoyed both it and working together.

Miriam, one of our volunteers, was a home economics major. She was teaching twelve teenage girls how to use a sewing machine and a washing machine. She didn't have to demonstrate stitching by hand; they were already proficient at that.

At the end of our first week, one of us, Ruth Pheeney, had a birthday. We decided to celebrate by inviting a few Inuit we had gotten to know, so we could have two dance squares. We ended up with the two accordionists, and, at one point, I counted at least one hundred people dancing reels. We didn't have enough cake or drinks to feed them all, but it was hilarious fun.

After work each day, our little group had Bible study and discussions. We were not there to convert anyone. We spent hours talking among ourselves about the future of the Arctic and the lifestyle of some of the government people from southern Canada who worked there. Were they idealists, wanting to help, or was it the only well-paying job they could get? We objected to the many *Qallunaat* (non-Inuit) spending their evenings getting drunk and encouraging the Inuit to do the same. We learned about permafrost and why Apex's houses were built on stilts. If the houses were set directly on the ground, the heat from the buildings would melt the layer of ice below, and ultimately, the whole structure would collapse. Years later, I learned that melting permafrost would have more dire consequences than that.

We discovered that the government identified the Inuits by numbers, not names. Many of them only had one name. I don't remember any discussion about the government sending the children off to residential schools run by churches elsewhere. We

71

probably accepted that as necessary and were not aware how poorly they were treated there. Apex was full of school-aged children on vacation.

We had heard about elderly Inuit abandoned on ice floes to die when there wasn't enough food. Some of us decided that such a death was actually relatively peaceful, quick, painless, and preferable to prolonged confinements in southern hospitals. We met only one person there who had been treated in a sanitarium. Although our group was not always happy about the way the government was helping, we agreed that it was to be commended for its efforts to stamp out the disease.

Working together provided opportunities to make friends with the Inuit. It was difficult because few of them spoke English. We organized a field day for the children, and some of the campers played ball with them every evening. They were much easier to get to know than the adults. One of them, Paloosee, followed us around constantly. He would choose one Qallunaat and perfectly mimic every move, like a swagger or a wave of a hand. He was so amusing.

The hills around Apex were inviting to hikers because the thick moss and lichens made the rocky hillsides a delight to walk on. The air was pristine; however, mosquitoes discouraged much hiking, but armed with insect repellent and mosquito-net hats, we did venture forth. I especially enjoyed the lovely turquoise blue that seemed to be painted on the ice floes in the bay; silt from the seabed created that beautiful color.

A couple of our guys wanted to spend the night on the tundra and tried to load their gear on one of the dogs. Although one of their native friends helped them, the dog wouldn't move, and they had to give up. This was good for a laugh, but we had to be careful around the huskies. They were usually tied up and could attack us if freed.

Even walks around town were interesting. The tides rose and fell about forty feet twice a day. Once when the tide was high, we saw Simonee in a small boat, waving an oar and yelling. He was chasing fish into gill nets and managed to catch some Arctic char without falling into the water. I don't think he could have done that in a kayak. We never saw a kayak, the famous skin boat invented by the Inuit, because they preferred metal boats with outboard motors.

The Anglican minister, Reverend Corness, took two of us to the tent of his catechist. We felt uncomfortable not being able to say much beyond "Hello." The family didn't seem to mind. They knew us, and we could at least laugh together. One gave us a piece of raw seal to try. It tasted fishy, like seaweed, its texture like that of raw oyster, and wasn't unpleasant. I took some seal back to the others to try. One wondered about worms. The next day I didn't feel well, and the strong taste of seal lingered in my mouth for a couple more days, but I never did get worms. I don't remember any of us getting sick in the Arctic.

One day, I went with the government nurse, Sherle, to visit a sick woman in a camp twenty-five miles (forty kilometers) south by boat. I was thrilled by the opportunity to visit a genuine hunter-gatherer camp with people who lived off the land. Sherle was from Winnipeg. An Inuk ran the outboard motor for her while another stood precariously balanced on the bow of our small boat. He was looking for seals and shot at them when their heads appeared above the surface of the water. At first, I was nervous because we had been warned that the water was so cold we would only survive in it for a few minutes. No one else in the boat appeared worried, so I relaxed and enjoyed the beautiful ice floes and high, rocky coastline. I searched for seals, too. They were a large part of the Inuit diet, along with fish, caribou, and whale.

I learned about the dangerous curiosity of seals that day, too. Each time Tikavik shot at a seal, the animal would disappear under water, only to emerge to look for the source of the noise. The men tried to anticipate where the seal would surface and managed to kill two of the thirty inquisitive creatures that we saw.

The patient lived in a camp consisting of four canvas tents, their occupants, and an impressive number of tethered, barking dogs. It was set close to the water, mounted on rock, and sheltered by hills. The weather was too warm for igloos (snow huts).

We entered her tent. It had a dirt floor with a sleeping platform at one end; seal skins, raw fish, and dead seals lined the other; store-bought food, cooking utensils, and a Primus camp stove lined another. The family was not completely self-sufficient because it had amenities from the outside world. What did I expect? Whale-oil lamps? These people had been trading furs for Primus stoves and outboard motors for years. Tikavik interpreted for Sherle while she treated the woman.

The two men helped themselves to the pot of cooked clams by the door. Sherle invited me to have some. I hesitated and waited for an invitation from our sick hostess, but it never came. Sherle said that it was customary to help oneself to any available food. Everybody shared. Not being able to resist any longer, I joined the men. The clams were delicious, and the woman beamed when I thanked her.

This woman's world was amazing. We had seen no other camps, no other humans, since we left Apex. She was totally alone with no one nearby to help if a polar bear or anything else threatened her. Her husband had traveled to Apex to alert Sherle that she was sick. I admired her bravery, her faith in the white man's medicine, and in the isolated world that fed and clothed her. The Inuit people had survived that way for centuries.

Tikavik took two of our guys out several days later, and they brought back one seal, a dozen eider ducks, and a six-foot baby whale. They thrilled us with a tale of their two-hour whale chase, an experience that rich tourists in the future would pay thousands of dollars to experience. We watched squeamishly while children eagerly ate the raw eyes of the whale, a delicacy.

For the newspaper, I took a lot of pictures of our volunteers and the people in Apex but only one of me. I never saw an Inuk with a camera. These people had to carry all their belongings, ready to move at a moment's notice. Cameras were not an essential tool for living, and the Arctic had nowhere to process film into pictures.

Eight weeks went by too quickly. As our plane lifted up from the airbase, I wondered if it had only been a wonderful, adventurous vacation. Did we really achieve anything? Then one of the volunteers passed around a letter that someone handed to him just before we left.

> You have left behind a something which will last through all the years ahead, a thing which has not been strong in this community, and that is the idea of working hard to help some worthwhile project, with no consideration given to oneself. I am glad that . . . you have made us less selfish, and have helped us forget our own personal interests. . . . Because I like the north, and what I saw of you was good for it, I want to warmly thank you for the pleasant time you spent with us."

A lump came to my throat as I read it, and from then on, I clung to the hope that we had done something more than paint houses, fix roads, and teach some girls to sew on a machine.

After the strong, treeless landscape of the Arctic, it took a couple of weeks for me to get used to seeing trees again back in Toronto. They looked so flimsy. I took an anthropology course at the university about the Inuit and learned about their myths and their art. Their hunting skills were amazing; for example, they would put blood on the blade of a knife and stick it, blade up, in the snow. When wolves licked the knives, they would cut their own tongues and bleed to death. In the winter, an Inuk might wait outside an air hole in the ice for as long as twelve hours ready to spear a seal. They were resourceful wilderness survivors. Would they be able to adapt to the changes?

Alas, I lost touch with most of the members of our workcamp group. I never heard that any of them ever went back up north to work. I did try hard to find them, later posting the video we shot there onto YouTube with the title "Iqaluit Summer 1957." But then China became the focus of my life, and I was able to find aboriginal groups there, too.

In 2011, more than fifty years later, my husband and I spent five days in Iqaluit. We found a town of about seven thousand people. Iqaluit had become the capital of Nunavut territory in 1999 and was full of government offices, supermarkets, apartment buildings, a museum, a few schools, and a college. About 61 percent of the people were Inuit, many working for the government. Other residents were from elsewhere in the world.

The taxi drivers all seemed to be from the Middle East. My curious husband asked them how they timed their fasting during Ramadan. Would they starve because the sun never set during the Arctic summer? No, said a couple of drivers, "We take sunset time from a city in the south and base our fasting times on that." Five years later, the Muslims built a mosque in Iqaluit.

Apex was still there, not much bigger than before. It still had a few of the old prefabricated houses, plus some bigger ones. I couldn't find any of the houses we had painted or stayed in. I suspected they had been repainted several times since in different colors. Many houses had been moved closer to the airport where they could be more easily serviced with drinking water and garbage disposal. A store selling expensive fur garments was in the old nursing station. There was a stone monument to the Inuit who went south and died.

I took a report about our workcamp and gave it to the museum because we had been part of the area's history. The museum had a fine collection of Inuit art. We stayed in a comfortable hotel that had a swimming pool and a movie theater. The hotel and goods in the supermarkets, like disposable diapers and canned peaches, were extremely expensive because food and construction materials still had to be flown in or brought in by ship. Disposable diapers cost seventy-five dollars a box, and I hoped the Inuit were still using traditional moss or rabbit skin for their babies. We heard of attempts to grow vegetables in green houses. A few dogs were still around. Snowmobiles had largely replaced them.

Our visit was during July 1st, Canada Day. I looked for signs of the old culture during the four-day arts festival. Artists demonstrated stone carving. We watched a fierce tug-of-war like those we competed in during our workcamp days, but we saw no traditional Inuit blanket tossing that I had read about. "You can see those on July 9 during Nunavut Day," the mayor said when we asked her. In the museum, there was a free workshop on throat singing, a competitive Inuit game. Mathew Nuqingaq danced a story about the

Inuit with tuberculosis who had to go south to Hamilton, Ontario, to be treated or die. It was good to see that the culture was not lost.

I found it inspiring that both the mayor and the premier of Nunavut, whom we also met, were both women. Rock music and jazz, face painting, and a parade with screaming ambulances and fire trucks, their lights flashing, all had southern origins, as did the platoon of eight, red-coated RCMP officers marching with military precision. A car topped by a giant plastic fish and a truckload of waving children distributed maple leaf flags. The parade terminated with a feast of free hot dogs, chili, and then square dancing. The city was a cultural hybrid.

We saw Iqaluit's modern hospital. The sick didn't have to go south anymore. We learned that between 1958 and 1962, more than twelve hundred Inuit received treatment in southern Canada. Newspaper and government reports stated that tuberculosis was erased in the 1950s and '60s, but it had returned because of a poor diet and substance abuse.

In 1983, the European Union reacted to French actress Bridget Bardot's campaign against clubbing cute baby seals to death for their white, fluffy fur in the Gulf of St. Lawrence. It banned the importation of all seal products, including those from the Arctic. Inuit hunters lost a large source of the income they needed to continue even a token of their traditional hunter-gatherer lifestyle while they adapted to life in a settlement. They didn't have much left of their age-old culture except stone carving and work as hunting guides. Many were on welfare and worked for the government or the iron mines. The traditional Inuit way of life was almost all gone. The European Union boycott of seal products by Inuit hunters was stopped in 2015, but it was too late to revive a market for it.

One of the most satisfying aspects of our trip was taking some of my 1957 photograph collection to the Elders Center near the museum. About eight elderly women were enjoying a lunch there that day. I just walked into the building and asked if I could join them and was immediately welcomed with nods. No one was curious about me.

One of the elders was using an *ulu*, the old style knife used by women for cutting meat and stripping furs. The utensil out of the past made me think of the old legend of the elderly left to die on an ice floe when food was no longer available. I was glad these older women could live out their lives in more comfort now, in the company of friends.

The women looked at my pictures, and one of them, Martha Kilabok, said in English, "That's my sister. She's dead now. I never got a picture of her." Being able to give her the photo remains one of the highlights of my life. It was a very small gesture, and it added a little more satisfaction to the little our workcamp had done there.

By then, I was feeling called to work elsewhere. The Inuit and the Arctic were added to my list of urgent world-wide problems—when I had time.

In March 2019, Canada's Prime Minister Justin Trudeau went to Iqaluit and apologized to the Inuit for the forced relocations, the tuberculosis policy, and the residential schools. "The racism and discrimination that the Inuit faced, was, and always will be, unacceptable," he said. At the same time, Trudeau announced the beginning of the Nanilavut Initiative, a database designed to help Inuit find the graves of family members in southern Canada. The government also promised funds for relatives to travel south to visit these graves. It was a step in acknowledging racial discrimination and making amends.

Then scientists began to warn us that global warming in the Arctic was happening twice as fast as elsewhere. With higher temperatures, the ice cover was melting and not reflecting back the sun's rays. The defrosted land was collapsing and releasing more greenhouse gases than expected. Wildlife was suffering; polar bears no longer had ice on which to hunt. Sea levels were rising, and wildfires were increasing. Permafrost was disappearing, and some buildings were collapsing. People in the "civilized" south were destroying the traditional habitat and way of life even more. The Inuit, especially the young, have the highest suicide rate in the world. Much more than a government apology is needed now, and I could only hope that others would be led to respond to that challenge, as well as global warming.

A couple years after our first Iqaluit visit in 1957, our father died, sadly by suicide. His death was almost a relief. As we were growing up, he frightened us frequently by threatening to kill himself. It was a shock when he finally succeeded with a legally-registered gun that he kept in his basement office for protection. It was a gun he also used to scare away evil spirits, welcome the New Year, and alert our ancestors at the cemetery during the annual Ching Ming Grave Decorating Festival.

The restaurant was deeply in debt. My working in the restaurant wouldn't have helped. My siblings were there without me. I felt rootless and wrote a poem.

> I feel
>
> Like a leaf
>
> Caught on the edge of a wind,
>
> Sailing along with no will of its own except to try
>
> Vainly, insanely
>
> To cling—
>
> Here to a bush,
>
> There to a fence,
>
> But only for the lifetime of a breeze on a hot, sticky night—
>
> Moving, ever moving
>
> Unable to protest
>
> Against the force that sends it
>
> Whirling and swirling,
>
> Spinning and falling,
>
> Leaping from the earth
>
> Like a quail flushed by a hound.

Being at a juncture in my life, I decided I needed a profession, some actual training that I could put on a CV, so I could work overseas. Teaching English as a second language was a possibility, but I decided instead on social work, hoping to acquire some qualifications in international community development. The School of Social Work at the University of Toronto didn't have a course on community development then, so I studied case work. At least I could always get work processing relief checks if there were a recession.

Our studies centered on Freudian psychology, which was disappointing because Freud went out of style afterward. After getting another degree, I went to work with the Children's Aid Society in Sudbury, Ontario, saving money because I lived with Uncle Harry, Mom's one-eyed brother. I was also learning about Northern Ontario where I was supervising children in foster homes, a job I had also done as a student in Toronto.

One day, I brought a twelve-year-old ward for her last visit with her biological father. We were preparing her for adoption to another family, and this was the last time she would see her dad. She was weeping as she begged him not to drink any more. She didn't want to leave him, and she obviously loved him, but he didn't seem to care. I wasn't crying either. I suddenly realized that I had become the ideal social worker who was emotionally distanced from the people I was serving. I was feeling nothing so I could remain objective in such situations, but I didn't want to feel so detached. I really wanted to empathize with this unfortunate child and be angry at her alcoholic father. I decided I didn't want to be a social worker after that. Maybe I should go back to my original plan to be a journalist. Maybe I should have studied how to teach English as a second language. Social workers were important, but the profession wasn't a fit for me.

Chapter 7:
First Taste Of Asia:
Japan, Taiwan, Hong Kong,
Malaysia, Myanmar, 1960-1961

When I had saved enough money from my social work job for a plane ticket from Vancouver to Hong Kong and back, I felt ready to set out again. It was the summer of 1960, and very few foreigners were able to get visas to the new China, so I didn't count on going there yet. But maybe I could. Again, I left it to fate, to the Spirit, to God. I had plans to visit several other countries as well.

Hong Kong was close to my ancestral village in China. My case work studies had made me think more about the important relationship a child has with a father. The tragic death of mine was drawing me to find out more about him and the country he left.

CFTO-TV in Toronto asked for stories, and it would pay about fifty dollars for tape recordings and still pictures. *The Globe and Mail* was interested, too. It had published everything I had sent its editors about our Arctic adventure. It seemed that writing and photography were the way to go.

Newspapers often depend on reliable freelancers like me because they can't afford to pay the expenses and salaries of their own correspondents abroad. We freelancers were adventurous souls who had the nerve to go to newsworthy countries on our own and hopefully "string" for several different newspapers or media outlets. Freelance stringers could make enough to cover their own expenses if they were lucky. I also bought a few hundred dollars worth of traveler's checks in case I wasn't.

In order to get help from governments, tourist offices, or the military, freelancers needed to be accredited by some media. *The Recorder and Times* was still only paying five dollars a story, but its press card would provide invaluable access to press trips, press conferences, and probably some travel industry receptions that were renowned for their hospitality. Freelance writing is also a way to learn about a country because it forces a writer to ask questions. It can teach me and our readers about the world and encourage them to travel, too. As my stories were features and not news with deadlines, I could send them by airmail to Toronto and Brockville.

I joined the Quakers in Toronto before leaving. I wanted to have a spiritual anchor while I was traveling, and I was pleased they accepted me. By then, I had learned about its seventeenth-century founder, George Fox, and his rebellion against the official Church of England. The Quakers were early feminists and encouraged women to speak during worship services. Any of them could be a minister and share divine inspirations in meetings for worship or elsewhere. Although some of them owned slaves, as a group they opposed slavery. Quakers also refused to swear oaths in court because they believed people should tell the truth at all times. I didn't feel I could be one of those called to bravely speak truth to power, but I felt I could help those who did, wherever there was an opportunity.

The Quakers had a center in Tokyo, and it needed help with a workcamp. I would not be alone in Taiwan, either. A friend from college had invited me to visit her, and I knew I could stay with my half-sister, Mei Ting, who was living in Hong Kong at that time.

Our father had returned to China to an arranged marriage when he was eighteen. Canadian government regulations would not let him bring his wife to Canada, and he could only stay away for six months. She died soon after she gave birth to Mei Ting. An aunt raised our half-sister in our grandfather's house in Sun Wai (Xin Hui).

Daddy was finally able to get special permission for Mei Ting to visit Canada for a year in 1949 when Mei was twenty-nine, but she had to return to her husband in Hong Kong. It wasn't until much later, after more immigration laws were passed, that the two of them could immigrate together to Canada.

When I left Mom and my siblings, I only expected to be gone a few months, six at the most. Mom was determined to keep the restaurant operating and pay off its debts. She had a lot of energy, but she wanted family to be involved. She argued that I should stay to help because the restaurant had paid for my college education. I wanted to escape from working in the restaurant. I argued that I was trying to help humanity by reporting stories and fighting racial discrimination. This, in turn, would actually help her.

My sister, Val, was a schoolteacher, and she and her husband, Daniel, could assist with the restaurant during the busy summer months. Our brother, Joe, was in college in Ottawa and could help Mom on weekends. I didn't feel that she was abandoned.

I was still wondering about the "starving children in China." Were they still starving in the new China? And what about my identity? I had felt at first that the crew at the bowling alley in Toronto was my group, and during my Arctic period, I was part of the workcamp group. Maybe the Quakers were my group now?

A young man from Toronto Quaker Meeting was driving to the West Coast at the same time that I needed a ride. Ken was a British geologist and gave me an interesting running description of the landscape along the way. He chose to drive through Minneapolis in the U.S., and his car broke down there. In all, it took about six days. He dropped me off at a mini-workcamp in British Columbia, but I wasn't interested in more geology or anything else he had been teaching me. Asia was beckoning. I already had a plane ticket.

Creston was on the way to Vancouver, B.C. I had committed to assisting a Quaker there for a month. Barbara Bachovzeff was trying to help heal a rift between Quakers and a radical sect of the Doukhobors called the Sons of Freedom. British and American Quakers had made it possible for these pacifists to immigrate to Canada from Russia, but once in British Columbia, the Sons of Freedom refused to send their children to public schools. They wanted to maintain control of their own unique communal way of life and protested against the government by bombing trains and setting fire to schools and even their own houses. The police took their children away from them, and the women embarrassed the government by demonstrating bare-breasted. By 1960, they had complied and agreed to send their children to public schools, but they blamed the Quakers for betraying them. Barbara was trying to heal that rift.

Barbara rented a little cottage in the Kootenay Valley near Creston from which we tried to meet some Doukhobors. Barbara spoke Russian. I spent a month hoeing potatoes alongside Doukhobor farm workers but, unfortunately, was never able to make friends with any of them. They kept together in tight family groups. At least our wages helped to cover our meager expenses.

Barbara taught me survival skills, such as how to keep food from spoiling without a refrigerator. We kept our milk in a bottle that sat in a bowl of water. The water kept the cloth on top wet and cold, and this kept the milk cool, too. Barbara continued on with the project after my departure, as I headed to Japan and forgot about the dissenters. It was an interesting experience, learning about another group that wanted to maintain its traditional culture, but other adventures and opportunities were calling me.

In Japan, my assignment was with the American Friends Service Committee, the same group that sponsored our workcamp in Mexico. I was to help a two-week volunteer workcamp for about thirty high school students from Hong Kong and Japan. AFSC also invited me to an international seminar afterward with expenses covered for the month.

I worked with another wonderful Quaker couple named Dave and B.J. Elder, Americans from Philadelphia. A British teacher, Joe Whitney, accompanied the students from a private Hong Kong high school. They had spent a year raising money for their trip. Our job was to clear a field full of stumps, bushes, and wasps, so an extension could be built to a hostel for women with disabilities. They needed volunteer help because there wasn't enough money to pay for the clearing.

We all labored six hours a day, five days a week. On weekends, we visited shrines and Mount Fuji. The rest of the time, the students learned about each other's cultures, songs, and customs. They discussed problems such as whether the girls or the boys should bathe first in their only bathroom. The Japanese said boys should go first because males were more important; the Chinese boys may have agreed, but they were more gallant. The students ended up compromising, taking turns each day. It made them realize there were several valid solutions.

The Quakers were trying to help the children of two former enemies appreciate each other. The brutal Japanese occupation of Hong Kong had only ended fifteen years earlier. By the time our Hong Kongers headed home, they were all best friends. As their ship left Japan, the Chinese held onto long paper streamers while their new Japanese buddies on the dock held the other ends, trying to prolong the time they could feel in direct touch with each other. When the streamers finally broke, I was in tears, too. We were all friends. The same wonderful camaraderie also happened later with the seminar and its university-aged participants.

When the workcamp and seminar were over, I didn't want to leave Japan. It was full of stories to write. The Japanese had a different way of thinking. Why the frequent bowing to each other? And why a different bow of just so many inches/centimeters, depending on who was doing the bowing? What about *harakiri*? Why was suicide a ritual, always performed in the same traditional way? Why a special ceremony just for drinking tea? I found Ruth Benedict's book *The Chrysanthemum and the Sword* very helpful in answering some questions.

Traditional customs were changing. One Japanese friend complained that her parents and Japanese culture in general were pruning her like a miniature bonsai tree. On the other hand, another friend's parents encouraged her to learn English, attend university, and work abroad.

Many opportunities arose to help me explore. Yoshida-san was a member of Tokyo Friends Meeting. He was a carpenter with a passion for taking photographs of geishas and man-hole covers—two extremely different subjects. The man-hole covers were not hiding any illicit obsession; he just liked to study their designs and histories.

Yoshida-san couldn't afford to enjoy geisha hospitality himself, but he knew all about them. Each culture has a different criterion of beauty; for example, Yoshida-san said you have to look at the nape of the neck and the walk when judging a geisha. He arranged for me to meet the sister of two geishas. Masumi worked as a typist. Her tiny apartment was one small room serving as a bedroom, dining room, and parlor. She was happy to be featured in a newspaper abroad as a typical modern Japanese woman, and she invited me to stay with her.

Her sisters were a modern version of an ancient tradition. They explained that high quality geishas still spend several years training in make-up, music, and dance before they can work. They insisted that they were not prostitutes. They were professional hostesses who entertain guests in very strictly defined ways. They had a union arranging their appointments, protecting them, and making rules of behavior. If they married or prostituted themselves, they had to leave the profession, they said.

I could understand why these young women would choose to pour their energy into becoming geishas or into any art form. Photography and writing were my art forms, my escape from working in a restaurant. I learned that the traditional Japanese wife stayed at home, taking care of the children. They rarely, if ever, went out to socialize and enjoy themselves. Geishas at least had some decision-making powers over their own lives.

I also began poking my inquisitive nose into other aspects of Japanese life. I wondered why the Japanese hated the Koreans so much and vice versa. It seemed centuries of rivalry and actual invasions made them enemies, and they considered each other inferior.

The Koreans claimed the Japanese stole their pottery art. There didn't seem to be any way these two groups could be reconciled.

For two weeks, I stayed at a youth hostel in the ancient cultural capital of Kyoto. There, I met university students who spent as much time as possible "foreigner hunting." They were eager to practice their English, so they could get good jobs and travel abroad. They took me everywhere I wanted to go and acted as free interpreters. One of my highlights in Japan was a walk with them after dark, up a hill through a cemetery and by a Shinto shrine. They sang traditional folk songs as we enjoyed the curved roofs of Buddhist temples silhouetted against a full moon. We appreciated the same exquisite beauty.

The students also took me to a Pachinko parlor, a type of pinball hall, where I won a week's supply of chocolate bars.

During neighborhood festivals, I danced with kimono-clad housewives who made me feel welcome in spite of my clumsiness. Much of my time was spent just wandering around, trying to find reasons why these delightful, polite, hospitable people committed such atrocities in China and elsewhere. I decided that it was because Japan had a very small amount of land to cultivate, most of it covered with mountains. Meanwhile, its large, growing population needed more space and resources. Their leaders in the 1930s and even before that tried to solve this problem by invading neighboring countries.

Attacking people of other cultures meant that rules of polite society didn't apply. Once they were in uniform with their individuality masked, soldiers could consider other peoples as inferior. They used women in captured countries as "comfort women" for their troops. They did not hesitate to kill captives. War brought out the worst in people.

CFTO-TV and *The Globe and Mail* also published my stories about an anti-American student demonstration. I visited a Toshiba camera factory and wrote about Japan's superior technology, which now helped to solve its problem of feeding its people. Its rewritten, post-war constitution was exemplary. It said: "The Japanese people forever renounce war as a sovereign right of the nation and the threat or use of force as a means of settling international disputes." Japan didn't need an army to prosper, only a self-defense force and technological skills. It sounded like a good solution.

A graduate student needed help correcting his English on a thesis. It was an easy job because his English was good. He paid more than expected. I didn't have to worry about money.

It was December of 1960 when I thought about moving on. I was happy in Japan, but it was getting cold. A daily public *ofuro* (bath) warmed me up, but I didn't want to buy winter clothes. Taiwan was on the way from Tokyo to Hong Kong, and stopping in Taipei didn't cost any extra airfare. It was just before Christmas, and I intended to stay a month.

It was my first Christmas away from home. Taiwan is not a Christian country, and December twenty-fifth was not a special day. No Santa Clauses. No nativity scenes. No Christmas music. To stave off nostalgia, I stayed away from the few churches. I had always spent Christmas with family in Brockville, with presents, parties, and a freshly cut, eight-foot tree in the family apartment. Taiwan was very different until my friend Carol Chiam arranged a dinner with some Canadians who invited me to stay with them in a suburb of the capital.

Taiwan was better known then as Formosa. It is officially called the Republic of China; but it wasn't the China with the Great Wall that I wanted to visit. The only thing I knew about the place was that it was a beautiful little island off the eastern coast of China, and Canadian missionaries had worked there. Generalissimo Chiang Kai-shek and the Chinese Nationalist army had fled there after the Communist victory in 1949. Almost overnight, the island added about two million people, nearly all men, to its original six million.

The newcomers were intent on retaking the mainland, the homeland they had just lost. In the meantime, they had taken the governing of the island away from the people who had lived there for generations. The official language became Mandarin while the Taiwanese spoke the Fujian dialect of Chinese. They had been under Japanese rule for fifty years with a Japanese education system, so many also spoke Japanese. Their culture had developed differently, and they didn't appreciate the newcomers who had taken over. My Taiwanese friends called their homeland a police state. The newcomers considered the Taiwan-born inferior.

In a police state, would policemen follow me everywhere? Through my friend, Carol, I met many Taiwan-born people, who all hated and feared the Chiang Kai-shek government. Whenever I asked them about it, they would look around to see if anyone else was listening; then they would lower their voices and talk about the arrests and jailing of people who criticized the Nationalists or advocated for an independent Taiwan.

As a result, I was apprehensive when I went down to the police station to register, as was required of outsiders staying longer than a few tourist days. Outside, I took a deep breath and opened the door. The young policeman looked up and glared. I knew it wouldn't help if I showed fear, so I gave him a smile. It was a mistake. He registered me without trouble, but days later, he also began coming around to where I was staying. He wanted to take me out for dinner, but we really didn't have much in common. I had a hard time turning him down without antagonizing him; he had the power to make my stay in Taiwan difficult. While Quakers believe in always telling the truth, I lied. I told him I already had a boyfriend, and he gave up.

Actually, Taiwan really wasn't as bad as I had expected. I don't think any policeman followed me at first. The police state reputation was understandable. Taiwan, as a province of China, was still in a state of war with few civil rights. Some of my stories and letters never arrived home, but generally, I think, the press credentials protected me.

My hostess, Carol, had been studying at the Deaconess Training School in Toronto when we met. She and her mother, a piano teacher, were Presbyterians, and both were very assertive women. Carol had a lot of contacts and was determined to make me enjoy my time and prolong my stopover. She wanted to get me married to one of her friends. Michael was a nice fellow, who invited me to his brother's wedding where I was treated like one of the family. The wedding was full of traditions like matchmakers, a specific number of wedding gifts to the bride and her family with special cakes, clothing, and a red wedding chest. I remember the bride's elaborate procession in sedan chairs, the musicians, the couple jumping over flames together, and the firecrackers. It was fun but not for me.

Michael said the bride would serve ceremonial tea to the mother-in-law to show how subservient she would be. Yikes! He assured me that modern weddings could be different, but I couldn't see myself spending the rest of my life following an even more conservative set of Chinese family traditions than those I had escaped. I got the impression that families were trying to compete with their neighbors in how much they spent. In spite of being turned down, Michael still gallantly continued as my tour guide.

Carol arranged my stay at first with an elderly Canadian Presbyterian missionary in a big, old brick house outside the capital, in Tamsui. From its balcony, I could see the lovely Goddess of Mercy Mountain. Living in Taiwan as a missionary was not the great hardship I had imagined. She had two servants to help her.

Then Carol moved me to the home of the Canadian couple with their two little girls, a delightful family who spoke Cantonese, Mandarin, and English with each other. Alice Yang was a Chinese-Canadian from Winnipeg. Her family lived in the upscale, suburban Beitou hot spring area that seemed to double as a red-light district. In the evenings, I could hear the motorcycles ferrying prostitutes to their customers. I stayed there as a guest until one of my contacts from the Quaker seminar in Tokyo invited me to stay in his home in downtown Taipei.

We had called him "Taiwan Paul" because there had been other Pauls, but here he was just Paul. The U.S. Agency for International Development had invited Paul's father, Mr. Mao, to tour the United States. Mr. Mao was a banker and desperate for someone to help improve his English, one hour a day in return for room and board. I stayed for about eight months and felt like a member of the family.

One day, I happened to be interviewing the director of Taiwan Christian Service, Irving Pearson, for a story. This was an

American relief agency that distributed U.S. surplus food like flour, cornmeal, cooking oil, and rice to the needy. The "poor" included the Chinese Nationalist army. I accused him of subsidizing an army, and he admitted it, but he asked me to work for him, writing publicity and reports. I agreed to a half-time job for a month and ended up staying for eight months.

It was an ideal situation. Part of the day, I was doing my own freelance reporting with help from the Nationalist government, which was trying to show how the Taiwanese people appreciated its rule. The government was eager to help me with stories, and I got to know some of the mainlanders. The rest of the time, I was investigating slums and starving people to help Taiwan Christian Service appeal to U.S. churches for support. Taiwan's very existence, its freedom from Chinese Communist control, depended on the United States, which wanted to keep Taiwan from becoming Communist. At the same time, it didn't want the Nationalists to fight to take back the mainland.

The press card from *The Recorder and Times* meant invitations to Quemoy and Matsu, courtesy of the Chinese military. Quemoy was an island about two miles (3.2 kilometers) from the Chinese mainland. The Communists had been unable to capture the islands because of the intervention of the U.S. Navy.

Quemoy gave me my first glimpse of China, which proved to be a row of low hills with a few small houses. I guess I had expected drum rolls—a "ta-da!" moment. I had finally seen the motherland, a dream realized, but it was far away and quite ordinary.

Another foreign journalist and I were there for three days, visiting a hospital, schools, and gun positions. China shelled the island every other day. We heard the shells exploding and saw damaged villages. During our visit, twenty-eight rounds fell on the island. We weren't even in a shelter, and I wasn't afraid because no one else seemed concerned about it. Our hosts assured us that eighty thousand troops were defending us, and the shelling didn't seem to frighten them. The Nationalists were sending gift packages of soap, rice, cigarettes, and children's toys to the mainland by balloon. They said that Chinese people there were starving.

Matsu was the other off-shore island that the Nationalists still controlled. Our group of journalists there could see China, about twenty kilometers away. We were stranded there a week, waiting for transportation by ship back to Taipei after our official visit. It was during the Moon Festival, and the military laid on parties for us every night. We even went water skiing with navy frogmen and swimming on beaches that the officers assured us weren't mined. We visited a home for the aged, a school, and had tea with officers of the Women's Army Corps. All of this was so incongruous with a state of war.

It was rather nice being on an island with a dozen foreign journalists and twenty thousand soldiers. Their commanding officer entertained us, too. I don't think the Quakers would have approved, especially when one of the officers put a cord attached to a propaganda balloon meant for the Chinese mainland into my hands and took a photo. Too late, I asked what the Chinese characters on it meant. They were "Long live the Republic of China."

The officer agreed to my request not to publish the photo because, someday, I expected to visit mainland China. How would they treat me if they knew I had sent them a propaganda balloon? The officer promised he wouldn't publish the picture, but he did tell other officers and even Matsu's local commander about my plans. I squirmed uncomfortably, expecting to be executed as a spy for even thinking about visiting the enemy; fortunately, they were very nice about it and said going there would be dangerous. The Communists were "bad people," they argued. Finally, after the tenth sermon, I said, "I'm going there to welcome you when you return to the mainland." The general grinned and answered, "No, you'd better wait until we get there first. It will be safer for you."

He and his buddies were never able to launch a counter-attack. I didn't want to take part in their dispute or with the rift between the local-born Taiwanese and the Nationalists. The problems were too big, and China today is still threatening to take back Taiwan.

It was probably Michael or Carol who recounted the traditional story about the end of headhunting in Taiwan. The island has many aboriginal groups, one of whom used to present a freshly-acquired human head each year as a gift to their gods and ancestors. A government official named Wu Feng tried to end the practice in the eighteenth century. Although the tribespeople respected him, they refused to stop an annual ritual that was supposed to give them a good harvest.

One day, Wu Feng said to them, "Tomorrow at noon you will find a man in a red robe riding on a white horse beneath the tall tree at Shekou. You may kill him but not anyone else. Otherwise, Heaven will punish you."

The next day, the tribesmen did kill a man in a red robe. Then they found out that it was Wu Feng, and they understood too late why it was wrong to collect human heads. They never did it again, and there is a temple to Wu Feng in Taiwan.

It was the most beautiful story I heard anywhere because it represented the power of self-sacrifice rather than violence in making changes. Wu Feng's death made them realize the value of the people they had killed.

I had intended to stay only a month in Taiwan, but my friends were so hospitable that I kept extending my stay. My mother continued to be supportive and gamely handled my finances in Brockville. I shopped for Chinese curios for her to sell in the restaurant. I tried to learn Mandarin Chinese, which was the national language of China and most important for visiting the whole of China. Alas, I never mastered it beyond a few words.

By the end of spring, I had money to spare. I could afford to take a one-week trip to Hong Kong to visit my half-sister. The press card came in handy there, too, opening doors to a variety of Hong Kong events. I was invited to a modern beauty contest but wasn't interested in writing about it. My maternal cousin, Hong Man, took me to Hong Kong's border with China. I could see more of China from an adjacent hill than I could from Taiwan's offshore islands. The closest Chinese settlement, Shenzhen, was just a little village with one-story houses then. It was a step closer to seeing China. Today, Shenzhen is a city full of skyscrapers with a population of at least twelve million.

Hong Man was an English-speaking school teacher. In his spare time, he was my personal tour guide. I envied him because he lived in a lychee orchard; for us in Canada, dried lychees were a special treat. In Hong Kong, they were fresh and even more delicious.

Hong Kong was a British colony from 1842 to 1997, the result of a trade imbalance. Britain was buying a lot of tea, silk, and porcelain from China, but the Chinese authorities saw no need to buy anything from Britain until western powers successfully smuggled opium into the country, and many people became addicted to its feel-good qualities. Chinese leaders fought against the importation. Western powers attacked several Chinese ports and forced China to open up the country to foreign trade. The Treaty of Nanjing ceded Hong Kong to Britain until 1997. It wasn't until the 1950s that China's leader, Mao Tse-tung (now Mao Zedong), successfully banned opium from China.

During my visit, I saw no evidence of the opium trade, but it was important then for both sides to keep Hong Kong open to international trade. China and the outside world supplied Hong Kong with food and water, and the colony was China's only trading port. China's agriculture was failing because of natural disasters and bad management, and millions of hungry people were trying to escape starvation by fleeing to Hong Kong, some of them swimming in shark-filled waters to get there. Makeshift shacks housing these refugees covered the hillsides. China needed to import food and get foreign exchange through Hong Kong to pay for it.

I stayed with my half-sister, Mei Ting, and her husband, Chun Wing, in their tiny apartment downtown. Chun Wing was in charge of an elementary school owned by a group of restaurants for their children. Mei Ting was one of the teachers, and they had met while they were both refugees in mainland China, fleeing the Japanese. She told me how a Japanese soldier once beat our grandfather. I had no idea that this had happened during those war years. To me, Grandfather was just a picture in our parents' bedroom. Now the war became more than a newsreel on a Saturday in Brockville.

Luckily for me, they had a maid's room where I could sleep. While Chun Wing was fluent in English, I spoke with Mei Ting in a mixture of Toishan dialect and Mandarin. I had a wonderful time. They were very hospitable, and I enjoyed the stay.

The combination of Hong Kong's Chinese and British flavors made me feel right at home. Brockville had been settled by United Empire Loyalists who were refugees from the American War of Independence. Those refugees brought with them their British culture, resulting in Brockville's architecture being mainly British. Although most of the architecture in Hong Kong was Chinese, it had many British-style buildings. Its Chinese buildings had second stories projecting over the sidewalks, protecting pedestrians from the frequent rains. I thought it was a very practical idea. Signs were in English and Chinese, but the language in the streets was Cantonese. I enjoyed the combination of the two cultures.

In spite of its hillside squatter settlements, Hong Kong was beautiful. The main city is on one of 263 islands. Kowloon peninsula, a five-minute ferry ride away, is attached to the Chinese mainland. Hills surround its famous harbor, the air was clean, and it was not as crowded as it is today. The whole place was stunning, exotic, lively, and noisy, except for the welcome quiet of the Quaker meeting. That was held in a meeting room in the Anglican cathedral on Sundays.

The popular movie *Love Is a Many-Splendored Thing* had come out five years before with its romantic story about an American journalist and a Eurasian doctor in Hong Kong. It was based on an autobiographical novel by Han Suyin. Although it portrayed the prejudice against Eurasians, its sentimental theme song was still popular in 1961. I heard it in almost every restaurant and shopping mall. It was intoxicating and constantly in my head as I explored the city.

I was on vacation and attracted to the glamor of Hong Kong. A tailor made me a *cheongsam*, a tight-fitting dress with slits up the side—Taiwan had them, too, but Hong Kong's were more stylish. Hong Kong was the Manhattan of Asia. Hong Man took my picture seated in a human-drawn rickshaw near the Star Ferry. I was a tourist. I didn't think about the poor man who had to pull the cart through the busy streets to make a living. He could have been a relative from my father's village, less than a hundred miles (150 kilometers) away. I didn't think about serious matters like colonization and exploitation by imperialists powers.

Nor did I dream then that I would be married in Hong Kong six years later, with that song, *Love is a Many-Splendored Thing*, in my subconscious memory.

Back in Taiwan, I continued to enjoy myself, pleased to be able to help feed thousands of needy people. A big typhoon hit the island, and I learned that most victims of typhoons lived in low-lying areas near the sea, their homes smashed by high waves and winds. Poor folk like fisher families suffer most during such catastrophes. Wealthier people can afford to build their homes on hills.

England's newspaper *Daily Express* was looking for a stringer. I signed on. At last I could call myself a foreign correspondent, but before I could submit a story, I felt the urge to move on. I interviewed a group of anti-Nationalist dissidents. Soon, my Taiwanese friends were telling me that the police were asking them how long I was planning to stay on the island. I suspected I was being followed. I sympathized with the plight of the Taiwanese but not enough to join their fight for independence. My work with Taiwan Christian Service was satisfying, but giving out food to the poor was only a Band-Aid solution.

Murray Thomson, whom I had met at the Quaker meeting in Toronto, was with the American Friends Service Committee in India at the time, and I wrote to him. Murray answered with an invitation to attend the international seminar he was helping to organize in Malaya (now known as Malaysia). It was another opportunity for young Asian leaders to discuss their cultural differences and work toward cooperation and harmony. I couldn't resist, and I had enough money. Taiwan was feeling too provincial.

I flew to Bangkok and met some members of the seminar group in a hostel operated by missionaries. Then, seven of us participants took an overnight train south to Kuala Lumpur in coach seating, not a sleeping car. One student tried to sleep lying down in the luggage rack above our heads. The rest of us spent the time discussing our traditional customs and issues. In Penang, a Malaysian participant joined us and gave us non-Asians our first taste of durian fruit, a large, spiky, melon-shaped fruit that smells like rotten eggs. I did not like it. The Asians on the trip laughed and insisted it was an acquired taste, a test of one's ability to adapt to the continent. I never did learn to like it, even when it was served with ice cream.

Our discussions on the train were stimulating and so much broader than our discussions in Taiwan. One of my new friends argued that there was a tendency for some previously enslaved people to behave insensitively toward their own kin once they became free. They had no compassion and just took over the role of their former master. It was a strange topic, but it left me wondering if world peace was possible.

The seminar was two weeks long. AFSC had collected about thirty young Asians, two Swiss, two Americans, and a German. As usual, it was trying to overcome international barriers between nationalities and cultural groups. It was trying to make us think.

Our German participant, Johannes Glauche, was amazing. He was an East German who had escaped to West Germany. There, they drafted him, but he became a conscientious objector and had just finished nine months of his alternative service in Israel. His was a beautiful story, worth retelling, of a German trying to atone for what his countrymen did to the Jews.

Johannes recounted the details later in an email about his experience in a *kibbutz*, an Israeli communal farm:

> I was just myself. I had walked thousands of kilometers for three months to reach Israel overland. It was and is the Holy Land for me. I wasn't so stupid to believe that I could change anything. After reaching Jerusalem, I inquired which kibbutz had survivors of the Holocaust. So I went to the Kibbutz Buchenwald, now called Netzer Sereni, and asked if I could work there as a volunteer. The elected head of the kibbutz at the time told me that I should come back after two days. Meanwhile he would call a general meeting of all the members of

the kibbutz to discuss this. For them, it was an entirely unforeseen and new matter.

After two days, I went back to the kibbutz where they welcomed me warmly. The younger ones asked me lots of questions about Germany and Europe. There were no opposing votes, just two or three abstentions by people who did not want to talk to me. I was the first German they met after 1945. It was one of the most important times of my life. . . . No suspicion and no belligerence at all. Very open, friendly, and kind. Every day we worked very hard, side by side, in the Jaffa orange plantations. It was harvest time. Most people were curious, amazed, and loved to talk in German with a real German. They enjoyed speaking their language again, which they knew much better than Hebrew. I was invited into their houses every evening for talks, listening to classical music.

In India, Johannes also assisted Service Civil International in a workcamp, building a kindergarten near Ahmedabad, clearing slums in Kerala, and working in a leprosy camp in Orissa. He helped Tibetan refugees, too. I thought Johannes was a real hero to face people who had reason to kill him.

Seminar participants discussed the theme: "The Demands of the Future on the Youth of Today." It was an open-ended, all-embracing topic. We stayed in a beach resort just outside of Port Dickson, south of the Malayan capital. For years afterward, I lived with lovely memories of floating in the soothing tropical waters of the Strait of Malacca in the shade of palm trees. Discussing politics with a charming, distinguished British professor about China was idyllic.

Another topic was the recent riot between Malayan Chinese and Muslim Malays. Conflicting festivals ignited the violence. That year, the dates of Ramadan and the Chinese New Year were close together. For the Chinese, their festival was a month of lion dances, fireworks, and eating their favorite foods, such as pork. For Muslims, it was a month of meditation and fasting, without even water, between dawn and sunset. Pork, as always, was forbidden. It erupted in violence. At least our group of Muslims, Buddhists, Chinese, Malays, and Christians could discuss it dispassionately.

Several of us from that seminar remained friends for years afterward, and every one of us had an international life. Whenever I was in Bangkok, I stayed with Mini from the Philippines in her dorm at Chulalongkorn University. She was another amazing person. She had a prominent red birthmark on her face, but she never let it bother her. She was outgoing and friendly to everyone and was trying to hook me up with one of her Thai friends. She and Johannes were later married, and they live in his native Germany.

Other members of our clique were also amazing. I saw Anwar Kamel from Pakistan later in New York City after he was elected to the United Nations Committee on the Elimination of Racial Discrimination. I hoped the Quaker influence would help that organization. The very tall American man we knew as "Two-meter Tex" became a diplomat who helped expose human rights abuses in Argentina when thousands of people were imprisoned and killed. Murray, who had invited me to the seminar, married the beautiful Suteera from Thailand and continued beating swords into ploughshares. In 1990, he was a recipient of the Canadian Pearson Medal of Peace for his work in peace and justice. Walter Ebnother from Switzerland still does voluntary work with projects in Guatemala and Chiapas and with Amnesty International in Southeast Asia.

One of the other Americans, Norval Reece, who was working then in the Friends Center in India, wrote later to say that, "Taking part in multiple international seminars, workcamps, and hitchhiking along non-tourist paths in foreign countries increased my comfort in dealing with people from vastly different backgrounds. These gave me the courage to invest in a successful TV company in Communist Poland."

They were an amazing, internationally-minded group.

For me, the seminar was a life-changer. The director, Russell Johnson, offered me a job helping to organize the seminars out of the Quaker office in Delhi, India. This time, I didn't need to spend time praying for guidance. The offer to go to India to work at peacemaking seemed absolutely right. Besides, it would add another country to my collection.

Back in Taiwan, I said goodbye to friends and booked a flight to India's capital at Quaker expense. On the way, I thought about the conflict between the two different Chinese groups. The Nationalists with their military power and dreams of returning to the China mainland were still dominating the weaker Taiwanese, and I wondered about the future of my friends as I looked forward to learning more about the world.

Of course, I stopped in Burma, now known as Myanmar. It was on the way to India. Spencer Pan had been at the Tokyo seminar, and Burma had been on the list of countries I had wanted to visit. It was part of the British empire from 1824 to 1948 and was under Japanese occupation from 1942 to 1945. At the seminar, Spencer had joked about his famous uncle who was really named "Peter Pan," a name most of us knew from the British story of a boy who wouldn't grow up. Spencer had also demonstrated to much more laughter the various uses of a *longyi*, the Burmese sarong worn by both sexes to carry purchases, keep off the rain, and protect one's modesty. He was very funny. He had invited us all to visit his country, so I did.

In Toronto, I had seen a black-and-white Japanese film, *The Burmese Harp*, made in 1956. It was about a platoon of Japanese soldiers who find themselves prisoners in Burma at the end of the Pacific war. Another Japanese platoon refused to surrender, and the British killed all of them. One of the Japanese survivors decides to stay behind as a Buddhist monk to bury his dead compatriots. It is not a great film, but it is a powerful one with beautiful Japanese folk music and a pacifist theme. I loved the sound of the Burmese harp. I never forgot it. I wanted to see Burma.

Burma then had more than 135 officially recognized ethnic groups, many of them hill tribes. Some of the major ones were fighting the government for power, for control of the illicit drug trade. Some had been headhunters. The government was too preoccupied to be interested in encouraging tourism, and I knew of no one else who had visited the country.

Was I thinking of Spencer as a possible husband? That idea was always with me when I met any eligible men, but I didn't care if Spencer was married or not. I was more interested in seeing the country. Spencer's hospitable family lived near the capital. They wanted to take me to the highlands where it was cooler and more beautiful. A relative was an official there. The area was closed to foreign tourists, but they wanted me to see it.

Spencer said I could pass for a local. "You look Burmese," he argued when I protested. His sister lent me some local clothes and demonstrated how to tie the longyi with just a knot around the waist. We were in the Rangoon railway station when the knot started coming undone. A stranger laughed at me and pointed to the falling sarong. No one called the police about the obvious foreigner intent on getting on a train to forbidden parts. Spencer's sister tied the skirt again, and we completed an otherwise uneventful, happy family trip. Being polite, Spencer and his family never mentioned the embarrassing incident at all. I still don't know how to keep a longyi on without a safety pin or belt, but I knew living in Burma was not for me.

They were sweet, gentle people, but they were too conservative for my rebellious spirit. Many years later, I could not understand why these sweet, gentle people were so cruel to their Rohingya ethnic minority.

Chapter 8:
Discovering India and Mike,
1961-1963

AFSC paid for my flight from Taiwan and most of my expenses for almost the next two years. In addition, I received an allowance of ten U.S. dollars a month that barely covered the processing of all the personal pictures I took and the occasional lunches downtown. The pictures were mostly for my own records. But the stipend didn't matter. I loved the job, and I was too busy helping to organize the meetings to do much freelancing.

The Quaker Center in Delhi was in a big two-story bungalow in an area of India's capital called Civil Lines, a zone built by the British for its senior officers when they were in charge of the country. The center was old and luxurious compared to houses in the rest of the city. It had room for Sunday meetings for worship and diplomatic gatherings, overnight guests, and staff. Our lawn doubled as a badminton court, which we played only in the cooler weather. For exercise in the dry, hot summer, we went swimming at a nearby hotel or took a morning walk along a nearby ridge.

The Quakers have centers around the world, many of them started because of their work after the First World War, helping victims of war in Europe. In India, the Delhi center supported the nonviolent campaign of Mahatma Gandhi and, at times, mediated between him and India's British rulers, as the country moved toward independence. The center's directors were John Linton, who had worked for the BBC, and his wife, Erika, a former Jewish refugee. John was like the Quaker ambassador. Norval and I each had a room of our own with ceiling fans. Mine had a desk, so it also served as my office. From my balcony, I could reach the fruit on the top of a papaya tree. It made me feel I was in a very exotic tropical setting. It felt good to be back in a Quaker community again.

Living there was very different from sharing a room with the aimable daughter of my student in Taipei. Every day our *bearer* / butler brought morning tea, *masala chai,* to my bedside—a wonderful, luxurious way to wake up. Our cook was a Christian from Goa who had to cook for people of all religions.

We also had a Nepalese guard who patrolled our compound at night while armed with a *kukri,* the traditional Gurkha knife. It was most un-Quakerly, and we had lots of discussions about a pacifist organization needing an armed guard because the house was an easy target for thieves. We had a wall separating us from the road outside on all sides, but it was not high and could be easily climbed. Fortunately, we never had any intruders, except for a loudly bellowing cow that wandered into our driveway during meeting for worship one Sunday.

The Quaker ideal in confronting a stranger in one's house was to invite him or her to tea. I wasn't quite prepared to do that, partly because I couldn't speak Hindi, the local language, so I remained silent during the discussions.

My job was to help the two directors of the Quaker International Seminars Program in Southern Asia. In addition to AFSC, it was financed by British Quakers. It included going to diplomatic functions. In a letter to my mother, I mentioned an evening that had included wine, caviar, and blue cheese, all rare treats in India. Even though I passed on the wine, this was not what one would consider a hardship post, except for the temperature.

It took a while to get used to the heat. Before the monsoons, it was 115°F (46°C) during the day and never below 90°F at night.

The first summer, we didn't have air-conditioning. I tried to sleep outside on the balcony, but it was no use. I complained to Russell that the Quakers were wasting their money because we couldn't work after a sleepless night under a fan that merely moved the heat around. The next summer, my job included buying an air conditioner for our main office. I slept there happily on a cot at night.

Norval had been at the Port Dickson seminar. He was a cheerful, thoughtful, twenty-something American, who had been working and living at the Quaker Center for over a year. He organized "Challenge," a weekly seminar on international affairs for students from a nearby university. Speakers included India's Prime Minister Nehru, President Radhakrishna, cabinet ministers, and ambassadors. The Quakers were very highly regarded in the country.

Norval also organized workcamps, so the students could help poor Indian villagers and newly arrived Tibetan refugees. In 1959, the Dalai Lama had escaped from invading Chinese troops and was given asylum in India. Many Tibetans followed their leader, whom they considered a god. They needed help getting resettled. Norval's students were from wealthy, upper-caste families, yet he convinced them to help repair school buildings without the assistance of their servants. Manual labor was something upper-caste people never considered doing. I was very favorably impressed with what Norval had done.

To thank him for the help, the Dalai Lama gave Norval a private audience and an autograph on a ten rupee note. When Norval later showed the autograph to some Tibetans, they prostrated themselves head to the ground because they considered the signature to be a part of their divine leader. Norval never did that again; he was too embarrassed to find Tibetans bowing in his direction.

Norval was eager to orient me to the country, including to Indian movies, where I had to stand in the women's line for a ticket while he stood in the men's line. Movies were my introduction to classical Indian dances, specifically *Kathak* and *Bharatanatyam*. The term Bollywood was not used until later and applied to another kind of Indian dance. He also showed me how to get around by motorcycle rickshaw, but his introduction to some local customs were quite gruesome. We visited a crematorium to see some funerals. I watched while an eldest son cracked open the skull of his deceased father "to allow the spirit to escape." After the first shock, I thought it beautiful that a son would repay a father's love in this way.

An introduction to one of his favorite people, an elderly guru or religious teacher, was also on Norval's list. Rehana Tyabje was a Muslim who felt it was her duty to help people from different cultures understand each other. She got excited when I told her about making recordings and photographs and sending them back for broadcast in Canada. She thought it was amazing and hoped to see them someday. I felt I had met someone who shared my passion to experience everything, and she inspired me to keep looking for even more adventures.

She called Norval, "my son," with much affection. One day, she told him he had been a European Roman Catholic writer in a former life, and she had been his mother. She spoke English with a flawless British accent because she had been British in her previous incarnation, she said. She told fortunes and refused payment except for chocolates and Agatha Christie novels. I thought she was wonderful.

My comparative religion classes had covered Hinduism, but it was different experiencing it where the majority of people believed in it and especially in reincarnation. People here told stories about relatives being reborn after death as an animal, human, or spirit. We heard about a child easily finding important articles left behind in secret places by a deceased grandparent, presumably in his previous life. Being reborn into better circumstances, like a higher caste, depended on a person's behavior in their previous life; however, the Hindu goal in life was to escape from this continual cycle of rebirths.

People like Norval's friend Rehana made me think that reincarnation might be possible, but who really knows what happens after death. I was in no hurry to find out.

Norval refused to give money to beggars on the street. He said adults had kidnapped and maimed children to make them more appealing to donors. In addition, the money they collected didn't go to the children or their families but rather to those in control of them. Moreover, successful beggar children would never go to school and get out of their predicament if they could make a living begging. They needed to go to school, so don't give money to them, he insisted.

I think it was Norval who said that individuals shouldn't just distribute money to the poor indiscriminately. He said some "do-gooders" tried it and were so inundated by beggars that they had to leave town to escape the crowds.

Still, I remember later turning down a dirty teenager and then seeing her as my train pulled us apart. I felt her listless movements and tears were real as she stood alone in a far corner, empty-handed, because of me. What can anyone do about these unfortunate people? How do you decide if your actions are good or bad?

Norval also made sure I saw Rajghat, the place where Mahatma Gandhi, the nonviolence leader, was cremated. British Quakers had been directly involved with Gandhi, so we were part of India's history. Norval was a great guide, a nice guy, but not yet ready for a serious relationship.

After I got my license to drive in India, I went to see the Taj Mahal. Every visitor to India has to go there. This beautiful tomb was built by a Mughal emperor in memory of his beloved wife who died in childbirth in 1631. It was only a four-hour drive from New Delhi and a thrill to visit, but driving in India was a challenge, especially in a small car directly in front of an elephant. Fortunately, this only happened to me once. The elephant had a driver who steered it away from our little car, but the possibility of his stepping on us was always there.

Four of us organized the international seminars from an office in the Quaker Center. As assistant to the directors, I did everything from collating copies of speeches to chairing lectures to meeting people at airports. During my term, we convened two more seminars for young people, similar to the one we had at Port Dickson in Malaya. They were in Singapore and Thailand.

I helped arrange one of the diplomat conferences, too. Its main purpose was to create an atmosphere where people who differed politically, religiously, and culturally could grow to understand and appreciate each other. We provided a neutral setting, so they could discuss their differences as humans rather than as mouthpieces for their governments. Discussions were informal, and everything was "off the record." Each government covered the expenses of its own diplomats because countries felt their participation was important. We hoped the diplomats would get together and solve mutual problems and convince their governments to do likewise.

Our Indonesian conference was with medium-ranking diplomats at a mountain resort. We had counselors and secretaries from twenty-four countries, both East and West, including the U.S. and the Soviet Union. They came together for ten days to discuss subjects like coexistence, technical aid, and the prospects for international law. Our speakers included university professors and government leaders. For two of our meetings, we had Dr. Han Suyin, author of *A Many-Splendored Thing*. Her pro-Communist China views stimulated much discussion.

Did the conferences help overcome any major conflicts? I don't know, but it was gratifying to hear a socialist diplomat joke afterward to a western one, "Before the conference, you were my enemy," he said. "Now you are my friendly enemy."

The diplomats were very thoughtful and careful people. Although each country's politicians determined its foreign policies, diplomats seemed to have a lot of influence in the decisions. The Cold War between the U.S. and Russia was still being fought. I like to think we helped to end it. At least we tried.

The seminars with the younger people were more relaxed. They were basically like the one in Port Dickson. We hoped to make these future leaders aware that the problems in their own countries were similar to those in other countries in the region; for example, in much of Asia, the education system was geared toward examinations and memorization of facts with not much creative thinking. We invited scholars, journalists, and government officials to lead discussions on the value of minority groups, the prospects for regional cooperation, and the problem of overpopulation. We usually included the conflict between western values and traditional ones like love marriages versus arranged marriages. We, the organizers, did not take sides.

The results were very satisfying. It was really great to see a Pakistani and an Indian sit down and discover they had something more in common than their mutual disagreement on the Kashmir issue. Unfortunately, the Kashmir dispute still exists to this day.

It was also encouraging for us to hear a Thai delegate admit that she had altered her traditional hatred of the Chinese because she found some Chinese she liked. One of the most dramatic moments came when a Japanese student admitted he had come to Southeast Asia to tell people there about the shame some Japanese young people felt about the Japanese aggression. At our seminar, he met an actual victim for the first time. Hiroshi was stunned when he realized that his countrymen had killed the father of his new Singaporean friend. All he could say was, "I'm sorry. I'm sorry." The young Singaporean man tried to console him. "It wasn't your fault," he said kindly.

Alas, although some world problems, like the admission of mainland China to the United Nations and the wiping out of smallpox have been solved, many of the problems we discussed still exist today, but we must not give up trying.

In between international meetings, I tried to learn about India, at times spending hours or even days sitting impatiently in government offices, trying to satisfy bureaucratic demands. Getting a parcel out of customs required four different signatures from officers in four separate buildings. Just to get a refund on a train ticket was a struggle. Why? It was probably to give jobs to four people instead of one. Which was better? Creating jobs where no jobs were needed, or having millions of unemployed people doing nothing? Or was there another way? Here, as elsewhere, there were so many unanswerable questions.

A woman politician was campaigning for political office, and I followed her around one weekend, admiring her courage. While India was another male-chauvinistic country, some women were trying to assert themselves politically. I also met Indira Gandhi for a few seconds when the Canadian Broadcasting Corporation asked me to personally deliver a note to her regarding an appearance on one of its shows. I felt pleased when she later become prime minister.

I read books. Khushwant Singh's novel, *Train to Lahore*, was set during the partition of India after its independence from Britain, when Muslims were fleeing from India to the newly created country of Pakistan. I cannot forget the scenes of trains arriving in Lahore with every Muslim on board killed. Even though Hindu and Muslim had lived side by side for centuries, the British departure and subsequent separation of British India into Muslim and Hindu states unleashed feelings of suspicion on both sides. It was a terrible time: fifteen million people were displaced, and more than a million people were killed, primarily the result of fear of each other. The experience of Johannes, the German, who made friends by working and living with people who had reason to kill him, suggests another possibility.

Another memorable book was about a man who discovers how to make a statue of a god rise out of the ground by burying some seeds under it. After he pours waters on the statue, the seeds expand and push the statue slowly out of the ground. Gullible people watching this "miracle" believe the statue is a god and start to worship it, and the protagonist becomes a priest with a source of income.

Parts of Delhi were depressing. I did get relatively immune to the dirt and the maimed, begging children, the apathy and the fatalism. One has to, or one can't live in India. The plight of the "Untouchables" (now known as Dalits) bothered me. They were considered the lowest of the low, only allowed to be sweepers and garbage collectors. People of higher castes thought of them as "impure" and less than human. I saw one Christian church with separate seating for them and shuddered that even some Christians thought the same. Gandhi had fought against such discrimination and called these unfortunate people *harijans*, children of God. He tried to give them equal recognition in the new, independent India,

110

but he didn't completely succeed. Everybody seems to need to feel superior to someone else.

We had a Dalit at the Quaker Center. One day, I spilled my tea, and Norval wouldn't let me clean up my mess. "You are taking a job away from the sweeper," he said. It was sad that many Indians told us that the caste system didn't exist anymore. Decades later, when I returned to India, I still found evidence of it.

Most people were vegetarians. All sentient lives were sacred. Stories abounded about villagers who wouldn't kill rats; instead, they caught them for release near other villages. But it seemed to be okay for humans to kill other humans.

I took lessons in Hindi, which most people in New Delhi spoke. Only the educated knew English. One day, a newspaper advertised a discussion about Hindi as the official language in India, but the advertisement, ironically, was in English.

There were many different cultures in the city. Jain monks walked along the streets, wearing face masks while sweeping the ground in front of them; they didn't want to accidentally step on or breathe in and kill even an insect. I visited a leper colony where we spoke with people suffering from Hansen's disease, a disease that made others think of them as sub-humans to be avoided. The disease is curable, but many of its victims could not escape detection as it ate away parts of their fingers and noses. They had to isolate themselves.

I saw tent pegging, an Indian horse-riding sport of obviously military origin. Mounted cavalrymen with long spears try to stab a tent peg stuck seven inches in the ground. They attempted this at full gallop in an effort to collapse an imaginary tent on top of an enemy. It was something out of a medieval world and only played by the wealthy.

One weekend, I explored the Jama Masjid, the largest mosque in India. I suddenly found myself sitting in a balcony above at least a hundred men, preparing to worship. Many of them grinned at me, and a couple leered; Allah was apparently not on their minds. I tried to escape, but I was surrounded and had to remain until prayers ended. Then the prayers began, and when the men were knees and heads to the ground, they ignored me. I was no longer a distraction, and I felt a profound spiritual atmosphere, a focused worship. I have never experienced anything like it since that day, not even in a Quaker meeting for worship.

My favorite person in Delhi was the secretary at the center. Arjun was our solver-of-all-problems in this strange world. He wasn't a Quaker, but he was the kindest, most cheerful person I ever met. One day, I arrived back from a shopping trip by rickshaw and thought the driver was charging too much because I was a foreigner. Arjun heard us arguing loudly and came out to mediate. He asked for my money, held it in his hand, and kindly asked the driver to take what I owed him. The driver took less than he had first demanded.

Arjun seemed to solve all our problems, like the night our bearer got drunk and got into a fight. I was alone in the house, and we called Arjun, who gently took care of that, just by appealing to better instincts.

It was very thought-provoking to be in India during the autumn of 1962, when the Chinese invaded and took over land they considered theirs. For a few months, India woke up alive and vibrant because Indians had a common enemy, a common cause. People rallied in the streets, urging the government to fight the intruders. Unfortunately, it meant Indians were approaching me with "aap cheenee hain"? It meant, "Are you Chinese?" My unexpected answer, "No, I'm Canadian," seemed to confuse them, and they would leave me alone.

Big demonstrations in the country urged the government to fight the Chinese. People stoned some Chinese stores and restaurants. The Canadian High Commissioner suggested I leave for my own safety in case I was taken for Chinese, but I never had any trouble, though some Thai and Filipina visitors were not so fortunate; they were hauled off to police stations in Calcutta and Madras. Fortunately, police released them when they showed their passports.

Danger did come close one day as I wandered near one of the demonstrations. People were looking at me strangely, and I could hear angry voices saying, "Cheenee hain?" Fortunately, one of the demonstrators knew me from the Quaker Center. He invited me up on the platform where he was sitting. That proved I was a friend and not an enemy.

People were caught up in war, ignoring the voice of Mahatma Gandhi with his message of nonviolence. It was basically a border dispute and still is. Russell kept saying, "The first casualty of war is truth." We tried to look at both sides of the picture. It was not easy.

And then the war suddenly, inexplicably ended.

India was so fascinating. It was so different from any other place I had ever visited, but it could be a lot of fun, too. The Holi festival was religious in origin, and it meant a day of throwing colored powder gleefully at everybody else, including foreigners. Some men dressed as women danced in the streets. I was to learn more about *hijras* on a future trip.

It took a while to get used to the hot, spicy food, but I grew to love it. The Quaker Center attracted interesting people, and conversations were always stimulating. While they worked elsewhere in the country, both Indians and foreigners stayed there during trips to the capital. Many of my friends were Indian university students, and I was invited to several Indian homes as well as those of the expatriate community.

I traveled around the country, once with an American Quaker on the back of his motorcycle. It was pleasantly adventurous until that trip ended up with us hitting an empty oil barrel in the middle of a road in South India. We were not hurt, but the vehicle was too damaged to continue the trip.

Then I met Mike Malloy, a journalist from Chicago. His mother was visiting him at the time. She had always wanted to attend a Quaker meeting for worship and had heard about ours, a small meeting with about thirty people. Afterward, she introduced herself and invited me home to dinner.

Mike was working for United Press International. His mother said he was having trouble finding women friends in India because any date with a respectable Indian woman involved taking along a chaperone. She was quite frank about inviting me, a Canadian with no such restraints.

Meeting a real journalist who worked for an agency might be interesting, I thought. I only knew other freelancers. Real foreign correspondents never had time to talk with us. UPI supplied news to several thousand media subscribers around the world then and could afford to hire full-time staff.

Mike seemed like a nice guy that first evening. He was tall and good looking with a crew cut. Dinner went well. I think we talked about the India-China war. He had been to Ladakh in northern India to report on it, and he was generous with explanations. It had been freezing there, and he had stayed overnight in an officer's home that had goats living on the ground floor. He had heard the artillery but couldn't get close to the fighting.

The war stopped when the Chinese got what they wanted, he said. It was in the Himalayas, the highest mountains in the world that separated the two countries. At that altitude, there was no way the Indians could have gotten tanks and heavy artillery up there to push the Chinese back.

Mike had begun his journalism career in Chicago as a copy boy in a newspaper office and had learned the trade as a police reporter. When he was drafted into the U.S. Army, he was assigned as a rewrite man and feature writer for *Stars and Stripes*, the U.S. military newspaper. He had worked for it in Japan, Okinawa, and the Philippines before he joined UPI in Japan and Laos.

That he hadn't fought and killed people when he was in the army was a plus in my estimation. It wasn't a bells and whistles, love-at-first-sight meeting. I thought he was interesting, and I liked his deep voice and his blue-gray eyes, his international interests and knowledge. He knew a lot about what was happening in the world, not just small corners of it.

Mike's mother had received alimony from a recent divorce and spent it on a visit to see him. She didn't know how long she would be staying in India. I learned later that she was of Latvian origin, and her previous husband had owned a bar where she tried to stop people from drinking too much. She was also divorced from Mike's father who was known as a boxer; his paternal grandfather had been a veterinarian who was hired from Ireland to take care of the horses and dogs at a fire station in Chicago. That was an interesting bit of cultural history.

Mike phoned a few days later to invite me along on a story he was doing. A holy man had been buried for forty days and was expected that day to emerge alive. It sounded like a story I would research for my own newspapers. He picked me up in his VW bug, and it was the usual hot day before the cooling monsoons. Suddenly, I realized heat was coming from the bottom of the car.

"Do you have your radiator on?" I asked.

"What radiator?"

I had driven a VW Beetle before. I reached down and turned off the heater. This guy needs help, I thought, no longer in awe of a genuine foreign correspondent.

The disinterment was to take place in a huge field. When we arrived, it was filled with hundreds of people and a platoon of policemen in brown uniforms and turbans. A couple of elephants carried riders in *howdahs* strapped onto their gigantic backs. A friendly bystander on foot told us about another holy man, who had emerged alive on a previous occasion from such a burial. People worshiped him as a god as a result. We waited at least an hour to find out what was happening

Mike was skeptical. To stay alive, the man must have air, food, and water slipped secretly to him, he insisted. I was hopeful. I was more open than he was to miracles.

The crowd was getting restless. Where was he? Finally, the organizers admitted that the holy man was dead. They brought up the body to show us. He was small and scrawny and looked stiff and green. I took a picture of him, a picture now lost, alas, in a sea of thousands of pictures I took on my travels. Then we had to run. The elephants were starting to panic as the disappointed worshipers shouted and ran in all directions. The police began hitting people with their sticks to keep control.

Such was our first date. I hoped it might foreshadow some possible future adventures together. I liked Mike's broad range of interests and even his skepticism. Soon he had to go to Nepal, so I didn't see him for a while. When he finally phoned again for dinner, I accepted, mostly out of curiosity to learn about his trip. I had been to Nepal with Norval where I had been amazed and horrified at seeing porters without footwear each carrying a heavy airplane tire up a mountain to Tibet. It was not just the lack of protection for their feet on stony trails that bothered me but the use of humans instead of animals or motorized vehicles for carrying such heavy loads.

When I arrived at their apartment, Mike's mother was dressed in the saffron robe of a Buddhist monk. It was wrapped around her obviously naked body. I was shocked by her lack of respect for Buddhists. She was dancing for a boyfriend, a Sikh named Chun who was also there. I think she was barefoot, too, and I was too polite to express disapproval. Mike didn't seem embarrassed, and I guessed he was used to her ways.

He invited me along to a reception hosted by the president of India. By then, I had learned that much diplomatic business was done at such events, but Mike seemed bored by the formalities. Afterward, we had dinner in a Chinese restaurant. He told me about Mustang, the most difficult place to get to in the world. It was a Tibetan kingdom in Nepal that he had heard about during his trip. No roads. Only footpaths from an airport to its capital, a five-day hike. He wanted to go one day because it was in such a remote part that hardly anyone ever heard of it. It sounded intriguing to me, but I wasn't keen on climbing mountains. Then he had to go to Ceylon, which is now known as Sri Lanka.

My term with the conferences and seminars program was to finish in September of that year. I had been away from home for three years, and it was time to see my family again, too. I was getting ready to leave. The Service Committee gave me a travel allowance to return to Toronto by plane via its headquarters in Philadelphia. If I traveled by land as much as possible instead of flying, I could include more countries. We didn't think then about carbon footprints. Going by land was always more interesting than flying.

One of the Quakers living in North India was staying two nights at the Quaker Center. I met her over breakfast, and she invited me to drive with her to Dehra Dun, a five-hour car trip north. From there, I could get a train to Pakistan. I hesitated and said I hadn't said goodbye to a friend who was returning to New Delhi the next day. She seemed to guess what I was talking about. "If it's going to happen, it will happen," she assured me, and because she was such a congenial person, I accepted her offer instead of waiting a day to take a train from Delhi. At that point, Mike and I had just been platonic friends.

From Dehra Dun, I took the train to Lahore in Pakistan. As we passed through Amritsar, I could see the famous Golden Temple, the head temple of the Sikh religion. I thought about the trains full of murdered people on the same line many years before, killed because of religious differences.

Two-meter Tex from our Port Dickson seminar had explained how to hitchhike through the Khyber Pass into Afghanistan. From a certain hotel in Peshawar, one contacted a specific concierge who knew if anyone was driving to Kabul the next day. If anything adverse happened, at least there would be a witness, he said. I was always careful when I traveled. I gave friends, and sent Mom, my itinerary, including the names of my hotels.

Tex's advice worked like a charm. In Peshawar, I hitched a ride with a man who had a new, comfortable car. I think he was either an Iraqi or Iranian diplomat. I was fortunate: the man could have attacked me on that desolate thirty-three-mile (53 kilometers) road, but he was a gentleman. We passed isolated, walled villages made of sun-dried mud and saw very few people. All was peaceful and seemed meant to be, but I would not recommend that trip to anyone else, especially now with the Taliban in charge of the country.

Mike had told me about the flight from Kabul to Tehran on Ariana Airlines. I contacted the airline manager he had interviewed for a story. Fortunately, Pete Baldwin had a free room at a hotel usually meant for his flight crew, and he invited me to stay there overnight without charge. I bought a cheap but fancy Persian lamb jacket in the market.

In Tehran, I stayed in a hostel operated by American missionaries, relatives of David Elder with whom I had worked in Tokyo. Quaker connections, such as David's, were amazing. AFSC used a lot of church-run hostels like those of David's relatives during our travels in Asia. They were relatively cheap, adequate, and comfortable, and staff were always helpful. I felt I was among friends.

Then Mike sent me a cable, saying that he was coming to Tehran to ask me to marry him. I was certainly surprised because he hadn't even tried to kiss me. I didn't turn him down but explained that we had only known each other for a few months and gone on only three dates. We didn't know each other well enough to make such a decision. I cabled back a "maybe" to the proposal. It wasn't a "no." Actually, I was thinking about his mother. If I had said "yes," this shameless woman whom I had considered irreverent and gross would be my mother-in-law. I didn't ask if she would be living with us.

My journey continued by train from Tehran toward Moscow, past Mount Ararat, through Armenia and Georgia, and touching near the Black Sea and the Caucasus Mountains. It was an excellent trip. The train was comfortable, and the other passengers were friendly. Only a few could speak English. I tried to learn the Cyrillic alphabet and Russian songs like "Moscow Nights" and "Katyusha" during the three- or four-day trip. Everybody I met said Moscow was very, very cold. It was a sad trip, too. As we reached every border, travelers without proper visas had to leave the train, even though they said they were going to Moscow. I wondered if they were being arrested.

I spent four days in Moscow at a hotel I had to book through the Russian travel agency Intourist. I explored the city on my own, amazed by its elegant subway system. Whenever I needed directions, I would approach any friendly-looking person on the street. They would take me and my phrase book personally by the hand. They were all so congenial and helpful, and it wasn't all that cold. I felt quite comfortable in my new jacket and enjoyed the hospitality.

At the time, Moscow and Beijing were quarreling over the definition of communism and which country was the leader. One of the Russian women I met said, "It is only a quarrel between governments. The Russian people love the Chinese people."

Intourist chose a Chinese-style hotel for me. One night, I ordered soup, and it tasted awful. The waiter wasn't the least bit apologetic. "That's because it's Chinese and not Russian," he explained.

From Moscow to Paris, I traveled by train and was able to see a part of the Berlin Wall as we went through Germany. I thought of Johannes, the German, I had met in Malaya. He had felt compelled to walk to Israel and volunteer in a kibbutz. That gave me hope that some divisions in the world could be healed. In Paris, I spent a week with Danièle, my former Toronto roommate, as always trying to practice French while exploring that wonderful city for the first time. Danièle's parents had been antique dealers, and their flat was full of exquisite artifacts. She had put up a copy of one of my touristy Hong Kong pictures in a prominent place; it was a very hospitable gesture. Her husband Michel was involved in political demonstrations in support of Algeria, which was then trying to free itself from over a hundred years of French colonial rule. I remember meeting Algerian leaders in their apartment.

Then I flew from Paris for a week to Philadelphia where American Friends Service Committee debriefed me and offered me a job, but I was a foreign national, so the offer had to be withdrawn. I stayed with Doris from the Mexican workcamp. After surviving three and a half years in Asia without a scratch, I fell off a horse while riding in a Philadelphia park. I was recuperating in Doris's apartment when one of her friends knocked on the door. President Kennedy had just been assassinated, and she needed to talk with someone. It was November 22, 1963, and I felt upset, too. I had admired President Kennedy for starting the Peace Corps with its grass-roots attempt to learn and help people in classrooms and villages, somewhat like what we had been doing in Mexico. It seemed to be so much more effective at making friends and raising living standards than the shorter-term volunteer tourism trips, which were being promoted by charities primarily to raise money.

Back home in Brockville, while preparing for a talk to the local Rotary club, I figured that I had visited seventeen countries in the last few years. None of them were mainland China. I guess it was an achievement worthy of a speech to business and professional leaders, and Mom seemed proud of me, too.

After the speech, some Rotary members asked where I was going next. I had to get a job to save some more money. China, my ancestral land, had to be my next goal. It was the cause of much conflict and controversy, and I wanted to get answers for myself. Why was it attacking Tibetans? What would happen to Taiwan? Should Communist China be invited to join the United Nations? Why wasn't it feeding its own people? Was the Quaker nonviolent approach an answer to world problems?

Chapter 9:
Canada, Iranians, Pakistan, India, Cambodia, Vietnam, Mike, 1963-1965

The world outside of Canada was now my main interest, and it was relatively easy to get a job related to international affairs. Murray Thomson, who had invited me to the Malayan seminar, was now in Toronto. He knew about a job in Ottawa at the Overseas Institute of Canada. It didn't pay much, but it covered my living expenses, and I could leave any time. For four months, I helped organize the OIC library and kept track of Canadian overseas aid.

Living in the capital, which was only an hour drive from Brockville, was also a new learning experience. When I lived in Brockville, our family sometimes went to Ottawa just for a genuine Chinese lunch because it had the closest Chinatown. I wanted to learn more about the city. It was also special because my brother was living there, and it had a Quaker meeting. I already had friends there.

I later found a dream job that sounded more interesting, or so I thought. I became one of several public relations officers for the Department of External Affairs (now Global Affairs), working for the Canadian government as it hosted the Third Commonwealth Education Conference. Some of the other PR officers were aiming for careers as diplomats, and I thought that becoming a diplomat might put me in a peacemaking position, too.

The Commonwealth of Nations is a political association of fifty-four member states, nearly all former territories of the British Empire. For over a week that summer, Canada brought together educators and officials from all over the Commonwealth. We PR staff arranged press conferences and wrote press releases.

The government was trying hard to be hospitable. After the sessions, which were all focused on education, it arranged for the delegates to go on a special overnight train to the Shakespearean festival in Stratford, Ontario, and then, the next day, to see our famous Niagara Falls. Canada must have spent considerable money on that conference. There were a hundred of us on that trip. Alas, I did not always act as a perfect hostess.

Many of us slept on the train in upper or lower berths divided by curtains. One of the African delegates asked me to sleep with him. I tried to be polite and told him my culture would not let me sleep with people I wasn't married to. This might sound strange in the twenty-first century, but birth control measures weren't as prevalent then as they are now. I was also among the Victoria College coeds who prided ourselves on saving our virginity for marriage. For me, sex meant babies. They are lovely creatures, but I had to choose between having a family and traveling. Seeing more of the world was still important. As for the proposition, a real diplomat would have taken the African aside and answered him confidentially, but as it was, everyone nearby could hear my rejection of his invitation. The next day, his colleagues related how they had teased him mercilessly. The man was very embarrassed and avoided me. I couldn't be a good hostess to him.

I also bluntly told an Australian delegate who invited me to Australia that I wouldn't go because of his country's "white Australia" policy. His government was still trying to keep Chinese people from immigrating there at that time. I was pleased to embarrass him. I still had to learn how to be more polite with people I disagreed with.

And then there was the delegate from one of the smaller island nations. I suspected he wasn't an educator nor even from a department of education because he didn't seem to know anything about the subject. I wanted to expose him. Was he on the trip, paid for by taxpayer money, because he was a relative of some bigwig, I wondered? He agreed to my arranging a press interview for him. When a journalist asked him a question, he spluttered and said, "I shouldn't be here. I don't know anything about it." He got up and left while I suppressed a grin. It was obvious that I wasn't meant to be a diplomat. And it was so easy to forget about Quaker respect.

I didn't like being part of a bureaucracy. Whenever we wrote a letter on behalf of the government, we had to get that letter cleared by several layers of officialdom before we could send it out. Although I understood why this had to be done, I didn't want to work that way.

My apartment was a short walk away from Parliament Hill. After hours, one of the official government interpreters was having a losing battle, trying to teach me French in the parliamentary cafeteria. French is one of Canada's two official languages and necessary for government promotions. Some members of parliament and many of their aides ate there, too. They were from all over Canada, living far from their families, and I had to fend off some unwanted attention. They made me lose my high regard for politicians, civil servants, and the government. While I felt governments were essential in changing a country's laws, a job in it just didn't seem a fit for me.

Then one evening, I overheard some tired-looking women in our apartment building laundry room talking about retiring from the civil service after several decades of hard work. They spoke of the comfortable pension they had. I knew I didn't want to be like them, working in a stressful job in Ottawa for a pension and then too old to enjoy it. I wanted a more interesting life—one in which I was in charge—not anybody else.

Mike was still sending letters, asking when I would return to Asia to marry him. Once he sent flowers, but the letters were newsy about taking orphans to a circus and trying to quit smoking, which was making him feel he was covered with ants. One letter had a page in response to my question about the Colombo Accords and another urging me to keep trying to get a visa to China because of the demand for stories from China. "The thing I love about you, Ruth, is that you are as interested in the world as I am. . . . You are the only girl I have ever met who had the makings of both a wife and a friend . . . so come back. I'll send you the money. I'll even send you the cartridges if you have to shoot your old boyfriend." I assumed the latter was a joke.

In response to my question, he wrote about his goals:

> Life is an adventure. Adventures consist of running into something new and trying to understand it. If people are going to live together, they should adventure togeth-er . . . meeting new people and learning new things. Your Quakering business is a pretty good example . . . I like to think of getting you accredited as a part-time stringer for some Canadian newspaper. Then we could share the more amusing or exciting parts of my goofy job, which also happens to be my goofy hobby.

I decided my future was not in Ottawa or with a career job. In spite of the private tutor, I wasn't learning French. By then, Mike's mother, Lou, had married Chun, and they had moved to Bihar in another part of India. With Lou no longer living with Mike, I began to reconsider his offer. I had saved a thousand dollars, so I planned another trip to Asia.

As I was thinking about my options, a strange coincidence happened, which I like to think wasn't a coincidence. Was this an act of God? I had been trying to get a visa to China with no success. One evening, as I was passing through the lobby of my apartment building, a friendly stranger approached. Although she lived there, too, we had never met, and she asked if I was Chinese. During the conversation, I must have mentioned my desire to go to China. She was the secretary of the Canadian Minister of Agriculture who had just sold sixty million dollars worth of wheat and barley there. No other country wanted to deal with the Communist government. They were all afraid of annoying the United States.

Canada did not establish diplomatic relations with China until 1970; the United States not until 1979. Droughts in China in the 1960s and the failure of its agricultural policies meant that there was not enough food grown there for its people. At the same time, Canada needed a market for its wheat, so the two countries made a historic deal. To celebrate, the minister was having a dinner party with some Chinese officials and journalists. This woman, who happened to have an apartment in my building, invited me along.

That evening, I met the minister. I also met two journalists from China's Xinhua News Agency and told them I wanted to visit China as a journalist. They said they could help and wanted to know my itinerary. They suggested applying for a visa at the Chinese Embassy in Paris and then picking up the visa in New Delhi. They would inform their friends there. I couldn't believe it! It sounded so easy.

Mike had transferred to Vietnam by then. For years, the Vietnamese had fought for their independence from the Japanese invaders and then from the French colonists. Now they were fighting among themselves for power. The Americans were involved in the Vietnamese civil war, fearful that a communist victory in Vietnam would mean other countries in Asia would also become communist. By 1962, the U.S. military had several thousand troops in South Vietnam. It seemed that Americans were trying to show the French they could do what the French couldn't.

I planned my trip to include Vietnam. My friends with their secure jobs in Ottawa thought I was crazy, going off without any assurance of a position abroad. I was able to get *The Star Weekly* interested in a story or two on China. It had the largest circulation in Canada and paid well. The Canadian Broadcasting Corporation was also interested.

It was good to see Danièle and Michel and their children in Paris, and it only took a few minutes to apply for a visa at the Chinese embassy. I could pick it up in New Delhi, said the friendly officer. I took a train to Munich in Germany and then a bus from there to Tehran in Iran. That eight-day, 2,600-mile bus ride was amazing. I had chosen it because it was cheap: a hundred dollars for transportation, food, visas, and hotels. We were one American, eleven Iranians, and me. Most of the Iranians were going home after studying or working in Germany. Three of them, including a doctor, spoke English fluently. The American was a man in his sixties, intent on traveling the world until he died. The trip turned out to provide examples of racial discrimination, Iranian hospitality, and a lesson in nationalism.

One of the Iranian passengers, a young student, was obviously a little unbalanced. He kept calling the German conductor a "whore" for no apparent reason. As a result, he and the German driver had a fistfight, and once in Austria, the police were called. It was a "misunderstanding," said the other Iranians, and the police told us to go on. In Bulgaria, the student continued his obnoxious behavior, and the driver put him off the bus and threatened to drive on without him. At that point, most of the other Iranians started leaving the bus and refused to get back on without the student. The Bulgarian police said the student couldn't stay in their country because he didn't have enough money. Fortunately, we changed buses and drivers in Istanbul and no longer had a conductor; the student caused no more trouble.

Our best hotel was in Bulgaria where the government seemed to be putting on a special effort to attract tourists. It was the only country where a local tourist guide got on our bus to tell us about the country. Bulgarians beside the highway waved at us, and we passed big signs advertising its famous yogurt.

After arriving in Turkey, we had a day of sightseeing on our own in Istanbul. Then, through the bus window, I watched as wealthy green Europe changed into arid Western Asia. There, the villages had mud houses, and the economy seemed dependent on angora goats and broad-tailed sheep. Even large communities were without electricity.

We passed Mount Ararat, streaked with snow and squatting like an old woman hiding an ancient secret. Did Noah's Ark really land there? The bus rolled into the hearts of the towns as we stopped for meals in restaurants, tea, and souvenirs. When I didn't like the food the bus provided, I snacked on cheese and dried apricots I had bought in Germany. I took photos of camels, veiled women, and crowded markets.

When we reached the Iranian border, the Iranian women all put on *chadors*, the cloak that covered their heads and most of their bodies. Once past Iranian customs, I smiled as a huge sigh of relief permeated the bus. I understood the feeling because no one needed to pay duty on their newly acquired cameras and record players. After we arrived in their homeland, the Iranians gleefully showed each other their German purchases.

Our hotels were modest but adequate except for our last night together, when only two rooms were available for all of us. By that time, we had become one big family, and no one seemed to mind sleeping dormitory-style. We had a party to celebrate. In Tehran, the offensive student disappeared. A fellow passenger explained that none of the other passengers actually supported the student, but they could not leave him at the mercy of the police in a foreign country. Much as they also disliked him, they had to support their fellow countryman. It was a lesson for me in the power of nationalism.

I received invitations to stay in four Iranian homes. Two of them came from people who could not speak English. Alas, I had no time to accept. It was hard to say goodbye to these friendly people whose lives I had shared, and I went back to the Christian guest house and flew the next day to Karachi in Pakistan.

That night in Karachi, I slept in a small hotel someone in Canada had recommended. I was a woman by myself in a country where women needed protection. The manager had told me to lock my door and not open it to anyone. That night, someone banged on it. I was frightened and tried to ignore the noise as I heard male voices arguing. Then the noise stopped. The next morning, I realized that the night manager had moved his bed to block my door. I was very grateful.

Before leaving Ottawa, an official at the government aid agency had offered to pay for photos of Canadian aid projects in Pakistan. One of these was the Mangla Dam. Once at the dam, I took a lot of pictures, so the Canadian government could see where its money was going. I was invited to spend the night with Dr. Frank and Midge Philbrook from Toronto, a medical team helping with the project. They were wonderful hosts, and Frank later spent five years as a member of parliament in Canada.

On the way, I saw a perfect picture-taking opportunity. The whole story was there in one compact setting. A cart had over-turned on the road. A man and a horse were dead. A woman was crying. Other people were around to help. But it was too private and tragic a scene, and I couldn't take the picture.

India and Pakistan were almost at war with each other, and I should have known better. I was on my way to India, which could have used pictures of the strategically-located dam. My pictures could have helped the Indians. In Lahore, where I was staying in a hotel with Quaker friends I had met before in India, a policeman came and confiscated all my films, including my pictures from the bus trip. They could have put me in jail as a spy, he said.

In an effort to get my photos back, I decided to stay. I contin-ued researching stories and managed to visit a Muslim home where the women wore *burkahs,* the black robes that covered their bodies except for the eyes and feet. One of the women was a university professor and spoke English. Even though I disagree with the se-questering of women, it was a pleasure to spend time in their world, so different from mine. The women and girls were very friendly and eager to meet a woman from another country and talk about their lives. Their interests were not all that different from ours in the West. They knew about fashionable European and American name-brand make-up and clothes. They wore these under their burkahs. None of them seemed to envy my freedom, nor did they show any curiosity about me.

A Pakistani man told me later that he could tell the age of a woman by her walk and her feet. A burkah was no protection, he said.

An officer from the Canadian Commission in Karachi came to Lahore to help. After he said he would try to get my pictures back, I took a train to New Delhi. At the border, customs officers expected me. They searched my luggage and took away more film, including tourist pictures of Lahore and those of the sequestered women. For a while, they seemed intent on keeping me in Pakistan. Although I liked the country, it was a relief to get back to India. It took several months before Canadian officials returned the pictures. The photos of the dam were out of date by that time and useless. I did not get back the unprocessed rolls of the bus trip from Munich to Tehran.

In New Delhi, I obtained my visa for China. Officials at the Chinese embassy predicted that I would be followed by Indian police as I left. They were right, but the police didn't do anything except stare at me as their car stopped beside my taxi. I stared back, and they seemed embarrassed and went away.

I met one of Mike's former Indian colleagues at UPI and told him I would be meeting up with him in Vietnam. He told me I should forget about Mike because Mike couldn't control his own mother. I wasn't sure how I should take that advice; besides, I still hadn't made up my mind about him.

The Abbott family were Quakers from Toronto. Ed and Viv were doctors working in rural India for ten years, an unusual place to bring up their five Canadian children, ages seven to sixteen. I went to visit them, and their fascinating story ended up in *The Star Weekly*. While Ed was inventing birth control devices and digging wells, Viv was treating people for malaria and delivering babies. Daughter Franie, who was about sixteen at the time, was giving penicillin shots to a cow; fifteen-year-old son, Bill, was climbing up hydroelectric poles and repairing the wiring. They all spoke Hindi fluently.

My former boss, Russell Johnson, was still in India, organizing another conference for diplomats. He invited me to help with an upcoming one in Cambodia. I was in no hurry to get to Vietnam. His wife, Irene, and I flew to Bangkok in Thailand, and, to save money, we decided to go by land from Bangkok to Siem Reap in Cambodia, a distance of 250 miles (400 kilometers). After crossing the border, we discovered that the last bus to Siem Reap had already left for the day. There were no hotels or taxis in that tiny border town, so we went to the police station for help. The police had a new building, as yet unused, and we slept there on bare desks that night. It was my only night in a police station, and it felt quite safe.

The conference was at a hotel near nine-hundred-year-old Angkor Wat. The temple covers 154 square miles (four hundred square kilometers) and is considered the largest religious monument in the world. It was in excellent, artistic condition except for the trees that grow through its ancient walls. That temple and the presence of Prince Norodom Sihanouk were more than enough to interest diplomats in joining the conference.

Russell had supported the prince who was trying to keep his country neutral in the Indo-China wars. As a result, the prince made sure the conference went well. Our opening night featured a platoon of boy scouts lining the bridge to the main temple with flaming torches. The prince's daughter, Princess Norodom Buppha Devi, a famous classical dancer, led a troupe of lavishly clad performers in the silhouetted building, which was lit with torches as well. With slow, deliberate movements, punctuated by metal gongs, drums, and xylophones, she and her dancers took us back to ancient times. It and the conference were a rare and beautiful event.

Russell later said that the prince was appalled that Irene and I had to spend the night in a police station. I didn't agree. It was a wonderful adventure. In spite of the Pakistani police, my trip had been great so far. I guess I was meant to go to Vietnam. Russell went on to a speaking tour to promote U.S.-Russian relations before he retired to make maple syrup on his New England farm.

Mike met me at the Saigon airport and greeted me with a shy kiss on the cheek. With his crew cut hair and informal clothes, he hadn't changed since I last saw him in New Delhi, except for the addition of a mustache. He was with one of his Vietnamese cameramen, and, as Ly drove through the strangely silent and peaceful city, it felt strange meeting him again after almost two years. I tried to look hard for signs of war: a few soldiers, army trucks, and barbed wire enclosed military buildings amid beautiful, tree-lined boulevards.

Mike was delighted to hear about the Chinese visa. He took me to a hotel, offered his own apartment when I wondered about the cost, and then went back to work.

That night, the constant noise of firecrackers made me think that the Viet Cong had invaded the city. Mike had said it was Tet, the Vietnamese New Year, and I figured that Tet was the reason for the racket and that the hotel was safe. The next day, I went outside cautiously to explore a main street full of flowers for sale. Flowers in the middle of a war! Many people were also ignoring a government order not to explode more noisy firecrackers. For forty-eight hours, Saigon sounded like a war video game.

Mike was busy. I tried to convince myself that I hadn't come to marry him. I had come to get to know him better, but I didn't have money to stay very long in a hotel. My Quaker connections led to cheaper rooms at the International Voluntary Service (IVS) hostel near the airport. This was a nongovernmental agency that the Quakers, Mennonites, and Brethren had helped to start.

Staying with American and British volunteers for a month was almost like being back in a workcamp. All were pacifists working in agriculture or community development. Some were teaching English in several parts of the country. "Teaching English," said one volunteer, "was a way to teach other things like cooperation, work, play, community spirit. That's what the Vietnamese lack." About seventy volunteers were in the country, congregating in the Saigon hostel from time to time, where they shared their stories and could relax.

Unlike most other foreigners in the country, the IVS people learned to speak Vietnamese. Les Small, an American agriculturalist, introduced me to the local food in a simple, outdoor restaurant. Taking me for a Vietnamese person, the waiter kept looking at me as he asked for our orders. Les answered in Vietnamese, which of course, I didn't know. The waiter was bewildered, and although his assumptions were based on race, we found it amusing. Les seemed to be very close to the people he was trying to help. His wasn't just a job; he genuinely wanted to help. Although I had no intention of going into a battlefield, there were a lot a human interest stories to write, some of them inspired by idealistic young people like Les at IVS. I wanted to write about alternatives to fighting.

One of its volunteers, Marybeth Clark, took me by public bus to the Mekong Delta to meet IVS volunteers there and to learn about the Summer Youth Program where Vietnamese university students, funded by USAID, worked together under IVS supervision. They were repairing war-damaged village infrastructure and building facilities like latrines and schools for refugees. There, Vietnamese students shared their problems with us, their concern about corrupt government officials stealing from the projects, and the wide divisions between the educated and uneducated. They talked about the conflicts between their paternalistic family system and the new westernized values. Some of the students worked enthusiastically, but some were lazy. Some seemed to have genuine rapport with village people. Others were indifferent. Many students complained about the "vagueness of freedom and democracy" as goals. Can corruption, nepotism, and inequalities in opportunity be eliminated? These were subjects we had also discussed at every Quaker seminar I attended in Asia, except here in Vietnam, it involved many human lives.

The country had over forty political parties, and one student, the son of a Vietnamese diplomat, bluntly stated, "I want to be a politician like my uncle. I want to start a new party. I want to be famous and be a leader like my father and uncle."

Back in Saigon, Mike was busy covering the war as bureau chief. He asked me to do some short radio clips with information from UPI. I did one by telephone for his editor in the U.S., who said UPI couldn't use a woman's voice. Too soft. It had to be a man's voice. Today, things have changed, and many broadcasters are women; however, I was actually glad to be rejected. I knew I couldn't think fast enough with the appropriate information to answer any questions.

It was a war unlike any other, much of it fought in the outskirts of Saigon. Occasionally, the Viet Cong, the Communists, would blow up one of the hotels or a restaurant frequented by Americans in the capital. Mike didn't support one side or the other at first. His job was to report objectively on Vietnam. He complained about the visiting American politicians on "fact-finding tours," who said the U.S. was there to defend and build freedom. He got the impression that they were actually there to get their pictures taken with the sons of their constituents fighting in the war.

Getting press accreditation with the Brockville newspaper's press card was easy. It meant that I could hitch rides with the U.S. military to other parts of the country. One time, after we had landed safely back in Saigon, the helicopter gunner said we had been shot at. I hadn't heard a thing over the noise of the thumping propellers. I was glad we were back on the ground.

Mike invited me along on some of his interviews, and we went out for occasional dinners, but he usually left me alone because of his work. There was no further mention of his interest in getting married. I began to date other journalists. The war attracted other interesting men.

Another journalist invited me out to dinner in a fancy French restaurant. I think Mike told him I had a visa to China. He was a little drunk when he arrived, but the conversation was not about China, even though he had been a teacher there for several years. He had started a newspaper in Bangkok years before. The Thai government had asked him if it should send some women to help the morale of its troops in Korea, but he didn't think General McArthur would have approved. He asked what year I was born in and said a fortune teller had said he should marry someone born in 1932, 1922, or 1937. I was amused but didn't tell him. The next day, his chauffeur arrived at IVS with flowers and the change left over from buying them. I handed back the money with a note, "Thanks for the flowers but not the money." I thought it was funny and told Mike about it, hoping it would make him realize I wasn't there waiting for him to make up his mind.

Another American journalist asked me out, too. Even before the first course, he talked as if all Asian women were prostitutes. I got up and asserted as I left, "I'm not that kind of a girl!" I knew such men didn't make good husbands and were a waste of my time.

I hung around the UPI office where I received my mail. By this time, I had gotten to know some of the other journalists. One day, I asked Ray Herndon who was the best foreign journalist in Saigon. Ray said it was Mike. Maybe Ray knew why I was really there, checking Mike out as a marriage prospect. Another reporter mentioned in passing that Mike didn't go out to get drunk like the others. That was important for me, too. I discovered Mike had an amazing mind, a vast knowledge about the world, not just about Asia. I knew I could never be a foreign correspondent like him. I didn't have that kind of memory; and I found out later that Ray was right about Mike.

A couple of days later, Mike announced that he wanted me to go to Laos. "Are you trying to get rid of me?" I asked. He said he was taking a vacation. He knew Laos, the country adjacent to Vietnam, because he had spent eighteen months there, covering that war before going to India. He thought I would like it. I had never been to Laos, and it didn't have a war at the time.

We stayed in the same hotel in Vientiane where Mike had lived before on an expense account. Maurice, the manager of the Constellation, was so surprised that Mike was paying with his own money this time that he didn't charge us. Mike talked about the Laotian war, the Plain of Jars, and his first motorcycle, bought in Laos, which he smashed into a truck on his first day with it. He never rode a motorcycle again. Smoking opium was legal. Martin Stuart-Fox, who was working in Laos for UPI at the time, took us to an opium den for a try. Martin was the only one affected. It made him vomit.

We flew to tiny Luang Prabang, the ancient royal capital, over 190 miles (three hundred kilometers) from the current capital. It is where the Mekong and Nam Khan Rivers meet, and it was full of glittering, little temples decorated with snakes with flaming crowns and gilded dancing spirits. Their roofs cascaded gracefully down in layers. We visited caves full of tiny Buddhas.

That evening, as we sat in one of its parks, farmers were burning the fields on the hills across the river, weaving an arc of fire in the sky. Mike proposed marriage again. It was too romantic. I did not need to think twice about it this time. I said yes because it seemed to be the right thing to do. Then he gave me our first real kiss. It was beautiful and worth waiting for.

Mike urged me to go to China. He repeated that it was a rare opportunity, and few Western journalists were able to go there at that time. It was obvious that he had been thinking about our future together. He said it was not wise for us to be married before I went to China. Radio Peking was always quoting him as "Imperialist journalist Malloy."

"We should get married in Hong Kong after you get out," he said. "You shouldn't go to China as the wife of an imperialist journalist."

Of course, I agreed. I liked his foresight. It would take some time to get permission to marry in Vietnam, and I had been desperate to go to China ever since I was in college. I suggested he write to my mother. I still have the letter, written on UPI stationery, that said:

> I make $140 per week plus about $50 more on certain commissions which go with the job. I have got $3,000 squirrelled away in the bank, a mother in India, and a married sister in Chicago. . . . My prospects and plans are wrapped up with those of my company. That makes them pretty vague because we generally go where or when the bossmen decide, usually on pretty short notice. However, I like Asia, have been out here for six years, and have little desire to move back to the States, short of being called on to become president of the company (most unlikely). . . . I will do my best to be a good husband for your daughter. I know she will make a wonderful wife for me.

He talked about a diamond engagement ring, but I didn't want to support a tradition based largely on De Beers's advertising campaigns. I opted for jade, which is very important in Chinese culture, although it is not usually used for an engagement. He promised to learn something about the Canadian version of the War of 1812 between British Canada and the U.S., a subject we had once

135

disagreed about. While he himself was an agnostic, he had no objection to my Quaker pursuits. We both agreed we wanted to have children. I said I wanted at least one kiss a day, and he pretended it might be a problem.

Mike later bought a solid gold smuggler's bracelet, only available in Laos. It was too heavy to wear as jewellery. We joked about it being a bride price, which I could use if we broke up. It is a custom in some Asian countries. We watched the value of the gold go up every year.

I decided to keep my Chinese maiden name but added Mike's family name to mine. At that point, I did not want to give up being Chinese. I still had a connection with the country.

Chapter 10:
China at Last and
Hong Kong Wedding, 1965

When I went to buy a train ticket to China at China Travel Service in Hong Kong, the ticket seller said overseas Chinese didn't need a visa. After all my trouble of going to two countries to get one! But I learned that a visa had advantages.

"Oh," I said, "What is an overseas Chinese?"

"It is not a matter of your parents being Chinese, it is how you feel that makes you overseas Chinese," said the clerk. I didn't hesitate to say I felt "partly Chinese."

This seemed to satisfy him, and I booked my ticket, a hotel and a taxi from the Guangzhou railway station. Soon, I was on a train to the border, apprehensive yet eager about my first trip to that much-feared land of my ancestors. I couldn't help wondering how Chinese I felt. At that point, it was probably between 5 and 25 percent.

I was surprised by the special treatment. At the border leaving Hong Kong, I was sent to the VIP lounge while officials stamped my passport. Although there had been crowds on the train, I was the only person in that room.

The same thing happened on the other side of the covered bridge that separated Hong Kong and China. I was singled away from hundreds of other travelers who also looked Chinese. Over tea in a private lounge with the latest editions of the government magazines, *China Today* and *China Reconstructs,* I tried to relax while pleasant young officials in wrinkled uniforms took care of the formalities. My fears were allayed somewhat by their friendliness and the enthusiasm of their welcome; however, a group of young people in the customs compound were having target practice with revolvers just outside the window. It was puzzling. At that point, I was glad to be rescued by a young woman, who officiously showed me which train car to take.

I sat alone in a comfortable seat as we passed by rice fields and villages of identical, one-story houses. Two hours later in Guangzhou, an overly inquisitive official reminded me I was in a very nervous country. Comrade Lowe took me to the Overseas Chinese Hotel. During our first few hours together, he asked innumerable questions about my relatives in China and Hong Kong. He wanted addresses. Having noted the stamps from those countries in my passport, he was also curious about my impressions of India, Pakistan, and Vietnam. He was probably trying to figure out exactly who I was and what to do with me.

How much had the Chinese journalists in Ottawa told anyone about me? Unlike the other travelers from Hong Kong, I had an actual visa.

With a smirk, he asked, "Were you in Saigon when the American Embassy was bombed?"

"Yes," I answered, reacting to his smugness. "I was three blocks away. I thought it was a sloppy job killing twenty innocent Vietnamese bystanders to get two Americans!" The grin faded. I still had to learn to be more Quakerly.

How should I act with Comrade Lowe? In self-defense, I asked him about himself, but his responses were vague. Lily Howe had warned me about nosy people like Lowe. She was a Toronto school-teacher who had visited China a few weeks before and had been distressed by the persistent questions and cross-examinations by officials. She and two friends had traveled without a guide in several cities. On their return to their hotels each evening, the women were separated from each other and officials asked them where they had gone, whom they had seen, and where they originally met. I wondered if the officials thought my friends were spies and if Lowe was wondering if I were an intelligence agent as well. I was worried, too, because other travelers had said Chinese customs had seized their films as they left the country. If they did that to me, I wouldn't have any photos to publish with my stories.

Three more officials visited my hotel room that first evening. Each one welcomed me "back," even though I had never been there before. They offered help to make my stay pleasant. That was fine, but why three officials? I felt like going back to Hong Kong.

The next day, Lowe returned. He asked for my impressions of Taiwan and wrote down the name of the magazine I was writing for. When I asked for directions to the home of a friend's friend, he hastily pulled out a scrap of paper and scribbled something down. Was I getting the friend's friend in trouble? Hong Kong's newspapers were full of stories of people fleeing China, afraid for their lives. Some said relatives in China had been kept as hostages, so visitors would say nothing bad about the country.

Much to my relief, it seemed that I passed the interrogation phase. China had an Overseas Chinese Commission (OCC) to look after visitors of Chinese origin like me. Its tone changed. No more threatening questions. I suspected that the Canadian wheat sales and the Chinese journalists in Ottawa had something to do with it. The OCC was a branch of the Chinese government, so I was unable to relax completely.

It was 1965, the year before the start of the Cultural Revolution that was to change China even more than its unsuccessful Great Leap Forward campaign. The Great Chinese Famine was over by then, and it seemed that China wanted more overseas Chinese to visit and contribute to the country.

The OCC offered a much appreciated interpreter / traveling companion to accompany me everywhere I went. I didn't speak enough Chinese to manage the logistics on my own. These guides—perhaps they were minders—asked where I wanted to go. I said Beijing, of course, Shanghai, Hangzhou, a visit to my relatives who lived in our ancestral village, and Guangzhou. I included Hangzhou because my favorite restaurant in Toronto was named Sai Woo (West Lake) which was in Hangzhou. They took me to Hangzhou, and it did not disappoint. It had the classical temples, moon bridges, curved roofs, water lilies, weeping willows, and the giant goldfish of famous Chinese paintings. It was stunning.

The OCC also provided a private car to places in Beijing like the Great Wall and the Forbidden City, and also invitations to my first Peking duck banquet and Peking opera. My guide, Comrade Liu, was a charming young man with a great sense of humor. He was a Communist party member but unexpectedly candid and fun. I expected Communist party members to be very serious. I was getting the V.I.P. treatment.

Liu arranged for me to attend the big parade in Tiananmen Square on May Day, International Labor Day. We stood just outside the Forbidden City, the former imperial palace. I watched hundreds of laborers in their work clothes march together, waving flags without enthusiasm. The Communist revolution had been based on workers, but the ones on display looked uncomfortable, as if they had been forced to be in a parade in their honor and didn't know how to behave.

That evening, Comrade Liu took me to dinner with Premier Chou En-lai (now spelled Zhou En-lai), just us and forty-five hundred other guests. It was in the Great Hall of the People, China's equivalent of Parliament. It seemed that Premier Chou had invited every foreign visitor in the city. I could barely see the premier because I wasn't important enough to get a table close to him.

The logistics of feeding forty-five hundred people was mind-boggling, but the servers were well-trained, like an army. We were in a room decorated with banners and flags, the largest room I have ever seen. The food was northern-style: Peking duck, dumplings, noodles, lamb, chicken, fish. One dish was decorated with a tiny fruit Liu called *goji* berries which were supposed to be "good for eyes." The dishes kept coming in an endless flow. Flavors were mild, like Cantonese food, but not as sweet. Food styles in each area of China were so different. Musicians played instruments that I had seen in Taiwan. Lively acrobats and dancers in long, filmy sleeves entertained us. Afterward, as we left the hall, fireworks shot up all around us. It was, indeed, thrilling.

The OCC paid for much but not all of my trip. One official companion lent me money to pay my expenses when I erroneously thought banks were open on Sundays.

"We are not like Europeans, out to make money," the guide answered when I protested, and I suspected ulterior motives. "We want you to know you are welcome and that you have a home here. We know how hard you have worked and suffered."

I took the opportunity to point out that most Chinese in Canada were not suffering at the moment. In fact, we liked our country very much. They accepted this without question, and I wondered about pressure on the overseas Chinese by the government. In denying it, one official answered, "Have we demanded anything of you?"

They hadn't, and they never have.

The Overseas Chinese Commission arranged a visit to meet my relatives. Yuet Yuen lived in Guangzhou. Her father, Kenneth Lor, was my father's first cousin whose home was in Gananoque, Ontario, a few minutes drive from Brockville. Because she was my age and also university educated, I kept thinking that I could have been like her if my father hadn't married my mother in Canada. Yuet Yuen lives in Toronto now and says my visits to her in China did not create problems for her. Yuet Yuen was and still is conge-nial, always smiling. She wore her hair with a slight curl to it. Her husband was an engineer; she was a medical doctor.

On my first look at her apartment, I almost wept with gratitude for having been born in Canada. Yuet Yuen, her husband, and one child had one small room with a kitchen in an old building connected to her hospital. They shared one bathroom with about ten other families. I probably could have adapted to that standard if I had to.

Yuet Yuen took me shopping and sightseeing in the large city where she lived. Its buildings were old and dumpy, but I was favorably impressed by the people in the streets. They looked adequately dressed, clean and healthy, and there were no beggars. The streets were swept three times a day, she said. People seemed to have time to lounge around in parks or play table tennis. Guides, who took me to see factories and kindergartens, explained that couples now chose their own spouses. Communes had replaced private ownership of land. This was not the China my grandparents left to find a better life in Canada.

Yuet Yuen was able to accompany us to our paternal grandfather's house in a town called Xin Hui (Sun Wei). He had left Canada before I was born, and upon his return to China, he had built a large, two-story, black brick house near a huge fishpond. Relatives still lived in the house. The deed was still in my grandfather's name, so my aunt called it "your" (that is, "my") house. It was a few meters from my father's sister's house. I didn't know my father had a sister, and I didn't know my grandfather had been a fish peddler.

Distant relatives were living in "my" house. Upon entering the living room, I found a picture of my Canadian family, taken years before in Brockville. I remembered when that picture was taken to send to relatives in China. In it were my parents, siblings, cousins, aunts, and uncles who were living in Eastern Ontario—Gananoque, Cardinal, Iroquois, and Brockville—each with a family and a restaurant in different little towns. And there I was—finally in China—staring at that picture, surprised to find that my China relatives actually knew everyone in that picture by name. Before this trip, they were just a blur on the other side of the world.

Did our house have electricity? I didn't think to look. I was so excited to finally meet my Xin Hui relatives. I remember an open skylight inside the front door and the dark interior of the living room with its bare, black brick walls because they were unusual. A half-dozen uncomfortable, plain wooden armchairs lined the room, and, near the ceiling, paintings of flowers and landscapes injected a bit of color. The kitchen beyond was small; the stove was big enough for only one wok, the huge, flattened bowl-like Chinese frying pan. Water came from a stone-lined hole in the ground, hauled up by a rope attached to a bucket.

The bedrooms were upstairs, surrounding an open space with what I assumed was the ancestral tablet, completely in Chinese. High up near the ceiling was Grandfather's picture. He looked as if he were waiting for his descendants to appear and bow to him. I recognized his picture from a similar portrait in our parents' bedroom in Brockville.

Our guide only allowed a two-hour visit before our taxi "was needed by someone else." Too soon, we had to leave. As I left, I could not help but feel a closer tie to my family in China.

Government guides also arranged the trip to the capital of Taishan county, but they said it was not possible to visit our father's village. It was difficult to get to. I was disappointed and wondered if the village was in trouble politically or if the road was really bad. Two nights were spent in a charming guest house beside a pond full of water lilies in the middle of town. "Volunteers had built the pond," said my minder with pride. I enjoyed hearing the local dialect, the same dialect spoken by my relatives in Brockville.

The buildings in the shopping area across from the hotel were all three stories tall. Like many buildings in Hong Kong, their second stories jutted out over the sidewalk. Small stores at street level were full of poor quality goods. Emigrants from Taishan county had built these structures, about the same time Grandfather returned to China in the 1920s, with money they made overseas. The decorations on their roofs all looked somewhat European, as if the owners wanted to show those left behind where they had made their fortunes.

Our ancestral village was close, only about twenty-five miles (forty kilometers) away, my guide said. I realized I hadn't completely arrived in China. I still needed to see the village where my father had come from. It was not enough to see other villages in the area as we drove around the county. Many of them had three-story watch towers too, lookouts for roving bandits. Our father had talked about spending nights in them.

I grew to like the officials from the OCC. They were intelligent and spoke good English. We discussed subjects like China's isolation, the Sino-Soviet split, the Cuban missile crisis, and atomic annihilation. One of the guides thought it hilariously funny that a twenty-four-hour hotline was necessary between the White House in Washington and the Kremlin in Moscow, in case a misunderstanding set off a nuclear war.

Our discussions usually ended in a draw with neither of us conceding because we realized we were basing our opinions on different sources of information. On some matters, I felt I had a stronger position because I had traveled, and they hadn't. I had visited villages in Vietnam and had personally seen that Americans were trying to help Vietnamese people. They were not going around mercilessly killing women and children, as the Chinese claimed. I told them about the IVS volunteers.

But that was before the American military increased its presence in Vietnam, the infamous My Lai massacre by U.S. forces of over five-hundred Vietnamese civilians, before the American bombings of Hanoi, and before Agent Orange. That was before the war got bigger and bigger.

From my guides, I learned that the Chinese government was discouraging the old custom of yearly visits to bow at ancestral graves. It was trying to get people to plant trees instead. I predicted in my *Star Weekly* article that the old custom would die, but I was wrong. It still exists in China, in Canada, and even in Brockville, where my siblings and I still burn incense at our parents' graves. In China, I was later to find stores selling paper cars, houses, and money to burn to keep ancestors happy.

I think I convinced my guides of the necessity to travel. I kept telling them to come to see for themselves that Canadian workers were not as oppressed as they thought. Working conditions were better in Toronto than those I saw in China, where the lighting was bad, and some workers, including my relatives, had to sit on low stools on the floor to weave baskets. I told them I had worked in a garment factory in Toronto. I had been a worker, too, like those in the parade in Beijing.

New fears replaced my old ones. I was in Guangzhou during a mass demonstration with thousands of workers and school children marching eight abreast in the streets shouting, "Down with U.S. imperialism," and "U.S. imperialism. Get out of Africa and Asia." While I agreed that imperialism is a bad thing, I found alarming the parroting of slogans without thought, without all the facts, and with no room for questioning. I was especially horror-stricken when children in a nursery school repeated the same slogans and pointed their little fingers upward, pretending to shoot down American planes. When I asked about their future, the older school children responded, "I want to serve the people. I want to do what Chairman Mao wants me to do."

Their desire to serve the people was admirable. I couldn't argue about that, but the worship of leader Mao Tse-tung was appalling, reminding me of religious fanatics. Everyone read slogans from Mao's little red book, like a prayer, before every meeting. Mao was the founder of the new China, a perfect being, a god. The guides dismissed criticism of the regime as "imperialist slander."

In a street play, a sniveling Uncle Sam with a big nose trembled before the guns of the People's Liberation forces. The spirit was no different from the campaigns I remembered from my elementary school days as the government urged us to buy war saving stamps and support the war against the nasty Nazis. I remembered drawing pictures of Lancaster bombers, but when I mentioned to my guides and my relatives that I was marrying an American, they wished us well, and one of them gave us a wedding present.

In the overseas Chinese hotels where I stayed in each city, I kept meeting other foreigners of Chinese origin. They were from Southeast Asia, Germany, and South Africa. They shared stories of their experiences in the "homeland" and how difficult it was to travel around China. U.S. citizens were not allowed to go to China then.

I was apprehensive as I got on the train back to the Hong Kong border. Would the Chinese confiscate the hundreds of photos I had taken? I had no need to worry. Leaving China went smoothly.

Back in Hong Kong, I prepared for our wedding. My mother had given her permission for us to marry, although she told Mike she would have preferred I marry someone Chinese. In spite of her Canadian upbringing and her acceptance of other mixed-cultural marriages, I think she felt that she would have more control of her family with a Chinese son-in-law. Of course, the request for permission was a formality. Now that I had made up my mind about Mike, I would have married him no matter what she said. I was delighted that she came to the wedding.

We were married in the city hall near the Star Ferry pier by a woman magistrate in a bright red cheongsam. Mike and I teased each other as we noticed that the vows didn't include the word "obey." We didn't have many friends in Hong Kong then, so the reception was fortunately small, about a dozen. The best man was an American business acquaintance of Mike's. Guests included Toronto friends who were living in the colony, my brother-in-law, Chun Wing, and his daughter, Theresa, then about four years old. My half-sister, Mei Ting, was too shy to join us, but my cousin, Hong Man, and his fiancée, Sue, were there. I wanted a Quaker connection at the wedding and was pleased the clerk of the Hong Kong Friends Meeting was able to join us.

I had met Canadians, Dorothy Plant and her nephew, Frank, Hooper, on the press trip to Matsu in Taiwan. They were living in Hong Kong in one of the few real houses left among a forest of tall apartment buildings. They were both working for Dr. Jim Turpin's Project Concern, a medical charity, and they hosted our reception in their home. They arranged for a volunteer from the British Army to bake and decorate a cake. Frank kept a pet monkey in their garden. It was an ideal place for a wedding reception and came with a romantic-sounding address, which Mike loved: The Garden House, Blue Pool Road, Happy Valley, Hong Kong.

My dress was a simple, white lace cheongsam. I knew white was the color of mourning in China, but it's the traditional color of western wedding dresses, so that's what I wanted. I brightened it up with a red corsage. I made sure a barrage of noisy firecrackers would accompany our departure and bring us good luck

Chinese-style. In Chinese tradition also, niece Theresa was included in some of the official pictures, signifying a wish for children. The limo had a doll attached to its hood. Such was my version of a Chinese-Canadian wedding.

We spent part of our honeymoon at the famous Repulse Bay Hotel on Hong Kong island. It was only a short distance from Happy Valley. There, on the hills above it, I discovered that my dashing husband was afraid of heights, but it didn't matter. From that hotel, we took a ferry to the nearby Portuguese colony of Macau and then returned to Hong Kong to a much less elegant hotel on one of Hong Kong's other islands. I enjoyed the variety. Our first week together was lovely, and then we went back to Saigon and the war.

The Star Weekly published two stories about my first trip to China, much of it quoted here. My editor surprised us by also publishing our wedding picture, which made me feel even more Canadian because *The Star Weekly* was distributed with newspapers in several major Canadian cities. *The Recorder and Times* also published a picture of the wedding. I felt Canadians cared about us.

Did I think of myself as Chinese at that point? As I showed my pictures from China to Mike and friends, I knew the answer. It was still a resounding "partly." China and my relatives there were still largely foreign to me. Chinese-Communist culture and Chairman Mao were completely foreign. I felt more Canadian than ever. I suppose it would have been different if I had been able to handle the language better, but I felt a connection to China that other Canadians didn't have. I couldn't completely dismiss my ancestral tie to the country.

Chapter 11:
Vietnam War and the U.S.,
1965-1973

One morning before I went to China, I heard a loud explosion near Mike's office. The Viet Cong had car-bombed the U.S. Embassy. I ran with my camera toward the noise and the smoke. Throbbing sirens indicated that ambulances and fire trucks were on their way or already there. I found first responders carrying bleeding, broken bodies on stretchers and putting out the fires. Bewildered, I felt I was in a disaster movie. Was there anything I should be doing besides take pictures? I thought about it afterward and felt guilty.

Photographers have to record events. That's what we do. However, should I have laid my camera aside and helped with the wounded? Should I have remembered Mike's warning about a possible second bomb aimed at people there to help? Should I have gotten so close? Fortunately, no second bombing occurred.

The embassy bombing was my closest personal experience to the bloody violence of war. Even now, my conscience has never let me forget an elderly Vietnamese woman sitting on the ground, obviously in pain. She was beckoning to me for help. Was she thinking I was Vietnamese? I watched the ambulance people carrying out wounded Americans, not Vietnamese. Could I have done anything for her? Since I couldn't speak Vietnamese, I couldn't even give her a few words of comfort. I don't remember if she was bleeding. Should I have stopped taking pictures that showed readers what the bombing looked like? It was a dilemma.

After our honeymoon, we lived with a cat in Mike's apartment above the UPI office in downtown Saigon. Mike and his reporting crew sometimes went by taxi to the battlefield in the suburbs. From our third-floor apartment, we could see the tracer bullets at night and feel the thud of exploding shells. We taped up the windows to keep the vibrations from shattering them. Every morning we had to straighten the pictures on the walls.

Being married was a new adventure for me, and it took a while to get used to giving up my independence. Having sex was new, and Mike was a considerate teacher. It didn't take long for me to thoroughly enjoy the intimate side of our relationship. Fortunately, he had enough self-confidence and intelligence to adjust to my needs, too.

Accurate news reporting was more important than writing features like mine. I tried to help make Mike's life easier. I supervised our maid Ah Som. I was the only person who could talk with her since she was Chinese and spoke the same dialect as my father. I still remembered some essential words from my childhood as she cleaned and taught me skills like how to bait the mousetrap. Unfortunately, it only succeeded in trapping our cat. Ah Som was a Buddhist and refused to kill anything. In the Saigon Market, I could only buy chickens and crabs that were still squawking or waving their claws. When I brought them home, I couldn't kill them either, but she was willing to take them downstairs to Mike's office for someone else to do the job.

For the Saigon market, I wore local pajamas with my hair braided, pretending to be Vietnamese, so the prices would be cheaper. I also didn't want to be a Viet Cong target. My disguise worked until I opened my mouth. I published a story about how foreigners lived in a country at war.

Having been brought up in a restaurant, I never had to cook anything beyond Kraft dinners, boiled eggs, and steamed rice. We had four cooks, and I had to learn to cook. One of them had taught me the basics of Chinese stir-fry while I was in Ottawa. As an accredited reporter, I could shop in the PX, the Post Exchange, the U.S. military supermarket, which had pretty much the same goods as supermarkets in the U.S., plus Japanese cameras, but at much cheaper prices. It had a copy of *The Joy of Cooking*, which taught me the rest. After years of eating in restaurants, Mike was pleased to have home-cooked food. Outside of the U.S. military, I probably made the only cheesecake in the city with a genuine graham cracker crust.

We tried to have a relatively normal life in spite of having to boil and filter our drinking water and work by candlelight when the Viet Cong blew up a power station. The whirling noise of frequent helicopters and the sonic booms of fighter planes became routine. Sometimes my Chinese appearance was a disadvantage. Mike and I were in a night club full of professional hostesses for a story once. A couple of them danced close to us and kicked me. Were they thinking I was trying to compete with them? On another occasion, some children threw stones at me while I walked with Mike on the street. Like everywhere in Asia, good girls didn't date American soldiers. Those who did were considered prostitutes.

For recreation, we went swimming occasionally at the former French Le Cercle Sportif de Saigon even though the presence of American officers made it a prime Viet Cong target. As we headed for home, I usually gave a huge sigh of relief to be still whole and alive. In the early days, there was water skiing on the Saigon River, but that was before some skiers went around a bend and didn't come back. The evening before we planned to go there, the Viet Cong attacked our favorite floating restaurant, the My Can, located a couple of blocks from our apartment. They killed forty-two people, some of them Americans, but mostly Vietnamese. We avoided restaurants after that, especially those with ground floor access.

When things were quiet, we invited other journalists for dinner in our apartment. The conversation was about the war, fire fights, and a brilliant but reckless Japanese photographer who walked backward through mine fields to capture the faces of advancing

U.S. soldiers. Kyoichi Sawada won a Pulitzer Prize for his photographs, but then his luck ran out. He was one of several friends who were killed or wounded.

But the conversation was not exclusively about war. Ray Herndon married about the same time we did. He and Annie had three wedding ceremonies: Catholic, Vietnamese, and French. Annie was beautiful. Ray told us about asking her family for permission to marry her.

"Why do you want to marry Annie?" asked her grandmother. "She can't cook."

Ray didn't care if she couldn't cook. "I'll do the cooking," he said. He was still doing the cooking when we visited them in the U.S. decades later.

We loved Annie's story about her wedding night as she told it, laughing. Ray had sprained his back the night before the wedding and was in hospital. Annie had never slept by herself until her wedding night! She had come from a wealthy, conservative, Franco-Vietnamese family, and every night, a servant accompanied her. Alone in a hotel for the first time, she was scared. Fortunately, she found a copy of *Time* magazine with the Pope on the cover, and, clutching it tightly, she managed to survive the night.

Making decisions without consulting my husband had to be learned. Even after discussing times and dates with him, his work frequently interfered. Something newsworthy would happen, and UPI was in competition with other agencies to be the first to report it. One time we planned on six or so friends joining us for American Thanksgiving dinner. He appeared just as they were leaving to go home. I had to be flexible.

Then the Americans started dropping bombs on the North Vietnamese capital of Hanoi, which was more than a thousand miles (1,609 kilometers) north of Saigon. I remember Ray Herndon yelling up the stairs to our apartment on several occasions, "Mike, they've bombed Hanoi again!" and Mike would stop eating and get to work. A Saigon byline was important. More American troops began arriving in the country by the thousands. Occasionally a tank chewed up the streets close to our apartment. I would groan my disapproval. More armaments were not the solution.

As the war escalated, a dozen reporters and photographers joined the UPI bureau. Mike was too swamped supervising them to see any more combat. I was relieved but worried about our friends.

One journalist, Martin Stuart-Fox, recounted later how Mike probably saved his life.

> One of the stories I wrote was about an operation I was on describing how U.S. Marines had stormed a village killing women and children. The Marines were furious. A few days later I phoned in another story to Mike and mentioned casually that I had been told that if I went out on another Marine operation I would not come back alive, adding that I didn't take the threat seriously. But Mike certainly did. He ordered me to take the next flight to Saigon.

I continued to write features. One of Mike's journalist friends, Ed Neilan, was looking for a stringer to write for *Copley News Service*, which was based in California. *The Star Weekly* wanted more stories. I was available to do both. One of my *Copley* articles was about the children of American business people going to school in Saigon. After it appeared, one of the mothers objected to its publication. Now the Viet Cong would know where they could kill American children, she complained. I had to apologize for my thoughtlessness; fortunately, the Viet Cong never attacked the school.

I wrote about how the U.S. government was seriously trying to help Vietnamese farmers with good quality livestock, seeds, insecticides, and loans for fertilizers. I followed a couple of American doctors, one of whom was taking two months of his vacation time for an adventure and to find out for himself what was going on in Vietnam. Dr. George Lowe was working in a provincial hospital where patients slept on wooden beds with no mattresses. He also got satisfaction from such achievements as getting the only X-ray machine to work, teaching a technician how to develop the film, and helping a three-year-old victim of a grenade. His hospital had two hundred beds and was serving mainly war victims. It was the only hospital for 500,000 civilians.

Although I had one amazing story that I never published, I didn't want to write about the fighting or soldiers. I didn't believe the American military should be in Vietnam, but on one trip to research how the U.S. was trying to capture "the hearts and minds" of the people, I found myself surrounded by about forty friendly American soldiers. One of them, a captain, had a badge with the name "Wong" on his chest. He looked familiar, and then I remembered. The last time I saw Bob, a refugee from North China, he was working in my father's restaurant in Brockville as a waiter. He once asked for a date, which I refused because he was a waiter. After I left for school in Toronto, I never saw him again.

Bob and I didn't have much opportunity to catch up because the soldiers around us were listening curiously to our strange conversation. Two friends from a tiny Canadian town were meeting accidentally in the middle of a war in Asia! I knew that Bob couldn't give me a contact address while his commanding officer was watching and listening. I never saw or heard from him again and have often wondered how he joined the U.S. Army and what happened to him after that encounter.

Frank Hooper, one of the Canadians who had helped to host our wedding reception in Hong Kong, was then in Dalat in the highlands of Vietnam with Dr. Jim Turpin with Project Concern. I spent a couple of nights there as Jim did his medical rounds among some Montagnard people. In spite of the possibility of being kidnapped and although other members of his team did, Frank refused to carry a gun. "If I was going to worry about it, I wouldn't have come here," said Frank matter-of-factly. "Doing medical work, training local staff to carry on, and then moving on—this is what I've been wanting to do all my life. We are not here to fight but to help. If they are going to attack us, they want us alive because medical people are useful to them. I prefer kidnapping to death." Fortunately, no attack occurred while I was in Dalat. Frank's attitude was reassuring. He was another hero of mine, and I saw him years later in Hawaii.

The Quakers had made headlines when a Baltimore Friend, Norman Morrison, self-immolated at the Pentagon in November 1965 to protest U.S. actions in Vietnam. He seemed to copy the suicide by fire of a Vietnamese Buddhist monk two years earlier who was objecting to Vietnamese government corruption. Other efforts against the war by Friends followed. In 1967, a Quaker group sailed to North Vietnam in the yacht *Phoenix* with medical supplies for North Vietnamese wounded by the American bombing. Canadian Quakers were helping young American men who were refusing orders to fight in the war by fleeing to Canada.

Among the Quaker volunteers in Vietnam was Masako Yamanouchi, who had been in our workcamp in Japan. She was then teaching in a Buddhist school, and I admired her courage. A Quaker delegation from the U.S., including clergyman A.J. Muste, met with some Vietnamese peace activists in Saigon to assure them that some Americans were supporting them. While I was making compromises when I traveled with the American military, the Quakers refused to fly in U.S. military aircraft.

I satisfied my conscience by writing in the hope that someone else would feel moved to do something about the situation. Mike, on the other hand, was no crusader, and he was, therefore, a good newsman. He kept saying that he didn't have the faintest idea what the U.S. should do about the Vietnam war.

After we had been in Saigon together for nine months, Mike won a Ford Foundation fellowship for journalists at Columbia University in New York City. He hadn't finished college, and now he saw the necessity of getting some formal education if he was to get a better job. He wanted to report, not administer. He was spending too much of his time trying to get some Vietnamese government department to pay money that they owed UPI. The fellowship was a good move, but it meant going back to North America.

We spent a few months in Thailand first, where Mike was lead correspondent for the whole of Asia. We suddenly found ourselves in another world, a city without war. We arrived there before UPI could arrange for money to cover our living expenses as we looked for a place to rent. We had no traveler's checks, and credit cards were not generally used then. With only a few dollars to spend, we had to eat as well as live in the Erawan, one of Bangkok's fanciest hotels, charging the room and meals to Mike's expense account. For a week, we could only dine on escargot, truffles, smoked salmon, flambéed steaks, and Thai curries. Desserts included cherries jubilee, bombe Alaska, and crêpes Suzettes—all them flaming. Of course, we didn't complain, but by the end of the week, we were sick of rich food. On our last night, we ordered boiled eggs with plain toast for dinner.

We traveled upcountry, looking for communist guerrillas and U.S. planes intent on bombing Hanoi. There we ate in dinky, little local restaurants. Mike wrote the stories, and I preferred to be the photographer. I got angry at him once because he didn't seem to respect photographers; he didn't give me enough time to carefully take pictures. It was one of the few times we ever quarreled, and I'm ashamed to say I lost my temper and hit him.

Then we were in New York City where I studied Mandarin for one semester, but we couldn't afford more. Our first child, Linda, was born the following year. We didn't have much money to pay for an obstetrician. Mike's stipend was only four hundred dollars a month, but my doctor just happened to have lived in Brockville and gave us a discount. This was another amazing coincidence because Brockville's population was only about 10,000 at that time.

The birth of a first child is a very special event. I felt a kinship with all the mothers in the world; all the babies were like mine. I was glad we could give Linda opportunities I didn't have and wrote in my diary that she could be what she wanted to be. I should have remembered that my parents didn't have many choices. I tolerated Mike's occasional beers, but he got drunk one evening. I made it clear that I didn't want to live with an alcoholic like my father and took Linda to spend the night in a hotel so that he knew I meant business.

When college finished, Mike didn't want to go back to cover a war now that we had a baby. I breathed a sigh of relief because I didn't want to either. Dow Jones hired him to write for Newsbooks / *The National Observer* from an office in Silver Spring, Maryland, a suburb of Washington, D.C. He wrote about horse racing and the federal elections. Linda and I went along with him to racetracks. With Quaker groups, we picketed our objection to the Vietnam war in front of the White House with Linda in a stroller.

We spent the next ten years living in Maryland, where more children were born, and I was a busy, full-time mother and wife. One day, as Mike and I played with Martin and Linda, I said, "They are so cute, but they grow up so quickly. Do we want another one?" and he agreed. Then we had Terry, and I wanted to try natural childbirth. Mike was in the delivery room as a breathing coach, a relatively new concept in the U.S. then. We learned techniques that minimized birth pains like breathing exercises, and he wrote about it for *The National Observer* with one-hour-old Terry in a picture with me.

In Maryland, our children had their closest connection with Quakers. Mike went to the very welcoming Adelphi Quaker Meeting where our children attended First Day School. In addition, I made sure they learned some Bible stories like Noah and the Ark and Joseph and his multicolored coat. I bribed them to learn the books of the Bible. This was an important part of North American culture then, and I wanted something to balance what Walt Disney was teaching them. Our home was a bungalow with a basement. Mike was a great father, and he put up a trapeze and mattress. The children and their friends spent hours there.

Being a parent helped me grow up. I could no longer make any decisions by myself. Linda reminded me recently that I grew bean sprouts, made yogurt, and baked granola, trying my best to be an ideal American mother. I took the kids to swimming classes and birthday parties. We walked to nearby playgrounds almost daily, and as they grew older, we took them skiing. I sang songs to them every evening before they went to sleep. When they were babies, the songs were mainly lullabies, and then they were songs I loved like *Moon River, You'll Never Walk Alone*, and *Old Man River*. I occasionally found time for myself. After I started writing guidebooks, I took a course in making pottery because I wanted to find out how pottery was made. We drove at least once a year to Brockville and Toronto to see my family and to Chicago to see Mike's.

Visits with my youngest sister, Gloria, were especially fun for our children. I had left for college when she was five and never got to know her until later. While skating professionally with the Ice Capades during their shows in Maryland, she arranged free tickets and thrilled our children by inviting them to join the skaters in their fancy costumes for a few minutes out on the ice. During our visit to Los Angeles after she retired from touring, she made sure our children saw Disneyland and Universal Studios. With her long eyelashes and makeup, she didn't look at all like me.

Mike agreed with my suggestion that we should give our children Chinese lessons. We arranged for Linda and Martin to go to a Mandarin class at a nearby Chinese church. Unfortunately, the other children considered them "half-breeds" and called them other derogatory names. We stopped the classes.

Life for me became quite middle-class and ordinary. I continued to bring Mike coffee in bed every morning because I was a morning person, wide awake early. We had our daily morning kiss, and he read three newspapers with breakfast. When he came home from work, he would put the youngest baby on his shoulder while he read the evening paper and I prepared dinner. With Mike making plans that I usually agreed with, my searches for the will of God were not so necessary anymore. I knew what I had to do: take care of our children and my husband. However, confined to home most days when the children were very young, I occasionally felt trapped. On one of the worst days when all three of them made life difficult, I even felt like killing them. I ended up weeping and hitting my head against a wall instead.

Ever thoughtful, Mike encouraged me to hire neighborhood preteen girls to play with the children while I wrote. They were cheaper than teenage babysitters. Writing was my therapy, and I wrote articles for baby magazines—about babies, of course. It helped me feel better, and I could quickly respond if the eager young helpers had trouble with the children.

Relatives like my wonderful niece, Judy Wark, came to stay and take care of the children while Mike and I went to France and Spain on one of his reporting trips. Mike's mother, Lou, happily came to help on other such occasions, especially when I started writing guidebooks. Lou was an ideal grandmother. She loved playing with the children, and they loved her. Being exceptionally resourceful, she made up great games for them to play.

Lou was back in the U.S. By then I had learned that she had brought up Mike and his sister largely by herself and made sure they were well-educated. Mike was later to define a good school as one where most of the students wanted to learn, and she was able to get him the occasional scholarship to study at some. With her limited education, she could only get jobs like waitressing and child care. Mike remembered having to move frequently because they couldn't pay their rent, sometimes skipping out without paying at all. He had frequently been the new kid in his class at school, the outsider. It was a painful position to be in. I learned later from his childhood friend, Bob Bower, that the two of them used to skip school and explore museums in Chicago. He was eager to learn but not in schools. He had dropped out of college after the first year.

Lou said she agreed to marry one of her American husbands because he promised to pay for Mike's schooling. It was alimony from that husband that paid for her trip to see him in India. In India, she and Chun started a school for Sikh children because she had developed her own theories on education. After Chun was able to get an Indian passport, he was able to immigrate with Lou to the U.S. Unfortunately, Chun's mother wanted grandchildren. Culture won out, Chun and Lou divorced, and he married a younger woman, an Indian.

Lou struggled on alone and worked on a college degree, living on government assistance in an apartment overlooking the Puget Sound in Washington state. She taught English as a second language. She was amazing, but she was also a busybody mother-in-law.

I was lucky that she didn't stay long when I was home, because she criticized the way I was bringing up the children, keeping house, and cooking. I found myself frequently arguing with her, even when she wasn't around.

In 1975, the Viet Cong forced Americans to leave Vietnam. Some South Vietnamese soldiers and people who had worked for the Americans found themselves suddenly airlifted to American aircraft carriers in the South China Sea. Next thing they knew, they were in the United States as refugees. Many Americans volunteered to help Vietnamese families get settled. Along with another Quaker family who did the same, we adopted two former Vietnamese paratroopers until they were able to live on their own. No one wanted to help them. We felt they were just ordinary people caught up in a war. I never asked how many people they had killed. They slept in our basement and taught us Vietnamese cooking. They couldn't go back to Vietnam because the Communist government considered them enemies, which meant years of prison if they were caught.

We enjoyed Khiem and Go. They would jump off the roof of our bungalow for the amusement of the neighborhood children, and they rode canoes while standing on the gunwales. I learned to cook pho, the now popular Vietnamese noodle soup. We had Nước Mắm, fish sauce, as a condiment with our turkey dinner at Christmas. It was delicious.

Go was illiterate, but a survivor, a fisherman. In spite of knowing no English and having little education, he got a well-paying job painting houses. He managed to acquire a driver's license by having a friend take a test for him. Khiem had eighth grade education and spoke English, so he worked as a bus boy in a local restaurant for minimum wage. The last we heard, Khiem was unhappily married and under the thumb of a Vietnamese father-in-law who had given him a better job.

I told my French friend, Danièle, about them. She had been a victim of war and said she would not have been able to do what we did. Paratroopers to her were S.S., the Nazis from whom she, a Jew, had once been hiding, fearful for her life. Although she knew we didn't support the U.S. involvement in Vietnam, she felt that taking them into our home seemed to support it.

In Maryland, where I was mainly a mother and a wife, Kheim and Go brought the outside world to us, the world beyond my own culture, whatever that was.

Chapter 12:
China with Five-Year-Old Linda, 1973

The year after I visited China, its Cultural Revolution began. To understand what was happening there, I took a course on the subject at the University of Maryland given by an American named Gerald Tannenbaum who had lived through it.

Chairman Mao Tse-tung had led China's Communist Revolution, but now he was losing control to rivals. In 1966, he organized the first of several massive Red Guard rallies in Beijing's Tiananmen Square. Speaking to crowds of over a million each time, he urged high school and university students to travel around the country "to continue the revolution to the end." He closed the schools. Over a million students took part, riding free on trains and sleeping in school dormitories. Municipalities fed them, and teenagers suddenly realized they had power over their elders.

Chairman Mao urged the young people to attack the "Four Olds"—old ideas, culture, customs, and habits. The youngsters happily obeyed and destroyed religious statues, buildings, Bibles, and ancestral tablets. They changed the old, dynastic street names to the likes of "the East is Red" and "Liberation." They attacked women who wore tight Western-styled trousers and makeup and cut off their long hair. People who used precious water to take more than one shower a week were criticized. Such "bourgeois" ways kept them from "serving the people," the young people proclaimed.

They tried thousands of people in court-like trials. They actually executed some whom they found "guilty." They sent professional people to the countryside to "learn from the peasants." Doctors and teachers cleaned latrines and bent over for hours while transplanting rice in flooded fields, just as the peasants had to. Everyone had to memorize the little red book of quotations from Chairman Mao, such as, "A revolution is not a dinner party," and "All reactionaries are paper tigers."

It was a bizarre era. Chinese young people are traditionally taught to revere their elders. During the Cultural Revolution, with unusual power in their hands, the youngsters caused havoc and terrified their elders, accusing many of loving foreign ways and being insensitive to peasants and workers. Thousands died.

By 1971, the worst of the Cultural Revolution was over. The United States allowed its citizens to travel to China. The following February, U.S. President Richard Nixon went to China for eight days to begin talks toward reestablishing relations with China for the first time since 1949.

I wanted to find out what had happened since my previous visit. Were my relatives still alive? What had happened to them during the upheaval? In 1973, with Mike's blessing, I took five-year-old Linda to China for a month, expecting that a visit centered on our cute, outgoing American daughter to that strange country would be an unusual angle. *Star Weekly* and Mike agreed. He was working then for *The National Observer*, a weekly national newspaper. It could use a story about it, too.

Arrangements were made with friends to help Mike take care of our other two children while Linda and I flew off to Hong Kong. How many husbands would do that in that generation? I felt so fortunate. Mike gamely kept working and taking care of the two boys in his spare time. He handled unexpected disasters like a rain-flooded basement with humor: "I'll let it evaporate or stock it with fish," he wrote. He also tried to toilet train our youngest.

It was relatively easy getting tourist visas this time, but once we were in China, it was delay after delay, getting tickets to travel around the country. I organized some of our hotels, tours, and plane tickets in Hong Kong, but at one hotel, after we arrived, the room clerk insisted no rooms were available. When I argued, suddenly there was a room for us. Although I was no longer a V.I.P., and there was a shortage of guides to help, we did manage to get around. One day it took eight hours to cash a traveler's check. No bank machines existed then. The departure time of our flights kept changing. But on one flight, I found a former resident of Brockville, Dwight Fulford, then a Canadian diplomat. His father used to send my mother stamps for her collection from his travels. Strange coincidences were still continuing.

Relatives in China were eager to use my duty-free overseas Chinese import allowance. Their kin in Canada paid for a transistor radio, two watches, a sewing machine, bicycle, and thirty yards of cotton cloth. It was the least I could do to help them. Hong Kong prices were cheaper than in China, and Chinese government stores in Hong Kong arranged to ship these purchases; I didn't have to carry them.

Eight years after my first visit, I found the country more relaxed. In Guangzhou's schools, the Children's Palace, and the parks on May Day, the blatant anti-American dances were no more. Now the children sang about tractor drivers and carpenters, diligence and unselfishness. It was a nice change.

We traveled mainly on our own, but many of my relatives took time off from work to show us around. My cousin, Yuet Yuen, still lived in the same tiny apartment. She now had a second daughter, and the two girls slept in a partitioned part of the hallway outside their apartment. The space was just big enough for a dresser and a bed. On the roof of their building, they raised chickens and slaughtered one in our honor. She didn't wear her hair curled anymore. She didn't say why, but I knew that the Red Guards objected to displays of vanity like unnaturally curled hair.

My relatives were all alive, but no one wanted to talk about the Cultural Revolution. When I asked what had happened, they politely said it was none of my business. Two of the families were no longer talking to each other. I suspected they had reported about each others' "crimes" to save themselves. The Red Guards had especially attacked people living on remittances from overseas, like my relatives, who didn't want to work and learn from the peasants. It must have been very humiliating for the victims.

One group of relatives in Xin Hui took us swimming with their teenaged daughters. Their mothers half-joked about finding them rich husbands in Canada. In Xin Hui, Linda was fascinated by the open wells and drew pictures of them for her father. Her pictures were later published in *The National Observer*. I was pleased I had brought Linda to China.

There were still silly security restrictions: "Taking pictures on ferries is forbidden," said a guard who made me stop photographing Linda, playing innocently with her new doll on a bunk inside.

I finally visited our ancestral village in Taishan county. After taking a ferry from Xin Hui, Linda and I rode eleven miles (eighteen kilometers) on the backs of my nephews' bicycles, along a narrow road. Bamboo groves and rice fields surrounded our village. It had about fifty tiny houses, all neatly placed, checker-board style, with pathways and open sewers between the rows. My father's house had been made of mud, relatives said. Now it was black brick, small and dark. I climbed up one of the watch towers; intellectuals from the city had slept there during their stints of learning from the peasants. Except for the wives, everyone in the village was a blood relative, all with the surname "Lor." About three hundred people lived there, growing mainly rice.

The all-important family graves were just unmarked mounds of earth placed on hillsides. We had to ford a stream to see them. The Ching Ming grave-decorating festival had just taken place, and a few graves had slips of white paper "money" held in place by a stone on top. Uncle Tse-Tse pointed to my grandfather's grave. Grandfather had had enough money to build a big house in Xin Hui, so I had expected one of those fancy horseshoe-shaped masonry tombs, but it was just a thigh-high mound of earth. It could have been anyone's grave. I could not see any markers and wondered if this was really his. And what did it matter?

Later in private, Uncle Tse-Tse handed me what he called our copy of the family book. It listed all our male ancestors dating from the Song Dynasty, about eight hundred years ago. It mentioned the full names of the eldest males and included my brother Joe and his birthdate. It only showed the family names of the wives, as if individual women were not important. But Chairman Mao was now teaching his country that women "held up half the sky." Women were important in China, he had said. Times were changing. History was also important, and I eagerly took possession of the handwritten book with its flimsy pages and story.

Uncle Tse-Tse had hidden the precious book from the Red Guards. He could have destroyed it to save himself, but he didn't, and he seemed glad to get rid of it. He said to hide it in my luggage because it was illegal to take antiques out of China. Fortunately, I had no trouble doing so. Chinese customs were probably more interested in expensive Tang vases and Shang bronzes. That book made me feel that I had a direct link to China, even though it didn't mention our mother or any wives by their full names.

Linda rode a water buffalo, and we slept in a four-poster bed under a mosquito net. She made friends easily with the shy village children after she learned that tickling them under their chins made them laugh, and they invited her to play. She had more energy than her cousins, which made me wonder if it was her higher protein diet.

That day in our village, I saw a tinker surrounded by all the tools he needed to mend pots and pans. It was a good picture. I should have asked permission, but politeness would have made for a stilted pose. That evening at dinner with my relatives, a policeman came to the door. "Why did you take that man's picture?" he demanded. My nephew said he could handle it. For a moment, I was scared and wondered if I would be arrested. I hoped he would explain that I was a visitor from Canada and didn't know any better. It turned out to be inconsequential, but it made me feel obligated for their help. I think my feeling Chinese went up a few percentage points that day because I needed and felt the support of my family.

A relative in the village spoke some English. I had told them about my dinner with Premier Chou En-lai on my previous trip. A nephew brought a note to give to the premier, as I was planning to go back to Beijing. He had been ordered to work in a commune, and he didn't want to go. I told him I really didn't have any influence with the premier, having been only one of many guests at that dinner, but he insisted. He finally agreed to let me put the letter in a mailbox in Beijing, which I later did.

An old lady in the village asked if I could find out if her husband was dead or alive. She gave me an address in Texas. He had a mental disability, and I promised to look for him when I was home again.

On the street, even among our relatives, people called Linda *fan gwei nui*—foreign ghost girl. Ghosts were feared, but it didn't stop people from trying to make friends with her. She loved the attention. The phrase didn't seem quite so derogatory here because it was said with a little affection, but they were still looking at her as if she were a monkey in a zoo.

While there was no improvement in Yuet Yuen's accommodations, China was building new hotels, one of them twenty-seven stories. Department stores were getting better quality goods to sell. New buses and taxis were on the roads, but I didn't see any private cars. China was moving toward catching up with North America, and some people had money to invest.

We found Americans in our hotels this time. They were overseas Chinese and appeared lost. Where could they get plane tickets? How did they book a hotel? Was it safe to visit relatives? China was not ready for international tourism. There was little information in English, and hotels had no signs pointing to money-changing booths or dining rooms. Foreign visitors with no knowledge of Chinese languages needed a guidebook, and I started keeping notes. I interrogated the tour guides I hired and asked them for information. I questioned fellow travelers, travel agencies, and hotel personnel. One of the guides asked why I wanted to know the telephone numbers of hotels. "They keep changing all the time," he said.

This was still the period when anyone with just a map of China could be accused of being a spy, but I saw an opportunity. Mike and I had read a lot of guidebooks each time we traveled to a new country.

When I arrived home, I put together a fifty-four-page guidebook on China. I asked Uncle Harry, the sign painter, to help. He had studied in China, so he knew Chinese characters, and he put the words for "China" on the cover. He added a picture of a sailing junk, a ship. The title was *A Guide to the People's Republic of China for Travelers of Chinese Ancestry.* The book was in English except for some helpful phrases in both Chinese and English that friend Dorothy Plant helped get in Hong Kong.

Mike encouraged the book and agreed to pay for printing eight hundred copies. He was a real gem. Dorothy was happy to find a printing company in Hong Kong, which was cheaper than in the U.S., even with shipping. I wrote to many Chinese-American organizations and churches, and we almost sold out the whole edition.

The book included advice on tipping, drinking tap water, and the lack of bellhops. It said there was no air conditioning in the Guangzhou Overseas Chinese Hotel and no taxis at airports. To mail a post card, one had to put glue on postage stamps. When local people welcomed foreign visitors with applause, it advised them to applaud in return. What was the difference between a "hard" and "soft" class train seat? To cope with unexpected delays, I included, "Find other Overseas Chinese, exchange experiences, and share frustrations. These are good for a couple of hours."

The writing came easily, and I enjoyed it. It seemed to be what I was meant to do. I visited a big bookstore in Maryland and wrote down the names of travel guide publishers and sent a copy to several of them. A couple of publishers were interested, and I chose the famous Fielding brand. Mine was the first guidebook about the People's Republic of China for all foreigners in English. I was to continue updating it for a dozen editions.

In writing a guidebook, I felt I was doing something to help China and the English-speaking world. China needed to learn about the needs of foreign visitors; its foreign visitors needed information on how to get around the country. I hoped the book would help make friends both ways.

After the first book was finished, there was time to look for the husband of the elderly lady I had met in our village. It turned out he had died in a mental hospital in Texas. My Chinese-literate relatives wrote to Uncle Tse-Tse, asking him to give her the sad news.

In reaction to the male-dominated family book, I designed a family tree with only our Canada-based family, descendants of the relatives who had immigrated to Canada. In the Chinese-Canadian version were included the full names of both our male and female relatives. I designed it so that the women looked just as important as the men. Uncle Harry decorated it with dragons and the family name in Chinese, but it was otherwise in English. We kept a copy on the wall of our dining room for years. I felt like a revolutionist.

The ancient book, the ancestral graves, and seeing where our father was born did make me feel more Chinese. My family rescue from the village police helped, too. I was feeling 10 percent Chinese then, but that percentage would continue to fluctuate. I was to go to China frequently in the next thirty or so years, learning about its diversity and the development of its tourism infrastructure. I saw again how racial, sexual, and cultural discrimination and political power in unwise hands caused a lot of suffering. But I saw a few ways I, an insignificant individual in the scheme of things, could help. As opportunities to finance research came up, I began to feel that writing guidebooks was my destiny.

Chapter 13:
Guidebook, Embroidery, Boots, Tours, 1973-2008

Guidebooks were especially valuable in the 1980s and 1990s. Until the year 2000, travel websites like Expedia and Trip Advisor didn't exist with their free, up-to-date information and hotel reviews. Even today, it is important to read guidebooks before traveling to a new country. They have concise information on how to get around, places to stay, brief histories, and recommendations by trusted, experienced authorities. I am always suspicious of advice given without charge.

Mike encouraged my books and was pleased I could produce them as long as I broke even on the expenses. Calling myself a travel writer rather than a housewife was satisfying, and he proved that he could take good care of our children when I was in China. Then *The Wall Street Journal Asia* offered him a job, and we moved back to Asia in 1977 with our children. We lived for three years in the Philippines and four years in Hong Kong. It was cheaper and less time-consuming to fly from there into China to work on the book, and we had full-time help on the home front.

Mike's passion for archeology was helpful, too. After he retired, he spent at least ten summers in Jordan, digging up two-thousand-year-old artifacts on a team with Wilfred Laurier University. He wasn't interested in going on innumerable trips to China, but he always encouraged me. Though I enjoyed his company, our summer separation worked well. I could plan my own itineraries without considering his archeological interests. When he was home, it was not unusual to find human bones on our dining room table. He wanted to be the "bone expert" on his digs.

For each book, I received a five thousand dollar advance. It did not cover all the expenses. Writing articles for newspapers and magazines helped. Payment for freelancers in a major Toronto newspaper then was about one hundred fifty dollars for each article, including photos that, considering the time involved and travel expenses, put travel writers below minimum wage. But travel writing had perks and unusual opportunities, and there were other ways to pay expenses.

For next three decades, I had to be focused on financing, researching, and updating a dozen guidebooks on China while trying to keep my family happy, not always successfully. Keeping track of the developments in its tourism industry, witnessing history, and feeling I was doing something helpful, was very satisfying. I had a lot of unusual adventures and was lucky. While foreign journalists could not travel without restrictions around China, I was able to do so quite freely and plan my own itineraries. Although I did worry at times that I could be arrested for being a foreign "journalist" on a "tourist" visa, I usually felt confident that China's government knew it needed tourists. China's official travel agencies helped me.

My first book with Fielding led to requests for more. Fortunately, each edition was an update and expansion of the previous one, so it didn't have to be rewritten entirely each time. After the massacre of hundreds of unarmed student protesters demanding democracy in Beijing's Tiananmen Square on June 4, 1989, my editor suggested we stop for a while. The morning after the slaughter, I joined hundreds of Torontonians at the Chinese consulate in Toronto as they angrily voiced their disgust and opposition. Tourism to China almost stopped then because many outsiders supported the students. I did, however, accept China's invitation for a free trip with all expenses paid for me, my brother, and a travel agent friend as the Chinese tried to get tourists to return. I was curious to know how China justified the killings.

On that trip, we found bullet holes in walls near Tiananmen Square. At one briefing, Chinese tourism officials asked our group for criticisms and suggestions. Toronto travel agent, Gloria Serafico, pointed out that the soldiers guarding tourist sites had their fingers on the triggers of their guns. That was not a good message for tourists, she said. That evening, the fingers were no longer quite so ready to kill.

Tourism has power to temper government policies like that—sometimes. Tourism is usually a big part of a country's income. When we asked officials if foreigners could put flowers at the Monument to the People's Heroes, where most of the students died, they said "no," but maybe we made a point. I was happy to let China pay for my trip, to pay at least a little bit for what they did to the students. I encouraged foreigners to visit China because ordinary people like waitresses, guides, and farmers were suffering from the lack of customers. I pointed out that no one boycotted the U.S. after the Ohio National Guard shot thirteen unarmed Kent State University students in May 1970.

Officials briefing us said that only "ruffians" had been killed, not students. Eye witnesses at the time told a different story.

To meet other expenses, I had to be open to all kinds of possibilities such as free hotel rooms. Some people feel writers can't be objective if we accept "freebies." Genuine travel writers do try our best to be honest and mention the hotels that helped. Five-star international hotels especially were happy to give hospitality in exchange for a mention, and there was no reason not to mention them. They were all international standard. Their public relations people were always generous with other information as well, like new tourist attractions and good local restaurants. They and travel agents everywhere all spoke English and produced a lot of tourist information in that language. My lack of Chinese was not a problem.

Except when I worked on a ship or taught English, I never stayed longer than two nights in any place where I wasn't paying, and I did pay for some of the cheaper hotels. Once the manager of a hotel near my ancestral village gave me a free room and meals for a month. It was lychee season, and every day I got a bowl of my favorite fruit, too. This was in return for teaching English to his staff. Of course, it wasn't long enough to teach anyone fluency in a new language, but I tried, and again, I felt I should have studied how to teach English as a second language. I was a terrible teacher because the class was too big and too diverse, but that job gave me Sundays off to visit relatives nearby as well as a chance to learn more about Chinese hotels.

How to finance research and travel is important if anyone wants to fulfill one's dreams of spending years traveling about the world. It has to be in tune with divine purposes, with serving other people.

Also, to make ends meet were jobs being paid to lead tour groups to and around China. It was a chance to learn about what North American tourists wanted—which was good food, minimal history lessons, and only one museum on each trip. The itineraries were exhausting. Tourists wanted primarily to be amused. Few asked questions about China's problems. Taking selfies weren't in fashion then, and they needed help to take a lot of pictures of themselves at the Great Wall and Forbidden City.

A Yangtze River cruise ship paid me to give lectures and act as a hostess for eighteen days. This was before the controversial dam was completed, when the Three Gorges were still especially dramatic, and its historic sites were not yet under water. I had my own small but adequate cabin, and it was fun. It included sitting at meals with tourists from many countries to make them feel welcome. I even got Japanese tourists to laugh. Being paid to cruise on the historic river was a dream job with an opportunity to explore what was once the only way to travel to inland China. If one looked hard enough, there were the remains of tow paths from which humans once had to haul boats upsteam before boats had engines. Taichi classes were on deck every morning, a ship's doctor gave acupuncture treatments, and every evening, an American piano player banged out a lively version of "New York, New York."

The Chinese were building the largest dam in the world then. I would love to see it now and study the dam's effect on the ecology. Did it accomplish all that it was meant to do like control the frequent flooding and produce more electricity? Was it worth uprooting a million people?

Frequent travel to China meant I was able to visit places the average tourists didn't go to like the former home of American author Pearl S. Buck in Jiangsu province, and in Yunnan province, the cottage of Austrian-American plant hunter, geographer, ethnographer, and explorer, Joseph Rock. The fourteenth Dalai Lama's birthplace in Amdo province and ethnic tribal villages were also on my personal list, as were the eastern and western ends of the Great Wall. I visited every province and region in the country, sometimes by myself but usually with Chinese-speaking guides. I traveled with personal friends like Joan Ahrens, Caroline Walker, Sarah Hall, and Francisca de Zweiger, who shared expenses and a passion for travel.

A special trip was with a couple from San Francisco who were taking their eight-year-old China-born daughter back to China for the first time to see the orphanage where they had adopted her. I almost choked with emotion as Mei Li pinned the letter she wrote in Chinese to her birth mother to the tree under which she had been abandoned. It said, "I am called Ai Mei Li. I just want to say hello. I want you to know I love you, and here are some pictures of me and my new family." Among the photos was one taken when she was three days old and bundled in a flowered blanket. I hoped that her mother would remember the blanket.

Said Mei Li's American father, "We just want to tell her mother she did the right thing. Her child is alive, happy, living in America, and learning Chinese. This is the most we can do." He felt "a karmic obligation to help remove a scar from her mother's soul that must certainly be there."

As we drove back to our hotel afterward, I saw a sad and tired-looking woman walking along the dusty road toward us. She looked like an older version of Mei Li. Something told me no, don't stop. If she was Mei Li's mother, she could be arrested for abandoning a baby, and so I kept my mouth shut. No one else in our car noticed her. Maybe it was for the best, and I hope her mother saw the note.

Chinese orphanages encourage adoptive parents to bring up children with some knowledge of their Chinese heritage, which Mei Li's American parents did. Today, Mei Li teaches Mandarin and is into Chinese brush painting, *taijiquan*, and salsa. She has also been studying Japanese in Japan.

From 1980 to 2016, China had a "one-child" policy. It was attempting to limit the expansion of its enormous population. Many Chinese parents preferred male babies because boys were expected to take care of them in their old age. Some still believed in ancestor worship where sons were like priests. Many believed that a female child would marry and be obligated to help her husband's aging parents. Such a belief meant that many parents abandoned their female and disabled babies and tried for a male child. State orphanages put these unwanted children up for adoption and mainly foreigners adopted an estimated 110,000 children, mostly girls from China. My own experience would later prove the Chinese tradition wrong.

This controversial practice also later resulted in another problem twenty years later, namely, a shortage of brides for the males.

Another memorable tour for me was one I helped to organize for alumni of the Shanghai American School (SAS). B.J. Elder, whom I had met first in Tokyo, had asked for my assistance, and I arranged to go along myself because I wanted to meet some more missionaries to China, or at least their children. Did they identify themselves as Chinese? Were they imperialists?

The boarding school was founded in 1912 in Shanghai by a group of Christian missionaries, so their children could receive a Western education. It later expanded to include the children of journalists, diplomats, and business people working in China. Most were Americans. The school closed in 1950 after the Communists took over China and expelled foreigners as spies. It reopened in

1980, mainly to serve the children of a new generation of wealthy foreigners working and living in China.

In 2004, our group of forty consisted of former students and some of their children. John Rawlinson took us to the spot on Shanghai's Xizang Street near the Nanjing Theater, where a Chinese pilot accidentally dropped a bomb in 1937 that killed his father. John described how his mother had to drag his body into their car because no ambulances were available. It was a privilege to hear his painful story at the spot where it happened.

During a question-and-answer session at the current Shanghai American School (SAS), today's students were keen to hear the alumni's experiences of settling back in when they moved "home" to the West. For most of the alumni, their childhoods were spent feeling a lack of identity, both in China and in the West.

B.J. was brought up as the only non-Chinese child in a town in Hunan province. She recalled the first time she felt she belonged anywhere was when she started classes at SAS. In her book, *The Oriole's Song*, she wrote that the school was "the place of our full belonging. . . . No longer suspended between two worlds, at SAS I fell into place."

Teddy Heinrichsohn's father had arrived in China as a missionary from Germany and later joined a trading company. He married a local Chinese woman who became Teddy's mother. When the Nazi government confiscated Teddy's German passport due to his mixed parentage (and therefore non-Aryan countenance), the family had to stay in China. Teddy said SAS was a haven of acceptance for him, too.

I felt this contact with Chinese missionary history was a rare opportunity. Their shared experiences illustrated the need for many people to belong to a group like themselves. I felt some of them were actually imperialists, as the Chinese claimed. They never learned Chinese even though they lived there most of their young lives.

Spending time in China didn't make me feel Chinese. Writing a book about China meant learning about its history and geography.

China became for me, no longer a country with a Forbidden City and emperors but a country with a culturally diverse population. I tended to identify with expatriates living then in China, and I had a lot of interest in its minorities.

In many places, I found racial, cultural, or gender discrimination. Tibet was one of my favorite regions of China. Its temples were not only exotic and beautiful, its ancient culture was still largely intact then, and its mountains were spectacular. What the Chinese were doing in Tibet was wrong. They were encouraging Han Chinese to move there, and they were turning Lhasa, the capital, into two cities: one Chinese and one Tibetan. They regarded Tibetans as barbarians and treated them as second-class citizens in their own region. I recommended that foreign travelers use Tibetan, rather than Chinese tour guides, and stay in hotels in the Tibetan part of Lhasa. These were essential for a Tibetan experience and to support these oppressed people.

Much later, Mike asked how I wanted to celebrate my seventieth birthday. "Kailash," I answered immediately without thought. Mount Kailash was a name that seemed to call to me since seeing a store with that name in India. It was a mountain in Tibet. I didn't know that it is a sacred place for Hindus, the home of Lord Shiva. It is also a sacred mountain for Tibetans who said that a one-day pilgrimage around the base meant the forgiveness of all one's sins. This only worked in the year 2002, a Tibetan travel agent said. I didn't think of going there to get all my sins forgiven. Kailash was my *Bali Ha'i*, although I didn't know why.

Mike agreed immediately and decided that someone needed to take care of me because of the altitude. Never having gone to Tibet himself, he said he would go with us. I had been to Tibet three times by then with no altitude problems, and this time it wasn't a hike. It was a caravan of trucks and jeeps to go from one end of the region to the other. I was happy Mike wanted to go, too, because of his knowledge of Tibetan history and his mind for dates and figures. He was my personal encyclopedia as well as my preferred traveling companion.

Unfortunately, at the time, India and Pakistan were threatening nuclear war over Kashmir, which is located just south of the Tibetan border. The day after Mike decided to go, the Chinese canceled all trips there, and he signed on to a dig in Jordan instead. The very next day, however, Tibet was open again. Was that fate? Instead, son Terry, who was thirty-one years old, came on our twenty-eight-day Tibetan adventure, along with my sister, Valerie, and two friends.

A Tibetan travel agent in Lhasa organized our trip. We ordered a convoy of two Toyota Land Cruisers and one truck for our tents and food, and we hired a guide, three drivers, and a cook, all Tibetan. The plan was to cross Tibet from Lhasa westward to Mount Kailash where we would book some yaks for three days of riding and trekking around the sacred mountain before continuing on westward to Guge. After exploring a historic monastery at the westernmost end, we would head eastward to Everest Base Camp and then back to Lhasa. On the way, we would sleep in tents or hostels, except for the only international standard hotels in Gyantse and Shigatse. Our crew would pitch our tents in open fields, of which there were many.

We started with four days getting used to the altitude in Lhasa. Then, as our caravan started climbing higher into the mountains, I got a lesson in physics. Our gasoline tanks overflowed as the air pressure decreased. We seemed to be adding more gasoline even though we weren't. How would this affect the human body? I warned Terry not to exert himself, but he insisted on playing ball with the children at every stop. We continued to climb higher into thinner air.

That evening at a hotel, Terry felt as though he was dying. Prickles of oxygen depletion moved from his fingers into his arms and toward his heart and lungs. He shouldn't go any higher. I had to choose between taking him back to Lhasa myself or sending him back alone. If I went with him, there was no way to catch up with the group later because there were no buses or taxis where we were going. It was one of my hardest decisions. What was God's will?

Then Terry said he felt well enough to take the only public taxi available that day back to Lhasa. I hoped that the higher power that was guiding my life didn't want to take my son away. We continued on without him. We had no cell phones then, and the next afternoon in a village kiosk, a call on the lone telephone assured me that Terry had managed to get back to Lhasa safely. I was so relieved I cried, grateful that he had survived.

As we went on, the other young man in our group got sick, too. Walter recuperated in a hostel after being treated with royal jelly prescribed by a Swiss clinic conveniently set up at the foot of Mount Kailash. We older women went on full of optimism, congratulating ourselves for outlasting our youthful companions. Altitude sickness tended to hit the young and muscular and not so much the elderly.

Tibetan pilgrims usually do the Kailash circuit in one day on foot; they are used to the altitude and can walk quickly. They believe the one-day journey is important and gives them much merit, good fortune, and help in stopping the continuous cycle of reincarnations. We three North American women had to scrap our plans to join them. Our yaks were big and fat under their saddles and not as comfortable as horses. I don't think my yak driver did a good job at tightening my saddle because, soon after I mounted, the saddle slipped off the back end of the animal, and I had to grab its hairy mane and scream for help to keep from sliding down its rump onto the ground. At that moment, our guides were busy tending to Valerie. Her yak had kicked her in the leg. Suddenly, the thought of three days with the unpredictable animals felt too long.

We compromised by camping that night at the foot of the magnificent snow-covered mountain that many consider the navel of the world. Kailash loomed alone high above us on one side like a giant pyramid. It was at least forty-five times the height of Egypt's tallest pyramid. On our other side was a stream, fed by springs and melting glaciers that formed the source of several major rivers, among them the Indus, Brahmaputra, and Ganges. I felt a connection with India, knowing that someday these waters would flow past the sacred Indian city of Benares (Varanasi), and the crowded city of Calcutta (Kolkata) and then to the sea. It would carry the ashes of many Indians and the bodies of dead babies, the final resting place for the very young.

With hundreds of Tibetan pilgrims passing our tents on foot and at least one doing the route with continuous full-body prostrations, it was a National Geographic Society video come to life. The women were all dressed in floor-length *chubas* with colorful aprons tied around their waists; the men wore knee-length robes and trousers, long sleeves dangling. Except for the determined prostrator, the pilgrims were a cheerful lot. A hundred must have passed us that day with smiles on their faces, their feet almost dancing with excitement.

The next night, we joined Walter in the crude Mount Kailash hostel and then continued on our way, stopping in every monastery and fortress, and turning back east after exploring the ruins of the ancient Tibetan kingdom just north of Dehra Dun. At that Indian city, I had caught a train years before to Pakistan. The Himalayas now separated us.

We continued our journey, spending several nights outside temples or in open fields, waking up surrounded by massive flocks of yaks, goats, and sheep. Fortunately, Terry was able to join us later at Everest Base Camp and the highest temple in the world. By then, he was used to the altitude.

When we arrived at Lhasa's airport for the flight home, there were three planeloads of Chinese troops on the tarmac. Small Chinese military groups had been within sight of our three hotels in the major cities. At checkpoints along our itinerary, our guide had to convince guards he had the right papers to continue our journey. But at the airport, there must have been a couple hundred soldiers. The Chinese were continuing to take over Tibet and its mineral resources in a big way. I felt angry and helpless seeing them but could do nothing except mention the invasion in my book, join pro-Tibetan, anti-Chinese demonstrations back in Toronto, and learn more about the nonviolent teachings of the Dalai Lama.

Today, alas, the Chinese have paved the road around Mount Kailash in spite of the objections of monks and religious Tibetans. Cars can do the thirty-two miles (fifty-two kilometers) in about an hour. The Kailash circuit seems to have turned from a sacred, spiritual pilgrimage path to a tourist-selfie opportunity. I felt sick when I heard about it. Our world needs sacred mountains.

The trip turned out much better for Terry personally. In Lhasa, at the Potala, the former palatial home of a succession of Dalai Lamas, Terry met a beautiful Finnish tourist who later became his wife. He and Anna married in Finland and gave us our first wonderful grandchild, Aaron. But was that the reason for the Kailash trip, another dream fulfilled? Or was it to make me even more vividly aware of what the Chinese were doing in Tibet?

Most foreigners on a group tour visiting China only get to know one Chinese person, an English-speaking guide whom they share with a dozen other foreign tourists. I was fortunate to know several guides and travel agents because I met them on many occasions, over a period of time. I followed some of them as they struggled with family problems or climbed the ladder from tour guide to tourism administrator. A few immigrated to Canada and the U.S., and I still try to keep in touch with them as well as some of my own relatives.

One of my dearest friends was Madame Song, whom I first met when she was a guide in Guizhou province. This was an area where many ethnic minorities lived, and she arranged for them to dance for our cameras. She was to spend years living in villages developing bed and breakfast accommodations for tourists, upgrading toilets, and introducing a wider variety of dishes. Up to then, the farmers mostly grew rice.

Buying and selling antique footwear was yet another good way to pay for trips, a special niche that probably doesn't exist anymore. I mention it as an example of unexpected possibilities to cover expenses. In the 1980s, I started collecting five-inch square pieces of fine, hand-stitched embroidery found for sale then in many outdoor markets in China. High class antique dealers didn't think these were worth considering, but it was hard for me to resist a bargain. Young girls used to make such samples of their sewing skills to show the family of a prospective husband that they could sew and make clothes for their children. Many of these ancient pieces cost only a few dollars each. Young girls no longer need to make them, and I bought a couple dozen because they were cheap and beautiful. I used some of them to decorate my own clothes.

Then I started collecting ethnic clothes, too. While most Chinese people are Han, China also has about fifty-four official minorities like Mongol, Dong, Gejia, and Hmong (Miao). Each group has its own unique language, religion, dances, and food. Each makes distinctive, highly decorated pieces of clothing. I could not resist buying handmade jackets, aprons, and shoes because they were very colorful, attractive, and affordable. North America has similar minorities: Cree, Ojibwe, Navajo, for example. I bought quite a few pieces and even wore a Hmong jacket on special occasions in Toronto, receiving compliments each time about how unique and beautiful it was.

As the collection grew, Mike said we didn't have room to store them. I tried to sell some at a "Christmas Sale" from our house, but no one was interested in such unusual pieces. The Museum for Textiles in Toronto accepted about a hundred of them. Museums in Vancouver and Edmonton took a couple and wanted more but didn't have room for them. The museums considered our gifts as charitable donations and gave tax receipts, which actually covered the price with some money left over for expenses.

Then the Bata Shoe Museum in Toronto wanted to buy antique footwear. It didn't give tax receipts, but I never needed to haggle with its wonderful founder. Sonja Bata paid cash for my footwear at international prices, which were considerably higher than the prices I paid. I felt honored when the museum put up my picture along with some of the footwear and considered me a "field collector."

Mrs. Bata was especially interested in antique shoes once worn by women with bound feet, another ancient custom. Wealthy families wanted their sons' wives to have tiny feet, both to show off their wealth and also to keep the wives from running away. They believed a good wife should serve her husband and his family and produce at least one male child. When a girl was about four years of age, female relatives would start to wrap the painful bindings tightly to stop growth beyond a few inches. Some men were turned on by the tiny feet and dainty steps. The Nationalist government banned the practice in 1910, but it continued clandestinely for a while after that.

In the 1980s, I started collecting these tiny shoes in street markets and even met some of the elderly victims. They were very shy, but a few allowed me to take pictures of their shoes and deformed feet. Some but not all could walk a few wobbly steps. After the women died, families could make a bit of money selling their discarded footwear. You can't find any of these women alive in China anymore. As I held their shoes and embroidery, I could feel a connection with these women who endured such unnecessary pain.

My favorite areas for collecting footwear were Xinjiang, Qinghai, Guizhou, and Tibet. Uyghurs once controlled the Xinjiang region, famous because of the Silk Road that connected China with Europe. This Turkic-speaking, largely Muslim group was the dominant culture. Han Chinese were a minority there, but the Chinese government was encouraging more Han people to settle there and take over the area. It is a huge region, one-sixth of China's land mass, and is rich in minerals.

My search for footwear there led to private Uyghur homes and invitations to meals under arbors of grape leaves. The hospitality was always warm and friendly. While the wives always served us, they never ate with us; Uyghurs are Muslim, and Xinjiang is more like the Middle East, like Central Asia. The boots and shoes were different, and I collected several.

On one trip to Tibet, I bought the boots off a man in a market and left him standing happy and barefoot, as he held the price of a new pair in his hand. On our twenty-eight-day trip in Tibet, we stopped at every monastery along the way. Some of them were largely in ruins from the Cultural Revolution's Red Guards, but some had been renovated with repairs to their unique domed stupas, which honored the remains of monks and other holy relics. At most were the religious storytelling thankas, the long embroidered streamers and the huge yellow hats that looked like they might have inspired the helmets of ancient Greek and Roman charioteers or vice versa. Large prayer halls were filled with low tables and pillows for monks to sit on. We paid the monks and nuns for prayers, and Terry recorded chants for his music collection. He was a professional musician.

At every monastery, our guide asked on my behalf for home-made boots that the monks and nuns no longer wanted. They preferred new machine-made ones and said they usually threw away the old ones. They were pleased to receive the price of a new pair. Our truck had room for them. Mrs. Bata later bought them all.

Mongolia also had handmade boots. This country was not part of China, but it was just an overnight train ride north of Beijing. It's one of my favorite countries, and I went there three times, even though it was not included in my guides except for a brief mention. Its countryside was much like Canada's foothills, the area between Calgary and the Rockies. It had prairies, rolling hills, snow peaks, and wonderful big skies. It also had throat singing. Except for Inner Mongolia and Tibet, it had everything China didn't, such as great herds of horses, sheep, cashmere goats, and yaks. It even had herds of camels, all freely roaming in unfenced grasslands. It is one of the few places where wild horses still live as they did centuries ago. Its nomadic culture was intact in the countryside, and cobblers, and even family members, still made boots there by hand. I photographed the process of making them with their upturned toes and fancy decorations and bought several pairs in markets and from cobblers. The Bata Shoe Museum bought my boots and my photos.

My best buy for the Bata museum was the boots worn by the last queen of Mongolia. I saw them in an antique store in the capital Ulan Bator, but the owner wouldn't sell them separately from an elaborate and very expensive robe and headpiece. The Stalinists in 1938 had taken over Mongolia and tried to destroy its Buddhist culture. They arrested the unfortunate queen one night because her husband had been the symbol of Buddhism in the country. Then they executed her and scattered her belongings.

I returned to the antique store the year after my first visit. No one had bought the set, and I was able to buy just the boots for the Bata Shoe Museum on condition that I could take them out of Mongolia legally and that the store owner could prove their authenticity. They were very beautiful as well as historical. They were not cheap, and I was taking a chance at their authenticity.

I had left my credit card in the safe of our hotel that day. Maybe that was a sign that I should forget about them. Fortunately, Joan Ahrens, my Hong Kong gem book co-author, had her credit card in her purse, and Joan was willing to pay for them until I could send her the money from home. I trusted Joan's judgment, and fortunately, she trusted me. They were over a thousand dollars, and it all turned out fine. Unlike those in every other country in the world, Mongolia's custom officers at the airport did not seize the historical relics.

A close friend, Dennis Jones, knew Gerald Harper, a fellow geologist working then in Mongolia. Gerald lived in Toronto, coincidentally in a neighborhood close to ours. He frequently flew home and generously carried several of the heavy boots in his luggage. It was another stroke of luck. I didn't have to pay for overweight baggage. The Bata Shoe Museum has since loaned the royal boots to the Victoria and Albert Museum in England with Bata staffer Suzanne Peterson personally carrying them on the plane.

I could write at length about these acquisitions. There was the fish skin. A curator at the Ethnological Museum in Beijing said a woman was still alive who knew how to make clothing out of genuine salmon skin. Before the Communist takeover, the tradition was unique in one of China's ethnic minorities, the Hezhen. After the revolution, it was easier and cheaper for the Hezhen to wear factory-made clothes, and they stopped wearing clothes that smelled of fish that made other people laugh at them.

After ordering two suits, I went to the Hezhen village near Harbin in Northeast China to pick them up. One suit was for the Textile Museum of Canada in Toronto, the other was for one of the University of Alberta museums in Edmonton. I published an article about them called "Pretty in Salmon" in the *Toronto Sun*. The seamstress made them to fit her grandchildren, and the Smithsonian Museum in Washington, D.C., paid to exhibit my picture of the three of them.

Canada now has some more unique Asian artifacts in its museums. For me it was a win-win situation. I had the fun of the hunt and the satisfaction of making enough money to help cover my travel expenses. The Tibetans and Uyghurs could buy new boots. I got to know some friendly Tibetans and Uyghurs and experienced parts of China few other foreigners did. I felt I was meant to buy handicrafts for Canadian museums. This is all to say that if anyone is meant to do something helpful, the means to do so will appear.

As for the Quakers, we had small meetings for worship only in Beijing and Hong Kong, which were not always convenient to attend. Several of the Quakers I knew in Toronto had worked as volunteers supplying medical relief and supplies with the Friends Ambulance Unit in the 1940s on the Burma Road. This road was China's only link with the outside world until the Americans joined the war. It connected the port of Lashio in Burma to Kunming in Southwest China. At the Quaker Meeting in Toronto, I met volunteers like Reg Smith, Bert King, and Francis Starr, who told stories about their work with mountain tribespeople, fighting local diseases and avoiding Japanese air attacks. They had to stop to fill up holes in the road made by the bombs before they could go on in their charcoal-burning trucks. It wasn't an easy ride.

A visit to Kunming meant seeing a bit of the Burma Road for a mention in my book. It was a largely forgotten piece of Quaker, British, and American history with narrow, winding, mountainous roads. My friends had spoken of the hardships and the work. Although the road was now paved, I was on a pilgrimage.

Aside from these, I was too busy researching Chinese religions to give much thought to my own spiritual matters. Unfortunately, I could find no trace of Mohism in China that Dr. Walmsley had talked about in his college classes. But I did find traces of Manichaeism, another obscure religion, and I wrote about Buddhist, Taoist, and Confucian temples; Christian churches, mosques, and Jewish synogogues.

Writing guidebooks then became too much work. My last edition, which was published in 2002 by Open Road, was eight hundred pages long. I figured that Chinese tourism no longer needed my help, and my relatives in China were no longer poor. When my sister and I visited Xin Hui, our relatives invited us to restaurants and wouldn't let us pay. One village relative had a motorcycle and an indoor toilet. Before then, we had to use the village's communal outhouse, which collected human manure for fertilizer. A super-highway was close to our village now. Another relative, living in Foshan, had built a substantial four-story building for his family, with space for a shop to rent on the ground floor.

Then my brother thought he could sell an e-guide to Beijing in time for the Olympics in 2008. That one would be much shorter, and I wanted to help him. I planned to go back to Tibet as well; however, Tibetans started rioting in Lhasa in support of Tibetan independence from China, the worst riots in twenty years. Although I didn't think that Tibet should separate from China, I felt China should be more thoughtful of its Tibetan minority, but alas, that didn't seem possible. People of the Han majority, like other majorities, still seem to think they are the center of the world.

Out of curiosity, I had hoped to go back to Tibet to try a new route from there through Sichuan province, to Chengdu, but again, Tibet was closed to tourists, this time long enough to force the cancelation of my plans. Tension was so high in Lhasa that Chinese soldiers had to guard the Olympic torch when it appeared there for only two hours. China wanted its first Olympics to show that it was now a major world power. It wanted the torch to be carried in every one of its provinces and regions, but the Tibetans didn't want any of it. I watched the opening ceremonies on television in Toronto with mixed feelings, proud of China but upset because of its treatment of Tibetans.

And then the Chinese started attacking the Uyghurs big time. At first it was just putting a few dissidents in jail. Then it forced thousands of Uyghurs into reeducation camps reminiscent of China's early brain-washing days and, alas, also of Canada's First Nations residential schools where children were beaten for speaking their native language. In February 2021, Canada's parliament at least voted to call China's treatment of its Uyghur minority a genocide, and sympathetic Canadians were advocating for boycotts of products made in the camps.

In 2021, Canadians were aghast at discovering unmarked graves of hundreds of children in its residential school grounds, a wake-up call to the injustices of that error, too. While many Canadians were involved in doing something about it, I was working on another problem.

Chapter 14:
Philippines, Hong Kong, Toronto, 1977-1984

In 1977, following the demise of *The National Observer* newspaper where Mike had been managing editor, *The Wall Street Journal Asia* offered him a job as correspondent in the Philippines. We sold our house in Maryland and shipped the essentials, eager to get back to Asia.

We rented a house in the city of Makati, which is in the National Capital Region, close to Manila. Bel Air was a gated community described by a Filipino friend as a neighborhood on the "lowest rung of the upper crust." We found it quite luxurious.

Although it was tropical and very hot, Manila was hardly a hardship post. A high wall surrounded our large house, and its garden had a fishpond and a live peacock in a big cage. We named him Buddy. The house included an office for Mike and four bedrooms, all air-conditioned. The two-story dining room, the kitchen, and the room for the maids had fans. Except for the frequent power outages and tap water failures, we were fine. We had a tank to store water. Manila's heat could be painful when the air-conditioning conked out, but we worked on manual typewriters then, and our driver delivered Mike's stories to the local cable office by car.

The cost of help was affordable. We had two full-time maids, and mail arrived continuously all day long. A local carpenter made some furniture out of our pine shipping crates for about ten dollars a day. He was so skillful, we are still using his bookcases, cupboards, and desks, as well as the rattan furniture we bought from a store there. We were fortunate that Dow Jones, which also owns *The Wall Street Journal Asia*, shipped our furniture whenever we had to move.

We were both careful about spending a lot of money, except to finance our passion for travel. By choice, I avoided hairdressers, and I was too busy to spend time on makeup. I still found cigarettes disagreeable and avoided alcohol because I didn't like losing control of myself. Mike drank in moderation.

We paid Kit, our driver, a hundred dollars a month, the going rate. Manila's traffic was terrible. Drivers would frequently try to squeeze five lanes of traffic into a space meant for three, and traffic jams were frequent. We needed an experienced, aggressive driver to go anywhere.

A maid walked our three children to school when I couldn't. At other times, the children were busy with homework, making videos, and playing with neighborhood friends.

The nearby international school was quite elite. A few of the very wealthy students had armed bodyguards who sat waiting outside the gate all day for their charges. Their parents feared kidnapping for ransom, but, fortunately, we were not wealthy enough to be targets. The country had extremes of wealth. I felt guilty paying our staff so little.

Kit drove us to a scuba diving resort most weekends, where we explored coral reefs and frequently found bright orange clownfish, like the star of the Disney movie *Finding Nemo*. We usually dove from a *banka*, the double outrigger Filipino canoe. We swam with sharks and sea snakes, which are the most venomous snakes in the world. Fortunately, the sea snakes and the sharks were friendly. Some fish were so friendly, they would eat food we held for them in our mouths. Even then we were aware the coral reefs were deteriorating and dying from pollution, warming waters, and the habit of local fishermen to use dynamite instead of nets.

Our son, Martin, was fascinated with sharks, and occasionally we would go together to the market to buy some baby ones for breakfast. They tasted okay, but then we learned about shark fin soup, the Chinese delicacy, which my relatives had served at weddings in Toronto. We discovered that local fishermen were catching sharks, cutting off their fins, and then throwing the live fish back into the ocean to drown. The sharks could no longer swim and needed air! The cruelty led to a limited boycott, even in Hong Kong, of the expensive Chinese dish. We stopped cooking baby sharks for breakfast and joined the ban.

Linda would bring home abandoned kittens, and then had to find homes for them among her schoolmates. She loved gymnastics and took horse-riding lessons. Terry, the youngest, was about seven and managed to get into trouble at school because he bought illegal fireworks to sell to fellow students. He seemed destined then to become an entrepreneur.

Language was not a problem. Most Filipinos spoke English fluently. It had been a colony of the United States from 1898 to 1946, and before that, a colony of Spain. Strangers usually addressed me in Tagalog, the local language, because they thought I was Filipina. The medical care was excellent.

I especially enjoyed proofreading Mike's stories before he sent them out. He was a careful writer, but occasionally I caught some typos. It made me feel he appreciated my professional judgment. Mike's stories were not only about the stock market and annual reports. He showed his sense of humor when he wrote a story about the time I naively gave in to Martin and Terry's nagging for a "friendly boa constrictor," like the one that belonged to one of their U.S. cousins. It only cost ten U.S. dollars in the market. Once in our home, the snake, a baby, sleepy from just devouring a mouse, gradually woke up. It started violently trying to attack anything that moved near its tank, and it wasn't the least bit friendly. It turned out to be a reticulated python with a hundred sharp teeth, a snake that grows two feet a year and can kill humans. Then it escaped. A maid found it in a bathroom and went hysterical. Mike bravely grabbed it. The snake peddler took it back and gave the boys back $1.36. We learned a lesson.

I planned my trips to China so I would be home for the children's birthdays. Mike's mother arrived to take care of them while I was away, and a dear American friend stayed with them on another occasion.

Two other Quaker families were in Manila, too, and we met them once a month for meeting for worship. Aziz and Raihana Pabaney were from India. Jack and Carol Urner were Americans. Both husbands were working for U.S. aid agencies, and it was good to have some Quaker conversations. After they returned to the U.S., Carol became an outspoken peacemaker and an activist with Women's International League for Peace and Freedom. She advocated for nuclear disarmament and the demilitarization of the Pacific islands, fought for women's and children's rights, and became a "Raging Granny." I admired her.

I wanted to give our children some spiritual education. From my own experience, I knew they had to do their own searching. I spent a great deal of time at a Spiritualist church trying to decide if psychic healing was real. A healer would stick his hands into a sick person's body and apparently pull human tissue out of the bloody depression he appeared to make. Martin thought he saw the healer hide the tissue in the palm of his hand and pretended it and blood came out of the patient's body. I wanted to believe that psychic healing, astral projection, and trances could be real. My mother and then brother-in-law, Ying Hope, who were visiting at the time, were convinced that the psychic healed their ailments.

The practitioners spoke in strange voices while in a trance, but I never did experience any of these apparent miracles myself. An American friend, Marian, spent a lot of time living with the healers who demanded sex of their female followers in return for the power to heal. The trances were frequently due to alcohol, she said, as she pointed out that they could put their hands in a pot of boiling oil without pain. I showed her that oil on top of boiling water is not hot because of different boiling points. I could put my hand in it without pain, too.

Linda was interested. She said she learned the value of meditation there. I didn't want to stop learning about the different ways that God worked and tried imagining a white light of healing flow into our children when they were sick. It could have been coincidence, as sometimes it worked.

Mike, however, had a strange fear of the psychic world. When he learned what Marian had been doing, he wanted her out of our house. Meditation was not a problem for him, though he was never comfortable with it himself and had joined us in Quaker meetings for worship in Maryland. The psychic world was something different, and after we left the Philippines, there were other things to explore.

The officer in charge of the 60th Battalion of the Philippine Army didn't like one of Mike's stories. For several months, Mike was on the verge of being arrested and jailed for "libel and rumormongering." President Ferdinand Marcos of the Philippines happened to go to Honolulu at the same time, talking to American and Canadian newspaper editors about press freedom in his country. Mike's boss and other important American publishers were dining with Marcos and his minister of defense, whose department was suing Mike. Foreign publishers like Katharine Graham of *The Washington Post* didn't want their journalists sued either. Needless to say, the matter was resolved at the highest level, and we breathed a sigh of relief.

Mike was fortunate. Today, many journalists around the world are imprisoned or killed for trying to report the truth.

The whole family was involved with one of Mike's stories, which coincided with my interest in aboriginal cultures. Friend and photographer Joe Cantrell's beloved grandfather was a Cherokee who once had land in Oklahoma. Joe remembered his grandfather crying when he saw the flooding caused by a dam built by the U.S. Corps of Engineers there, and, as a result, Joe took a personal interest in the Chico River project. He invited Mike and other foreign journalists to cover it.

Communist guerrillas were recruiting fighters from local tribes who were upset by government plans to build a dam to increase

Manila's electric power supply. The dam would flood their fields and burial grounds, but the Kalingas did not want their ancestral lands destroyed. Assassins killed Kalinga leader Macli-ing Dulag who was opposing the government.

Mike didn't want the government to know that he was visiting the late leader's village and a nearby guerrilla band. His cover was a family vacation to see the famous Ifugao Rice Terraces. Kit dropped him off across the river from Macli-ing Dulag's village, leaving him with men in loin clothes, bare-breasted women and slippery mountain trails. Then we went to see some of the two-thousand-year-old, hand-hewn terraces that were built on the mountain slopes, a magnificent and beautiful monument to the human creativity of growing food in extremely difficult terrains. That night, the children and I stayed in a hotel in a nearby town.

The plan worked except that the villagers had destroyed the only bridge from the road to their village in order to keep other assassins out. Mike and Joe had to swim across the narrow river while villagers carried his gear. Then they had to climb up a steep slope.

Of course I was worried because of the killing; I also thought about the Kalingas' headhunting tradition, even though the Kalingas had said they hadn't taken a human head for a decade. But it was at the spot where we had left Mike!

I contacted Joe about the story later. The Kalingas had told him, "We *are* this land. If they kill this land under the water, they kill us, so we might as well make it hurt them as much as we can." Joe wrote about how he and Mike fought their way across the river and climbed the hill.

> As we came over the top edge into the village, it looked like a scene from an excellent movie. There were silhouettes of people with spears and food bags atop their heads, huts on stilts, fires, all against a magnificent purple sunset. I'll never forget that sight, but I was too exhausted to pull my cameras out and take a picture. Sigh.

The people and Mike talked long into the night there. I can't imagine how he did it, having been so taxed by the climb up, but he did. And that story, Larry Cruz snarled at me, had immediately convinced the president of the World Bank to pull funding. Seems like it had been $1.7 billion, of which Marcos and cronies would have gotten a substantial cut.

Larry Cruz was President Marcos's press liaison officer at the time.

I am sure Mike's story wasn't solely responsible for the demise of the project, but it probably helped. Many people were fighting the dam. In recent years, Filipino politicians have accepted the help of China to revive electricity-making efforts on the Chico and other rivers.

Conflicts between aboriginal peoples and hydroelectric dams and other projects can still be found all over the world. If we are to believe Google, most of the electrical power in the Philippines now comes from coal, which is also controversial. Can't we just minimize our use of electricity?

Aside from Mike's conflicts with the ruling elite, we enjoyed the Filipino people, their informality and friendliness. They called each other, and even strangers, nicknames. They had a rare gift of remembering people's names long after a brief introduction.

All of us had to fly to nearby Hong Kong every two months to renew our Philippines visas, a welcome vacation paid for by Dow Jones. Hong Kong had interesting museums and a new sprawling ocean park with cable cars and a huge fish tank. Its live orca whale show was set against a backdrop of the real South China Sea, one of the most beautiful theaters in the world. That was before the popular 1993 film *Free Willy* made many people aware of the hardships of captive whales and led to freeing some back into the wild. Our children loved Hong Kong for its fancy floating restaurants and its shopping, too.

After three years in the Philippines, Mike was transferred to Hong Kong to become his newspaper's managing editor, supervising reporters around Asia. We were happy to move there. Shopping was very convenient; we could find everything we needed at prices cheaper than elsewhere in the world because it was tax free and very competitive. But it had some of the highest rents in the world.

Fortunately, Mike's company subsidized our apartment, which was in a three-story, Spanish-style building in upscale Stanley, one of the villages on Hong Kong Island. The apartment overlooked a bay and was within walking distance of the famous Stanley Market. Our backyard connected uphill to a huge park with good hiking along paved paths leading to the huge Taitam Reservoir that the British had built in 1888 to store rain water.

That Stanley apartment was my favorite home in the whole world because of the nearby hiking, its sparkling sea view, the weather, and its market, which had everything we needed. Then our landlord said he had to tear down the building to make room for something much higher, and we moved to Repulse Bay to a ground-level apartment with no view. There we had a garden with a couple of fruit trees, and we were close to the school and to a beach. From either apartment, it was about twenty minutes for Mike to drive to work. With eighteen hundred square feet of space, we had a lot more room than the average middle-class Hong Konger.

The feng shui of the apartment was good, I decided, after reading a couple of books on the subject. Feng shui is an ancient Chinese belief that the placement of one's home in relation to the topography of its surroundings influences one's fortune. A building at the base of a mountain was ideal because good luck comes from mountains. It was a complicated but fascinating subject and seriously consulted by just about everybody, foreigners included.

On some weekends, we hiked, climbed the mountains, and explored. Once we came across a spent shell case probably left over from the battle of Hong Kong. And once Mike had to kill a cobra that was on the path he was taking. On another hike, we came across some porcelain shards that the city's archeologist dated back to the Tang dynasty at least eleven hundred years ago. Once a year at New Year, we organized a three-hour company hike from our home, across the island, past the reservoir, to the high-rise apartments in Quarry Bay. We had a share in a Chinese junk, a thirty-nine-foot motorboat called *The Low Profile* that came with a driver. He took us to offshore islands for swimming and parties every other weekend. It was a life of privilege in one of the most crowded cities in the world, although at first, Mike worked from 3 p.m. to 1 a.m. to fit his paper's New York deadlines. When we could only get a part-time maid, I gave our children a choice of cooking or doing dishes. They all wisely chose cooking.

One day, Linda and her school chums were swimming in a pool in the hills above Repulse Bay near their school. She dived into a pond and hit the rocky bottom. Her friends carried her down to the road, and an ambulance just happened to be passing by and immediately took her to a hospital. Fifteen stitches later, her friends phoned us. We were very fortunate, and I wondered about feng shui.

Quaker meeting for worship in Hong Kong was held every Sunday in the Anglican bishop's personal chapel. The meeting was very small, and Mike preferred to stay home with the children since there was no First Day School for them, but as usual, he encouraged me to go. One of the Quakers was Gus Borgeest, a Portuguese-Chinese who had escaped from Shanghai to Hong Kong with his wife and child and then helped about six hundred other Chinese refugees learn to make a living on one of Hong Kong's deserted islands. For this and his work helping refugees fight opium addiction, he won the Ramon Magsaysay Award in 1961. One weekend, the Quaker meeting came with us to see Gus's island where he had helped so many. By then, Sunshine Island was abandoned and no longer operating.

Quakerism, and especially its service work, was still my spiritual anchor, countering Mike's skeptical agnosticism. My guidebooks on China continued to keep me busy, but in between editions, there was time to write and publish a novel, *Beyond the Heights*. It was a love story about a Chinese-Canadian woman and a Chinese Communist party member during the Cultural Revolution. My hero was based on my first guide in Beijing, a conflict between his idealism and his love for a foreigner. Writing it was fun as I wondered what might have happened if I had fallen in love with that guide. It did not become a bestseller.

Writing guidebooks on China was my main focus. I took our three children separately on trips to China while researching my books. Linda learned to play Russian poker with a group of Hong Kong tourists on a Yangtze River cruise. Only when the ship's loudspeaker announced a tourist attraction did the Hong Kong women look up from their cards. I made sure Linda saw the Giant Buddha in Leshan. Terry went with me to Xin Hui, where I suggested he take a picture of a policeman as we waited impatiently in a station to register our overnight family visit. I almost got us into trouble.

"It is illegal to take pictures in a police station," announced an officer sternly. My heart stopped. Then, after looking at Terry's passport, he said, "Since he's only seven years old, we won't arrest him."

Martin went with me to lovely Guilin with its many vertical limestone hills rising above the Li River. He was a curious child and fun to be with.

Dow Jones paid for home leave trips for all of us every two or three years. We planned those trips to include places like Tokyo, New Delhi, and Paris. We visited family in Los Angeles, Seattle, and Toronto. Traveling to the Olympic Peninsula was especially fun as Mike's brother-in-law, Bob, took us out in his boat to catch crabs and onto a beach to pick up oysters and dig up clams. We visited Mike's mother Lou, who was living nearby, and Mike's wonderful sister, Shawn, who arranged family reunions.

Shawn also had the benefit of their mother's interest in education. She completed a master's degree in urban affairs and worked in town planning. It was interesting that, in her family, three generations of women got pregnant at sixteen years old, and genetics became another of my interests. We enjoyed several family weddings.

Visits to the Chicago area included Mike's delightful Aunt Willie, the eldest of Lou's three sisters, and of whom we were especially fond. There was also cousin Doug who visited us in Hong Kong, where he bought a ruby ring for his fiancée, Raye, and Uncle Pat who always gave the children silver dollars. In Chicago, we usually stayed with Mike's cousin, Linda, an artist and art teacher. They were all very special.

We also joined Mom at the cottage in Brockville and went to more family parties. We were fortunate to have many compatible relatives on both sides.

Traveling with our small family was especially fun and educational. In India, Terry was about eleven when he discovered that he could haggle down prices in the markets. It's a skill he has continued to use to this day.

I don't know why, but we seemed to attract wild animals. Much to the amusement of the rest of us, a snake charmer in India was holding a cobra around Linda's neck when it defecated on her. She likes snakes and was upset by her family's insensitive reaction. A huge pelican in the Galapagos once did a job on Mike's head, and a peacock in New Delhi also thought Mike was a good target. Mike took these incidents with his usual humor. The kids thought they were hilarious.

While Mike worked with *The Wall Street Journal Asia*, I continued with my China guidebooks. When one was finished, I put together a book called *Hong Kong Gems and Jewelery* with American gemologist Joan Ahrens, whom I met at a lecture she gave on buying gems. I wasn't interested in buying any, but I found a great deal of pleasure just looking through a loup at each beautiful world inside Joan's collection. Mike bought me close-up cameras to photograph them.

Writing a book or newspaper article was my preferred way of learning anything, like the differences between topazes and sapphires, and how to tell a fake from a genuine gem. Joan was a knowledgeable and congenial collaborator. She and I appeared together at events to promote the book, which easily found a Hong Kong publisher. Interested buyers usually asked her questions while ignoring me. I assumed the slight was because of my Chinese face, but without me, there would have been no book. She did the research, and I did the writing. We were equal partners, but people seemed to assume only white people could produce such a book. Maybe they thought I couldn't speak English. It was an example of racism that is understandable in a colonial city. I was used to it by then, and sometimes I would say, "Hey, I'm one of the authors, too!" The book made the Hong Kong bestseller list.

Some of my Chinese relatives had moved to Hong Kong from Xinhui and were living in a tiny subdivided flat. There were still more opportunities in Hong Kong than on the mainland. Linda and I had referred to one of the children as "naughty Jang" during our visits to China. He was an obnoxious child who seemed to enjoy tearing apart live butterflies. With no fluent command of a common language, we couldn't really socialize with them beyond a few polite words.

We enjoyed meeting Uncle William Lore, half-brother of Uncle Henry, the doctor with whom I had lived in Toronto. He was a lawyer in Hong Kong and had wonderful stories to tell. He had been a lieutenant commander in the British Navy and told us about the time Phillip Mountbatten carried his bags since Uncle Willie outranked the future prince. We got a chuckle out of that one.

Uncle Willie was the first to enter one of the two prisoner-of-war camps to liberate Canadian prisoners taken by the Japanese during the battle of Hong Kong in 1941. I had to stifle tears when I thought about the end of a painful era for those people. I identified with the captives and their families, freed that day from their suffering.

Living mainly in the expatriate community, we had friends who had also lived in countries besides their own. Some but not all looked at the world globally, free of the narrow confines of their own countries. The friends of our children were primarily Americans. Alas, the only Chinese friends we had were the few at the Quaker meeting and those who worked with Mike.

In both Manila and Hong Kong, I toyed with the idea of sending our children to public schools so they would have local friends and learn Tagalog and Cantonese, but to turn down Dow Jones's often to go to the best available school was not wise as we considered their futures. As a result, they learned neither language fluently. In Hong Kong, they picked up swear words in Cantonese and could tell a taxi driver their home address. They managed with English in the Philippines.

I felt quite pleased when Linda invited her friends to our flat to hang out. Her group of about twelve different schoolmates varied each weekend. The door to her room was open, but I never listened to what they were saying. I wanted to give them privacy, and I was pleased she chose our flat rather than someone else's. I was obviously naive.

We were surprised when one of the school counselors invited Mike and me to her office. Some members of Linda's group were falling asleep in class, she said. The school was very concerned and suspected illegal drugs. The group had to be tested, and they could be expelled for using them. Mike seemed to react more calmly than I did; I was bewildered, angry, and very upset.

Linda was fifteen. She admitted that she and her friends were buying heroin and smoking it in her room. It was cheap, they shared it, and it made them feel good, she said. I discussed it with Mike. What had we done wrong? Were they just experimenting? Rebelling? We warned Linda about the school's threat, and we had some serious discussions with the other involved parents. They were mainly Americans, and the fathers were CEOs of international companies. Our twelve were the only students out of several hundred at the international school suspected of using illegal drugs. Mike saw strength in the other parents who all supported their children. "Maybe we can beat the odds," he said.

A British police officer visited us at home. He said he was more concerned about the dealer than the students. Linda told him about the dealer. Cannabis was hard to get and more expensive than heroin, he said. I didn't like doing it, but, urged by the school's counselors, I frequently searched her room. I discovered she was lying about giving up heroin, and I suspected her of stealing money. At times she was cheerful and apparently happy; at other times morose. She was going through what many teenagers experience as their bodies change. Once, when she was crying and in the middle of a tirade, I could do little to comfort her. Mike was home. He cuddled her, and she quieted.

We had to pay for the urine tests. The twelve of them were caught in a net, their friendship held together by a common interest that was making things worse.

I talked to Friends at the Quaker meeting, who commiserated. Meditation was helpful, but it was hard to concentrate. Ned Lyle was a school teacher. "It's the peer group," he said. "It's not the family, not the school; it's the peer group. She should be in a Chinese school," he added. "They have stronger families."

I was upset and afraid. On the verge of a nervous breakdown, I didn't know what to do. I wrote to other international schools in Asia, asking if Linda could go there instead, but boarding school prices were high, and we would have to pay it ourselves. I didn't like the idea of Linda being away from home. I also started attending Al-Anon meetings. It's the organization related to Alcoholics Anonymous that supports families and friends of alcoholics. Al-Anon was concerned with drug abusers, too. It reminded me to "let go and let God." Meetings ended with a prayer: "God grant me the serenity to accept the things I cannot change, courage to change the things I can, and the wisdom to know the difference."

Inspired by the testimonies of some of the Al-Anon members, I tried to convince myself that it was not my fault. There was nothing I could do about it. It was Linda's problem. I should stop reading her mail and searching her room. Linda would have to deal with the threat of jail and finding another school herself. She would have to figure out what to do.

Visits to a wise and wonderful Irish fortune teller named Marjorie Buckley were comforting. She said there are only two things you can predict in life: death and taxes. She recommended convent schools in her native India and predicted correctly that Linda would not be expelled. "Linda knows right from wrong," she said. "As she goes out the door, say 'Have a good time.' No reminders, no nagging. You have done enough. There is nothing more you can do." She also predicted that only Terry would give us grandchildren.

Linda told us later that she regretted causing Mike and me so much worry. The heroin gave her a lot of stress, too; she was constantly in fear of being caught. She knew that her addiction was unhealthy and controlling her life. She tried to quit several times on her own, but it was a struggle. Fortunately for us, the other members of her group left the school and Hong Kong. She was the only one left, and somehow, she passed the drug tests.

I appreciated other people brightening my corner this time. I was forced to add unexpected subjects—illegal drugs and Al-Anon—to my collection of interesting subjects to study. Mike wisely requested a transfer. Toronto was an option; he liked the idea of being in charge of Dow Jones's operation in Canada, his very own country; the alternative was to go back to the U.S.

Mike told me then that Dow Jones had a compulsory retirement plan for its staff, and we had some savings. We could afford a down payment on a house or pay for Linda's schooling abroad but not both. Fortunately, Mike's choice of Toronto turned out better than anything we could have hoped for. Linda told us later that, like most of her friends, she was unable to quit until she no longer had access to cheap heroin. Only one of her friends was unable to stop. He ended up homeless in the U.S. and died when he was forty-six years old. I wrote in my diary, "I cannot help but think that it has been the will of God, and I am grateful to God and/or feng-shui."

We moved to Toronto where we had family, a strong Chinese family.

Chapter 15:
Toronto, Kazakhstan, 1984-1996

I didn't want to leave Hong Kong, even after four years of living there. It was vibrant, full of writing opportunities, and sub-tropical. At times, the humidity would cause mold to grow on leather shoes, and we had to keep a light bulb lit in our closets. But the thought of Canada's cold winters made me shiver; however, it was the right thing to do at the time, and I've never regretted it.

Those were the days when newspapers made money, and we were very fortunate to catch the right wave. Hong Kong is no longer the same as it was then, politically or environmentally. It is much more crowded, very polluted, and its political freedom has been lost. Except for its cheap heroin, we were fortunate to have experienced this rare gem of a city during its best days.

On the way to Toronto, we included Truk (Chuuk) Lagoon in Melanesia, an itinerary Mike chose. I only knew that Truk was one of the best places in the world for scuba diving. It was there that U.S. forces had sunk about two hundred fifty Japanese ships and many airplanes. By that time, I had given up scuba diving because of sea sickness, but as I snorkeled in the warm, clear waters over the wrecks, I could see the shapes of ships only fifty feet below. Some had holes and were sculpted by the currents; all of them seemed to be covered with moss or seaweed or rust. The remains of Japanese sailors were still below, their lives destroyed because they obediently followed the decisions of leaders who convinced them to fight a war against China and then the United States. Such a waste of young lives! I felt more sad than squeamish while swimming over a graveyard.

Mike's choice of Toronto was good for us. We bought a house. Our children settled into its public schools, and Linda was no longer easily tempted by heroin. They did experiment clandestinely with cannabis, which was then illegal. Three of my sisters lived in Toronto, as did several of my Chinese relatives, including Mei Ting, Theresa, Chun Wing, and Yuet Yuen. Brother Joe lived in nearby Brockville. We were there when Mom sold the restaurant after working there for fifty-five years. It was good for me and our children to be close to family, to be in touch with some of our own Chinese-Canadian roots.

There were always parties at Christmas, Easter, birthdays, Thanksgiving, and Chinese New Year's, either in one of our homes or in a restaurant. Mike disliked the noisy Cantonese restaurants because he couldn't have conversations without shouting. We had the largest house and could accommodate thirty people without trouble. Our children got to know and enjoy the Chinese side of the family. I insisted on the children helping their then Uncle Ying Hope's campaign for city council, a lesson in government.

I had warned Mike that Canadian politics and life in Toronto were boring. Once you've seen the museums and Niagara Falls, there wasn't much else to do. Bars and stores were closed on Sundays then. I supported the closings because it meant families could spend time together. It was a custom that was soon to change.

Mike managed to find ways to make life interesting. His office produced business and stock market stories, but he also convinced his boss to send him to Resolute Bay in the Canadian Arctic, the starting point of expeditions to the North Pole. He came back with bragging rights and an article about an unexpected outfitter there who was from Madras in India.

Shortly after we arrived in Toronto, he took all of us to a four-day medieval war in nearby Pennsylvania, staged by the Society for Creative Anachronism. It was for another story. We found ourselves in a big meadow filled with tents and about three thousand other people dressed as Roman centurions, Renaissance cavaliers, Vikings, Japanese samurai, and characters from science fiction. Brewers sold mead, and monks offered "indulgences." Mike wore a caftan and pretended to be a merchant. We bowed a lot and used words like "forsooth" and "my lady." Every morning, someone would make the rounds of the tents shouting, "Bring out your dead!" Handmade jewelery was for sale along with shirts of chain mail and plates of mutton that had been barbecued all day on spits over an open fire.

Attenders each chose or invented a persona from the Middle Ages and wove a complicated story about their lives. The centerpiece was a bloodless battle between warriors from the eastern and western U.S.

Several of the participants chose to be mercenaries who could be persuaded to join either side. They seemed to be people with no ideals who just liked to fight and went with whichever side would pay them enough and give them a share of the spoils. They were like the merchants who sell weapons to whichever lucrative side of any conflict. The war came with symbolic fighting and rules like "no raping nor pillaging of camp followers." No one could hurt anyone else. The only casualties were from heat stroke caused by the heavy metal armor.

"We just come for the fightin' and the drinkin'," one mercenary soldier told Mike. I liked the attempt at historical accuracy and wondered if the excitement of a war, the craving for a fight and drink, real or imagined, was part of being human. But why did it have to be a war? Why couldn't it be some sports event? A concert? Organizers insisted that the participants were all ordinary, mentally-healthy people with day jobs in the real world. In spite of the unanswered questions, we all enjoyed it.

Back home, we did a lot of hiking along the verdant Bruce Trail which goes north from Niagara Falls to Tobermory. Mike wanted to do the whole 550 mile (nine hundred kilometers) hike on foot some day, in bits and pieces, but never did. Our kids grudgingly trudged along. We went canoe camping in Algonquin Provincial Park, portaging between lakes. In the winter, we went skiing in nearby resorts. Terry now takes his own son hiking, camping, and skiing, thus proving that some childhood complaints should be ignored.

At Christmas time, Mike took the family to pick out a tree at a tree farm. He was game for anything new, and he liked having his family with him. We all drove once from Toronto to the Magdalen Islands on Canada's east coast, which has the best windsurfing. He and I drove to Newfoundland and loved seeing wild moose and learning about a newly discovered sixteenth-century Basque whaling settlement in Labrador. Part of his job was an annual visit to the journal's bureaus in Ottawa, Calgary, and Vancouver, and of course I tagged along. He planned these so that we could spend weekends skiing in the Rockies.

Mike and our children officially became Canadian citizens, but they maintained their U.S. citizenships. It was a good decision because they can still vote in U.S. elections. Although I had the right to do so, I refused to apply for U.S. citizenship. While I didn't always want to live in Canada, I was glad to be a Canadian.

Mike's job was mainly administrative, and we vacationed in exotic places. During Linda's Trent University Study Abroad program in Ecuador, his mother, Lou, joined our family to cruise the Galapagos Islands. The brother of Linda's hostess had a small excursion boat there, just big enough for us. The Ecuadorian government very wisely limited the number of visitors to the islands. We had to have an official guide who enforced the rules that protected the animals and ecological uniqueness of this special place.

The Galapagos proved to be a favorite trip, as all of us swam with penguins and seals and almost tripped over nesting birds. We saw octopuses, sharks, and manta rays. None of them feared humans. Maybe they should have. We found a dead baby sea lion abandoned by its mother because, said our guide, some human petted it, gave it a strange scent, and thus made its mother stop feeding it.

It was interesting how the same species of birds evolved differently even from island to island. They were like cultures in isolated parts of the world, where people wore different style clothes and spoke dialects that were not the same as neighboring villages.

Unfortunately, we lost our son Martin to suicide when he was nineteen. I didn't have to go looking elsewhere to learn about mental illness; it came to us. He was taller than Mike and very handsome. He had always appeared cheerful, but he seemed unsure of himself. He was an excellent skier and windsurfer; and he liked to draw. His subjects were mostly unusual people, brains, and geometric patterns. He would have made a good designer.

He had cut his arm by accident while cooking, he said. The knife slipped. That should have been a clue, but I didn't catch it. I know now that self-harm is a way some people deal with emotional pain. But he was usually cheerful, and I never got the impression he was unhappy. I thought he was my friend.

The day before he died, he came home, as usual, at lunch time. He didn't like the bathrooms at school, he lied. We talked about his digestive problems, and he refused to see a doctor. Then he admitted that he had quit school six months before and had taken a job. I tried to discuss his future with him, suggesting art school. I was not happy that he had quit high school, but his father had been a college dropout, and I couldn't argue the point.

The next day when I came home from attending some chores downtown, I found Martin in bed, dead from a gunshot to the head. Somehow he had bought a gun and hidden it from us. I was so shocked and upset that I wanted to join him, but I stopped myself before I could get a knife. I called the police. Mike came home from work immediately.

We loved Martin. We are still not sure what happened. He left a note saying that he wanted to be buried cheaply without a coffin; he didn't want us to spend money on him. We all went for counseling, which helped ease the pain a little. The counselor said it wasn't anybody's fault. I wanted to move elsewhere to get away from the painful memories associated with the house, but Mike decided against it.

I like to remember that Mike said he dreamt of Martin one night shortly afterward, during which Martin apologized for what had happened. On our first trip to the tropics without him, clouds in the sky seemed to paint his portrait. No one else saw them. When Mike and I were in Machu Picchu in Peru, I felt something caressing my face on two different occasions. A fortune teller friend said that Machu Picchu was Martin's portal. I would know if he contacted me, and I like to think that he did.

I spent the following years trying to figure out the reason. Was it drugs? LSD? Was it irritable bowel syndrome? Had I not been a good mother? Linda and Terry assured us that they appreciated all the opportunities we had given them. They didn't feel I had neglected them because I was away from home so much. I was pleased that Mike and I were able to give the children the fun and companionship our own fathers couldn't; and Linda and Terry turned out to be thoughtful, caring adults of whom we are proud. Nevertheless, the death left a hole in my heart that was hard to fill. It helped me understand the suffering that other people endure when hit by similar tragedies.

By 1993, Mike no longer found his administrative job interesting. He read about a Fulbright Scholarship, teaching business journalism in Kazakhstan. Neither of us had ever spent much time in Central Asia, and I still loved going to places that none of my friends had ever heard of. He applied, was accepted, and left his job with Dow Jones. We tried to learn Russian, but he was fifty-seven and I was sixty-one. He did well with Russian, but I was never good at languages. We spent about eight months living in Almaty, the capital, our expenses paid by his grant.

By this time, Terry was making a living playing his guitar and touring with a band. They were fortunate to have found a patron who put them up in a house in Colorado when they weren't touring. Linda was living at home. She liked flowers and gardening while working in a plant store and applied for a job as a gardener for the city of Toronto. She worked as an administrator until she recently retired from the city's greenhouses.

Kazakhstan had been under Russian control in one form or other since the 1930s. In 1991, with the fall of the Soviet Union, Kazakhstan became an independent nation, the ninth largest in the world. The United States wanted to give it economic and political stability and security the American way. That meant a democratic system, private ownership, and a market-oriented economy. America had its eye on the country's mineral resources: natural gas, petroleum, and nuclear capability. It sent a lot of American advisers such as Mike to the country to help with tasks like rewriting the Kazakh constitution, reforming the economy, and setting up a stock market.

In September of 1994, the capital, Almaty, had a population of two million people. It was in the foothills of the Trans-Ili Alatau in the Tian Shan mountain range. The city was full of trees, and we could see the majestic snow-covered mountains from our apartment—except when the mountains kept the city's smog from blowing away. It was a multicultural city with mainly Kazakh people who were Muslim and looked Eurasian; and Russians, who were light-skinned, blond, and Christian. With my Chinese face, I had no problem fitting in with the Kazakhs. Friends told us that Genghis Khan and his Mongolian army were responsible for the Asian features when they invaded in the thirteenth century. Although Kazakh was the official language, Russian was the dominant one.

We found people of other cultural and racial groups like Koreans, Germans, and Ukrainians, along with horror stories about how, in the 1930s and '40s, Russia's Stalin forced these people onto trains to be dumped in Kazakhstan without food, warm clothing, or help. Today we would call it ethnic cleansing, deliberate starvation by depriving populations of land to grow their food. We could not escape hearing of the terrible things that humans did to each other here, too.

I was fascinated by the centralized heating system for the whole city, the pipes that snaked into every building around the city. The heat was turned on and off at specific dates each year, regardless of the weather. Power was in the hands of the government that controlled it. Amazing too were the technicians who quickly and efficiently set up our email system, so we could communicate with our children at home. At festivals, everyone wore traditional elaborate dress. I loved its museum with its even more elegant costumes and tall pointed hats. Once curators learned of Mike's archaeological interests, they showed us gold artifacts from its vaults.

We found that many of Kazakhstan's citizens were still suffering from the collapse of the Russian-built economy. People had made a living under the Soviet system by working for government enterprises. The rouble had lost most of its value, and now, people were scrambling to make any money at all. It was as if their father had died and left them floundering.

Among those hit especially hard were elderly pensioners. People who had retired after working for years for the government were trying to live on four dollars a month. We met a retired army colonel making eleven dollars a month, and a former KGB officer was selling his own insignias at a market in a park. He had been part of the much-feared Soviet secret police force.

Other people were not much better off. A teacher of English made about seventy dollars a month. We heard of a pediatrician who had to work as a chauffeur, and a brain surgeon was moonlighting as a security guard for the American embassy. Many local people survived by renting out their apartments to the Americans and moving in with relatives. We leased our flat from the accountant for the Transportation Ministry. It came furnished and included a thick carpet hanging on a wall for warmth. Because everyone needed money, every car became a taxicab. To get around, we merely had to flag down a vehicle, and it took us where we wanted to go. In return, we gave the driver cash.

As their collectives closed, workers with foresight had grabbed as many assets and power as they could. With the government no longer the employer, ordinary people were left with nothing. They had to grow their own chickens and vegetables and count on family to survive. Many people had to resort to bribery to live.

Mike hired an interpreter. Tanya was Russian, smart, and knowledgeable. She taught us a lot about the country. One day in the market, she ate a piece of raw pork fat and offered some to us. I was astounded, having been conditioned never to eat meat raw and especially not pork. I started to lecture her about life expectancies in North America compared to Kazakhstan. In America then, it was about seventy-five years. In Kazakhstan, it was considerably less.

"No one here wants to live that long," she said. I was startled by her response. That people didn't want to live as long as possible was a foreign idea. Tanya survived, though; we were still in touch with her more than twenty years later, and she said living conditions have improved.

Mike was expecting to find students who were eager to learn about business journalism or even Western-style journalism for that matter. Under the Soviets, journalism meant only the rewriting of government handouts. There was no such thing as investigative reporting. At first, they gave him six students who were about seventeen years old, some of whom spoke only Kazakh. They were not interested in learning anything about newspapers, so Mike taught them English. It was a waste of talent, but officials didn't seem to care to make any changes. I suspected the lack of cooperation was because Mike's job did not bring anyone free trips to the U.S.

It was not a complete waste of U.S. taxes. We met other American advisers. Fortunately, they used Mike to travel around the country, teaching local journalists about stock markets. I joined him on some of these trips and found elements of the old Soviet system still alive. It had tried to give power to workers, and much of this old habit was still evident; for example, passengers had to wait for the pilot and crew to get off a plane first. Elsewhere in the world, it's the other way around.

Our favorite example of "workers first" was a flight that arrived the same time each day in the town of Ust Kamenogorsk. Passengers then had to wait an hour to check into the hotel because the hotel staff hadn't finished lunch yet. This delay happened every day. No one thought passengers would be happier if either the lunch time or the flight time were changed. The needs of the workers, not the passengers, were more important.

We did have many pleasant times. After Mike's lecture in one city, we found ourselves in a private boat on the Ural River, the guests of a few officials. Asia was on one side of us and Europe on the other, a lovely moment for us lovers of geography. Our hosts treated us to champagne and black caviar as we cruised gently along. Kazakhs consider their caviar the best in the world, but being mainly for export, it's seldom available in Kazakhstan. The trip was a rare treat.

During Easter Sunday in another city, we met four priests and a woman on the street as we went to see what was happening in the Russian Orthodox church. They grabbed us by the arms and led us to their multi-domed building while loudly singing Easter hymns in Russian as we hummed along. The church was crowded with worshipers bringing their Easter bread to be blessed. They also brought food and vodka for the priests and beautifully painted Easter eggs to decorate the altars. While some of the priests splashed holy water on the crowd, others shared their wine and chicken with us. I hadn't expected to be served vodka in a church. A priest took us up to the belfry and showed us how they rang the bells. We had a merry time enjoying Russian hospitality that day.

Linda and Terry joined us for Christmas, and Terry played his guitar for a local orphanage in Almaty. We toured nearby Uzbekistan and saw Samarkand, Bukhara, and Khiva—old exotic cities with names I knew from my research of China's Silk Road that ended at the Mediterranean Sea. We explored huge, magnificent mosques, mausoleums, and monuments to poets, scientists, and mathematicians. As we tried to leave the country at the airport in Tashkent, an official tried to make us pay a bribe for not getting a "proper" receipt from an official hotel. We had stayed at private bed and breakfasts. Fortunately, another passenger distracted him, and we managed to get on the plane safely back to Almaty.

While Mike taught, I didn't want to spend my time playing bridge with the other expatriate, English-speaking wives. I wanted to do something useful. I tried to organize tours to China, the country next door. I managed to take one group of Americans to Xinjiang and Tibet before an American official ordered me to stop.

He said I was competing with Kazakh travel agencies. I argued to no avail that I was hoping to teach Kazakh travel agencies how to organize tours to China, which was next door.

Like everybody else, we carried around a shopping bag in case we found something we needed in a kiosk or the market. There was a shortage of things to buy. Near the market, a few women stood in line, each offering a few items for sale which could be just one pair of pantyhose or underwear. We searched for hours for envelopes, socks, and even bread or fresh garlic.

I joined a group of American women writing a guidebook for expatriates about Almaty. It was something useful, and I enjoyed, as always, working with other people. The city had no newspapers, telephone books, or directories in English to help foreigners find doctors, stores, transportation, and the latest news. We told them about the best shops for bread and to always carry a shopping bag. We explained how to find a place to live and where best to do their banking. We pointed out that a dish detergent named Barf was okay. "Barf" was the Iranian word for "light." We explained about local customs, such as the habit of many men to start the day drinking vodka at breakfast and that they rarely stopped imbibing until bed.

Almaty was not an easy city to research because of language. Our committee had conflicting opinions about what we should include, but we managed to get a book written before Mike and I left. I hope we helped the local economy and cultural understanding. Writing guides is a great way to learn about a city, and, as usual, we made some long-lasting friends.

When it came time to leave Almaty, I didn't want to go back to boring Toronto. I thought briefly and naively that I wanted to stay and start an English-language newspaper. It would be good for the foreigners as well as the locals. It would help the Kazakhs learn English and show them what investigative journalism was. Mike convinced me otherwise. My command of Russian never improved, and I knew I could never handle a bureaucracy dependant on bribery. He told me about Naya, an American, who was arranging to leave Kazakhstan and had to get permission to take her dog out with her. The customs officer said her pet was worth more than a thousand dollars, and she needed to pay a big export tax or give him a bribe. He was frank about the bribe. When she argued, the officer pronounced the dog a "national treasure." Now she couldn't take him out of the country at all. She responded by paying only forty-five dollars to another government ministry to write a letter, formally declaring that her basset hound was just a dog and not a national treasure. The ploy worked for her; I doubt if I had the smarts to think that creatively.

On the way home, we toured Turkey by public bus, stopping in ancient cities like Troy and Ephesus. It was yet another lovely honeymoon. Mike had to explain that the many balls on the chest of the statue of Diana of Ephesus were breasts. She was the goddess of fertility. I learned that pine nuts actually grew in pine cones and that the word "lesbian" came from the Island of Lesbos, which we could see one day in the distance. Today, that island is full of refugees. He explained the importance of the Ephesians, a name I knew from my Sunday school days, and the myths of Helen of Troy, and how to tell a reconstruction from an original ruin. As always, it was lovely to have my very own personal guide.

We took our time, spending nights in backpacker hostels. There was no reason to hurry home, or so we thought.

Chapter 16:
India and Hijras,
the Problem, 1995–1997

We were only back in Toronto for four days when Mike's former boss at Dow Jones asked if he wanted to work in Bombay, setting up a business news bureau with an Indian company. He said yes with no hesitation, and I agreed immediately. While we were there, Bombay changed its name to Mumbai.

We were living in the top-rated Oberoi Hotel on Mike's expense account for those first couple of months while we tried to find an apartment. I didn't have to think about cooking or cleaning. We didn't have to be careful about what we ate. We had a choice of six excellent restaurants, and we chose to eat mainly Indian food because it was so good. Our life was extraordinarily comfortable until Mumbai's air pollution put Mike in the hospital for four days.

We heard about a Canadian backpacker who had just died because she believed she could develop an immunity to germs by drinking the tap water. A guidebook on Mumbai might have been useful for newcomers like her.

Before I could begin exploring India again, I had to finish my latest China book. Then I joined INDUS, a women's club with a membership of well-connected, wealthy Indian women and a few foreign ones, all with Indian and international interests. It had a marvelous program of socials and lectures on subjects such as Indo-Chinese cooking, pranic healing, the Ramayana, and even the Macarena, all in English. With its congenial members, I attended the exotic Pushkar camel fair in Rajasthan, where camels of all sizes were bought and sold. It made me think of movies of pre-British India.

INDUS's many members were keen on learning about India, too. It was an excellent resource for writing a guide. Some members had meetings in their homes. When I asked about a mysterious palace Mike and I had discovered on one of our weekend excursions, one of its members said, "Oh, that belongs to one of our members. She's over there." And so we met a princess.

I also joined the American Women's Club, and Mike and I went exploring with some of them. Esther was an Indian Jew. Near Mumbai, there were many Bene Israel synagogues, so we visited several and learned some Jewish history. These Jews believed that they were descendants of the lost tribes who had been deported from their homeland twenty-seven hundred years ago. We met a rabbi who explained that many had migrated to Israel where they were not recognized as real Jews. Some had returned to India as a result.

There it was again. Many of the Jews had intermarried with Indians, but they still maintained many Jewish customs and considered themselves Jews.

We were finally able to find a small apartment. It wasn't easy. Landlords were reluctant to rent because it would take up to thirty years to evict tenants if the owners wanted their apartments back. Mike's company had to put up a guarantee of about U.S. $300,000.

The apartment was far from elegant, but it was adequate for the two of us, a ten to ninety-minute drive from Mike's office, depending on traffic, and close to the U.S. Consulate. We lived on the fifth floor, safely above what we later called the "malaria mosquito line." Servants and drivers slept in the open on the ground floor veranda, and many of them ended up with mild forms of the disease. I found and trained a bright, helpful Goan maid, who had just graduated from a Catholic high school. We had to pay a part-time sweeper because cleaning wasn't Leena's job. The caste system still existed, and supervising the sweeper was her job. Even though his work was sloppy, we couldn't fire him because he came with the apartment, and his caste guaranteed his livelihood.

Many people who had migrated from the countryside to the big city lived on the streets, some of them near the consulate. I was amazed that they seemed oblivious to the rest of us as they cooked, washed, and slept in public on sidewalks. Those near the consulate used a section of sidewalk to defecate at night because no conveniently located public latrine existed. We had to hold our breaths passing heaps of rotting garbage, too. Near a hospital, we could even see medical waste overflowing in bins.

Mumbai was a city of extremes, and I wondered how best to spend my time. Should I try to organize a neighborhood cleanup campaign the way the Quakers did in some U.S. areas? Would I be taking work away from someone? Could we just pay someone to clean the street every day? No, that wouldn't solve it. It would just continue after we left.

Mike had hired a car and driver to take him to and from the office each day. The rest of the time, I could use both to explore the city for up to fifty miles (eighty kilometers) a day at no extra cost. It was a travel writer's dream. It was now the monsoon season, and the rains came in the evening, cleaning up the air. It also made mush of the garbage and discouraged much walking.

I saw my first hijra at a stoplight, walking from car to car. They were begging, a scowl on an otherwise movie-star handsome face. They looked very unhappy, especially after a woman in the car ahead of us rolled up her window and turned her face away. They were wearing a white, floor-length sari decorated with flowers, and their hair was long and caught at the nape of the neck with a clasp. They moved on with resignation at the slight, their movements more masculine than feminine. I kept seeing more people like this as I explored the city. Some of them were going from store to store begging. I asked our driver who they were.

"Bad," answered Ashok. "Hijra. No good." He pronounced it "hij-ra."

What had they done to deserve such treatment, I wondered? India was a male-chauvinist country, where sons were preferred to daughters. To see masculine-looking people in women's clothing was bewildering. I had seen a few while living in New Delhi, too, but in Mumbai, there were many more.

I asked my friends in INDUS. They were all university educated.

"They're dirty," said one woman. "I can't stand them touching me."

Said another, "If they get angry at you, they lift up their skirts and show you. I hate them."

Our travel agent, Maya, had her own story. One day, she realized that her cook was a hijra. The cook wanted the evening off because of a full moon, a very auspicious time for hijras. Maya had a party that evening, so she was angry and fired them. The hijra cursed her and left. Shortly afterward, Maya and her husband both lost their jobs, and, as a result, also their house. Their two children got sick and died. Was it the curse or coincidence?

A two-paragraph item about the hijras in my guidebook would be an interesting sidebar, I thought, but who were they? I had to meet some. Why were they wearing feminine clothing? Why did people hate them? Were they criminals?

My Quaker connections helped. We had met the Pabaney family in Manila, and they were living now in Mumbai. One of their sons, Sahid, said his friend, Kamal Dhalla, could introduce me to some hijras, and his friend, Manisha, could translate for me.

Manisha was still in college, studying another language, but she had some time to spare. Unless she was busy with her job as a freelance interpreter of Russian, she could help me out, she said. She refused to take any payment. I was impressed that she could handle so many languages.

"I've always been curious about hijras," Manisha admitted later. "I've never had the nerve to talk with any before." She became one of our volunteers.

Kamal Dhalla was a successful businessperson. She seemed to know a lot of influential people and had once worked as an editor and a teacher of English in Iran. She had always wanted to help street children. Now that she had made sufficient money, she was taking a course on how to be a volunteer, she said.

Kamal was a Parsi, a follower of Zoroastrianism, one of the world's oldest extant religions. Mumbai was the world's Parsi center, with about fifty-seven thousand of them living there. Some people think one of the storied Three Wise Men from the East was Zoroastrian. From Hong Kong history books, I had learned that Parsi merchants had supplied the opium that the British forced onto China in the nineteenth century. The trade led to two opium wars and China's loss of Hong Kong to the British.

After meeting Kamal, I knew I couldn't dislike her for what her ancestors had done to mine in China. She was wonderful, and she introduced me to her teacher. Anaxi Shah worked for a Jain social welfare agency that was trying to help women and street children set up small businesses. She worked with drug addicts, too, but she was also interested in helping hijras.

Jainism was an ancient Indian religion. I had seen its monks in New Delhi, wearing masks over their noses and mouths and carefully sweeping the streets in front of them so they wouldn't breathe in or step on any insects and inadvertently kill them. Anaxi was not a monk. She did not wear a mask, but she believed in saving people.

Everybody seemed to have a different story about the hijras. Anaxi's information differed from those of the INDUS members. She said 90 percent of the hijras were victims of kidnapping. They were children from poor families who were taken to the hijras to be castrated.

I think my jaw must have fallen open at her description. "That's terrible," I gasped, shaking my head in disbelief. At the same time, I wondered if they needed help.

"They make money by blessing newborn babies," Anaxi continued. "They have friends in hospitals who tell them when babies are born. It is considered good luck for newborns to be blessed by hijras or, conversely, not to be cursed by them. So parents give the hijras about a thousand rupees to sing a song. They are invited to bless marriages, too. I can take you to visit some," Anaxi said.

Of course I wanted to go. So did Kamal and Manisha, and Anaxi said she would make the arrangements.

In the meantime, I walked into a police station and talked with a couple of senior police commissioners. Were hijras criminals? No. Were they castrated? Yes. Were castrations illegal? No. Had they been kidnapped? No. I didn't want to write about anything illegal.

"Hijra" means "third gender" or "neither man nor woman," said S. Chakravarty, additional commissioner of the crime section. "In English, they are called eunuchs," he said.

I learned later that the word "hijra" is derogatory, but it was a term they used themselves with us, so I have continued to use it here with apologies. I never heard them use any other word to describe themselves.

Commissioner Chakravarty arranged for a policeman to take me to meet one. They were eager to help journalists, and an officer in street clothes took me to Kamathipura, Mumbai's red light district. The policeman said to wait while he disappeared into one of the huge, multistoried, rundown buildings. It looked like a stage set with its crooked balconies. He came back with an older person who was dressed like a woman. When they spoke, their voice sounded masculine.

Sheila didn't really want to talk to us. "What's the use?" the hijra said. "Journalists have come before and promised help, but that was the end of it. All hijras want to work. We'd be happy with a salary of two thousand rupees a month. I don't want a job just for myself. I want jobs for all hijras."

That was all. Sheila asked for five hundred rupees for the interview. I offered thirty. They were not interested and made to leave but not before they gave me a firm handshake and a grin.

The head constable said that, without his help, we wouldn't have gotten that much cooperation. "Eunuchs are secretive. If anyone rapes or violates them, they won't complain to the police. They just go to a hospital." He also hadn't heard of any major crimes that the eunuchs had committed. The contradictory information and Sheila's accusation about journalists made me want to keep searching for the truth about these mysterious people.

Manisha and I met social worker Anaxi at her tiny field office. It was no different from the other shacks beside the railway tracks near the Mahim station. It was made of corrugated tin and was plain inside except for a desk and a stone statue of Hanuman, the monkey god. He was plastered with marigold-colored paint. A couple of social workers and a freelance journalist joined us. I grimaced because there were so many of us. I had hoped for an intimate one-on-one with an interpreter.

"Refer to them as 'she' and 'her,'" advised Anaxi. "And don't pay them."

Shouldn't they be compensated for taking time away from begging? I wondered.

The group of eunuchs we visited that day had their own little colony, a couple of shacks strung together behind the station. Two hijras appeared at one of the open doors. Anaxi introduced us and explained that we were social workers who wanted to know more about them, and the hijras invited us in. Their hut was made of straw mats and plastic sheeting. Since the weather was hot, the bottom of the mat walls was rolled up, apparently to catch the occasional breeze. Through this open area just above the floor, railway tracks a few feet away could be seen. The room was clean but cluttered with wooden or straw partitions and clothes hanging on lines. A small shrine with two goddesses was on the floor.

The hijras were all wearing clean, decent-looking saris. One was slight, about twenty-four years old, and like the rest, they were decorated with a necklace, earrings, and bangles. They had a green dot between their eyebrows and looked more feminine than masculine. Although I couldn't understand them, they exuded warmth and humor as Anaxi translated, and I liked them immediately. Another said they worked as a domestic servant. They were twenty but looked older and boyish. One of them looked like one of our daughter's boyfriends. A third had a round, cheerful, masculine face and wore a nose stud. They said they made fifty to eighty rupees a day begging. One of them had long curly hair tied with ribbons at each side. Some of their faces were unquestionably masculine and angular; the rest, androgynous. A couple of them showed traces of beards. They said they were women in every way, except for bearing children. Their names were female: Sumitra, Baby Dancer, Rita, Priya. They felt like women and wanted to be women. When they filled out government forms, they didn't want to check "male" or "female." They were neither.

About twenty minutes into our visit, they asked Anaxi if we would leave. I was beginning to suspect they were sex workers and that maybe we were frightening away their customers, but they did ask us to return any time and were pleased to pose for my camera. I promised them copies of the pictures. Their warm reception made me want to return, and we did the following week and for weeks after that. They were fascinating, but they kept telling us contradictory stories about themselves. They said to come back and meet their leader, Meena Balaji.

We met beautiful Selma, who lived nearby with another group. They said they were twenty-three years old. They wanted to be a doctor or a lawyer, but they also loved to dance. They said the others looked up to them because they were more educated; they wanted to continue their studies but didn't have the means. A doctor in Madras had operated on them three years before, and they couldn't go back to being male.

Selma felt attracted to men. They told us a few weeks later that they were a hermaphrodite. They had both male and female sex organs and didn't need to be castrated. I wondered if this were true because they had told us a different story a week before. Since I was in my social worker mode, I asked Selma if they and their friends would be interested if we could find them a tutor to help with their schooling. Selma said they would like that. Anaxi said she would help and later found a tutor who declined when they found out the students were hijras.

Meena Balaji was a big person who was obviously a leader. When we met the following week, they were wearing gold earrings, a nose stud, bangles, and a green house dress. We sat on the floor as Meena dominated the conversation. They had a strong voice and expressive hands and seemed to enjoy the attention. They said their family consisted of fourteen hijras.

Meena said they were from Bangalore and spoke several languages besides English. They had completed one year of a bachelor of science degree; but what was the use? All the boys made fun of them. They had dressed female since they were a child. At ten, they realized they were different and decided to leave home at sixteen. Tears filled their eyes as they talked. They were an embarrassment to their parents. Yes, they had had an operation for which they paid a doctor about fifteen thousand rupees. For forty days, another hijra had poured hot oil and hot water on their penis. Heat relieved the itching, and eventually, their penis swelled up and was cut off, they said.

Meena sent the others out of the room and lifted their skirt to reveal a triangle of black pubic hair that looked just like a woman's. Proudly, they showed us their swollen breasts, the result of abortion pills taken once a day for the last six years. Now in their late thirties, they had been in Mumbai for more than thirteen years, away from the teasing, the disgrace. Here they were anonymous. They asked me to take a picture of their body. Kamal said not to publish it. It would not be respectful.

Meena continued. About eight members of their family came back to the room. They listened to Meena as if they had never heard their story before. One fell asleep, and I wondered if they had been up all night with clients. From time to time, one would leave the room and then come back about ten minutes later. It was their turn, they said.

I gave Meena some Chinese bangles, but they didn't seem to like them. I heard someone say in English, "Give them some money," and I handed them thirty rupees, which they refused. Meena wanted us to come back to visit, any morning before noon.

"Many people come to talk to us," Meena said. "We see their stories in the newspapers, but that's the end of it. Journalists tell lies about us. They promise to help us get jobs, but they never do." I had heard that complaint before. We didn't tell them until later that I was a writer, but it was true: many journalists publish stories and then do nothing more. I wanted to show them that some journalists really cared. I was also curious to find the truth in what they were telling us.

Up to then, I hadn't promised anything except copies of my photos. We volunteers discussed our impressions after each visit. No one believed Meena had finished a first year bachelor of science course. A B.S. candidate would have better English and be more articulate. Anaxi said her agency was trying to help hijras re-join the mainstream and get them out of begging and sex work. She hoped they would manufacture things to sell.

Still unconvinced because of the conflicting stories, I looked up Dr. I.S. Gilada, who was considered the authority on hijras in Mumbai. His organization was trying to raise money for AIDs research and gave thousands of condoms to sex workers in Kamathipura every month. Dr. Gilada said that prostitution was legal, and there was no law requiring sex workers to have regular medical examinations. He said forced castrations are rare. He had never heard of children kidnapped by hijras.

"Castrations are usually done on the spur of the moment in remote places," said the doctor. "The patient is usually drunk or drugged, and the penis is cut off. A ceremony with a beating drum and music usually accompanies the operation. If the person dies, it is okay because they have achieved Nirvana or will come back in another life as a woman. They are prepared to die.

"Some castrations are done by doctors. Hot water and oil packing is done after the operation." Dr. Gilada disputed Meena's description of only hot oil and water for forty days. "A catheter is inserted, so a hole will remain for urinating. It takes forty days to heal, and antibiotics might be used. Cow's urine and dung are also used because they have antiseptic qualities."

Two of Dr. Gilada's workers took me into one of Kamathipura's brothels to meet more hijras. Inside this multistoried building were tiny rooms, each with groups of five or more people. Some appeared to be couples with children. They didn't all seem to be hijras.

Many doors were open because it was hot, and I could see ceiling fans. Narrow benches on which some people were sleeping lined the hallways. We had to step over tiny children and garbage. There didn't seem to be any privacy.

The people seemed reserved and suspicious. Some eunuchs recognized Dr. Gilada's workers and came for condoms. My guides said many of the people were from Nepal. It was the worst human habitat I have ever seen because of the crowding. It was worse than Kowloon's infamous Walled City, which I had also visited before it was demolished in 1994. I could understand why our hijras preferred their less congested housing near the railway station.

One of the hijras I met later that day with Anaxi said, "The operation proceeds once we have the blessing of the goddess. The timing depends on our mood. We must have a strong desire. We must wait for her call. If you feel the goddess possessing you, you dance joyously. You lose all sense of yourself and are only aware of her being inside you. Then you rush off and get it done. Ignoring her is like betraying yourself. Why not get rid of the organ?"

Another said, "The goddess disapproves of sexual activity. We go out in the morning, look for clients, and afterward, wash up. Then we ask the goddess to forgive us." Said another, "The goddess likes dancing and singing. We must dance in front of her. She likes us to be truthful, no lies, no stealing, no harassing and torturing of others. Otherwise, the goddess will send disease."

Anaxi told me later that their devotion to their goddess was stronger than that of the average Hindu family. It made her hopeful about working with them.

At the School of Social Work, its vice principal said that they did not teach counseling for sexually abused children because such abuse was "too common."

"Hijras are worse than animals, but they are human," she added. I was appalled by her lack of compassion and concern for the children. They needed someone to counsel them, too.

Many but not all hijras had been victims of abuse. They needed the support of a group.

Every policeman or doctor I interviewed gave me names of other professional people to talk to. I thought to myself, hey, whoa—was I doing a doctoral dissertation? Was I writing a book about hijras? Why was I so obsessed with finding out so much about them when I only needed a paragraph or two for my guidebook? I decided I was just trying to solve a mystery. No one seemed to know the whole truth about them. But I was enjoying taking pictures of their lives, their parties, and their worship.

Weekends and evenings were spent with Mike. We enjoyed hiking with friends around Matheran hill station where cars were banned, the food was good, and the views glorious. We awoke each morning to the thumping of monkeys jumping on the roof of our guest house. Also outside of Mumbai, we visited empty beaches, old forts, and the charming former Portuguese colonies of Diu and Goa. Friends invited us to a party on a boat to see the annual Ganesh festival. Ganesh is the remover of obstacles and is especially popular in Mumbai. Worshipers carried over a hundred thousand statues of the elephant-headed god to dissolve in the sea that year. The festival was spectacular.

I attended a four-day Vipassana meditation course in nearby Pune with Esther. It was four days of getting up at 4 a.m., having simple vegetarian food, and not being allowed to speak at all. Our leaders were people who spent at least two hours meditating every day when not teaching. This experience was also good fuel for a guidebook and for my spiritual development.

My meditation until then had been confined to Sundays at Quaker meetings. Now I learned to concentrate on feeling the air going in and out of my nose. It was amazing. While I had a hard time keeping my mind on my nose and sitting for hours at a time, I found the technique helped with the butterflies that choked me whenever I had to speak to an audience. It also helped when I was angry or frightened, and I started using it during Quaker worship.

Esther was an incessant talker. I wondered how she would manage with the "no talking" rule. She actually did well except to warn me to be careful because there might be snakes in the grass outside the door of our cabin. That bit deserved some thanks.

Linda and Terry came from Canada twice to visit us. We went to the Rajasthan desert for an overnight camel trek. The camel drivers pitched our tents and asked us the next morning how we wanted our eggs cooked. Camping in Ontario was nothing like this.

We spent two nights in a very elegant palace that a Rajasthani prince had built on an island in the middle of a lake. It was than a hotel. Ashok drove us between medieval walled cities. Once we came upon a pilgrim who was traveling like a rolling pin along a highway for two hundred fifty miles (four hundred kilometers), he said. He was going from one temple to another. His helpers laid down mattresses on the hot pavement and held an umbrella to keep him shaded. He stopped rolling to talk with us in fluent English, but he didn't want to say why he was doing it. He vaguely mentioned a problem in his family that should be resolved in this traditional way. It was more material for a guidebook. I was later to see people doing similar mortifications in Toronto at Sri Lankan Hindu festivals.

Back in Mumbai, we volunteers visited Meena again and again, and each time I brought them photos, which made us especially welcome. Some of them wanted pictures of themselves nude because they were proud of their bodies. By then, we had confessed that I was a journalist. Meena said I should publish their picture since they were senior. They insisted they wanted to get out of sex work because of the diseases. They said they could do housework, and Meena wanted to be a cook.

Meena was more articulate than the others. I always left a bit of money with them after every visit but no more than fifty rupees, which was about ninety Canadian cents. I always brought lipsticks and nail polish, soap and shampoo, which they all appreciated, although occasionally the lipsticks melted because of the heat. Members of my INDUS and American women's groups had gleaned these treasures from their stays in fancy hotels. Many of them were interested in learning more about the hijras. They wanted to help, too, but they never offered to join us.

Meena said that the hijra song celebrating the birth of a boy began with, "We are happy for a male child. We don't want this child to be like us. We invoke the goddess to bless him and give him life for one hundred years and be a proper man."

By this time, it was June 1997, and Mike realized that his joint venture partner in Mumbai wasn't able to keep its side of the agreement. Mike was threatening to go home. He hadn't left retirement to put up with the stress of operating a routine news bureau, he said. This meant my guidebook project would no longer be possible. If we were to help the hijras, it had to be soon.

Chapter 17:
Hijras, One Way to Help, 1997

One day while stuck in a traffic jam, I remembered that some of Toronto's beggars sold a newspaper to make money. It was not a direct plea for a handout. Maybe their Mumbai counterparts could do something like that. Maybe if the hijras sold a booklet about themselves, they would not only be doing a public education job, they would have another way to supplement their income. Moreover, they would not be competing with anyone.

When we arrived at Meena's colony, we discussed possibilities again. Meena said with a great deal of interest, "Give us things to sell, and we will sell them." I doubted if "handcrafted by a hijra" would be successful.

One of the other hijras talked about their attempts to sell vegetables on the street. Some "thugs" came along and smashed their cart.

A social worker we had consulted suggested they wear men's clothing to get a job. Anaxi was against anything that altered their appearance, especially cutting their hair. She said, "We have to accept them as they are, or they will never trust us if we say anything like that. They would be insulted." I agreed with her.

At home that evening, Mike, the ever thoughtful husband, asked as usual what I wanted for my birthday. He didn't always give me what I wanted, but this time he agreed to put money into our hijra fund instead of a lavish dinner at the ritzy Taj Mahal Hotel. Every day over dinner, he asked about my adventures. He was a good listener and very encouraging, although there were times when I joked about dedicating a book "to my husband, in spite of whom this book was written."

Finally, our little committee and Meena agreed to write a book the hijras could sell. It would be Meena's book with questions and answers. She would approve it before publishing, and it would be in English, the language educated people in India all knew.

We began to collect information. When Meena gave us contradictory stories, we would say something like, "Oh, I thought last week you told me that. . . . It looks like I misunderstood." Usually they had forgotten what they had said the week before.

One of them said they were all married; their husbands were in Madras. Why didn't they live with them? Answered another, "We want a man to be passionate and long for us. We have to create this by staying away."

It wasn't really a lie, I decided. It was an attempt at a respectable self-image, a fantasy that their lives were really not as bad as they were.

I began writing the book. We had a list of questions for Meena. Kamal translated her answers for me. Who are we? Why do people fear us? What is our religion?

The book started with, "Many men pretend they are hijras, but a real hijra has been emasculated. We have no male organs. Few people will give us jobs. We live by begging, dancing, and conferring blessings (or curses), and some of us are sex workers. We do not want to be sex workers, but we have no choice."

Somehow, Meena agreed on the text, but it took awhile.

One day, Meena announced a visit to their goddess, Bahuchara Mata, with whom they believe they have a direct connection. The temple was in nearby Gujarat state. I wanted to go, too. It would be great for pictures.

"Hijras ride the trains for free, but we won't be able to sit with you in your second-class, air-conditioned car," Meena said.

A railway official I had met explained later that hijras didn't ride free on trains. It was just that ticket takers were so afraid of them that they didn't bother trying to collect the fare from them.

Meena later told us a second railway story. One day, a hijra was riding on a train without a ticket. An inspector threw them off the train, but the train wouldn't move until he let the hijra back on. I checked that story with my friend also, and he disputed it, too.

It wasn't easy coordinating all the arrangements. We wanted to be sure we were on the same train, but when we went to tell Meena our dates, twice they weren't at home. It wasn't until the afternoon of our departure that we were actually sure we were going.

Mike came to Mumbai Central Station to see us off. It was an old train. The hijras looked happy and excited, especially on meeting Mike for the first time. They had arrived two hours early to get their seats.

Meena said, "I love him. He is so handsome."

"I love him, too," I said, and we both laughed.

Kamal showed up ten minutes before departure with our tickets. Mike confessed later that he was embarrassed because everyone in the station was staring at us. He found Meena amusing. It was unusual for a foreigner to be with such a group, but I was too busy talking to Meena to notice. Our new volunteer, Deepa, was translating.

How can I ever forget that trip? Meena gave us a delicious rice and yogurt dish to eat while she and the others rode in the other train car. I slept little on the train, worried someone would steal my camera. Our beds were on tiers with no privacy, not even curtains. We met up with Meena and her group of six the next morning on the platform in Ahmedabad. Strangers were pleasant and polite to them.

"They respect hijras here because they know the goddess," said Meena. "They call me 'mataji' or 'respected mother.' In Mumbai, everybody thinks we are prostitutes, but here we are like priests." I was pleased that they had a place where people didn't scorn them.

We stayed the night at a guest house across the road from the temple in Becharaji town. Anaxi had warned us to take a bed sheet to sleep on. Beds in such hostels had no linens; they were just dirty mattresses. The bathhouse had three cubicles—one with human feces on the floor and one with a sleeping dog. We used the third.

It took the hijras two hours to dress up in their best saris to greet their goddess. They all wore makeup and looked glamorous and very feminine. I felt like a slob in comparison.

For a temple that's not in any guidebook, I was surprised by how large it was. Once the palace of a king who was obviously very rich, it was seven hundred years old. It had many buildings with fancy domes and arches, gates, tombs, and pools. The main statue of the goddess Bahuchara Mata was covered with silver. Her vehicle is a rooster, and several live roosters roamed the grounds. Meena paid to set a rooster free: the act was a ritual prayer to the goddess. The hijras posed for my camera.

After the temple, we went to the local market. Meena bought a doll for seventy rupees and cuddled it. Meena wanted photos of themself and the others trying to nurse it. Their desire for a child they could not have moved me.

Deepa had bought a tape player, and back at the hotel, we danced. I tried to do a bump and grind. They seemed to appreciate my efforts. Meena wiggled her eyebrows, one up, one down in succession. We had a wild time.

Next day, we took two rickshaws to the birthplace of the goddess, about three kilometers away. Meena obviously had competitive hormones and urged our driver to race with the other cart. Kamal felt uncomfortable in Hindu temples and waited outside while the others prayed inside. Then, except for Meena, who had a pain in their abdomen, we all danced again.

We volunteers treated them to tea in a cafe. At first the waitress was reluctant to let them in, and we had to assure her that we volunteers would pay. It was almost like Dresden and Washington again.

Back in Mumbai, we accompanied Meena to a hospital. The registrars laughed with embarrassment because they didn't know how to classify Meena: male or female. Meena convinced them that they were a woman. Meena had high blood pressure. Everybody in the women's ward thought Meena was a woman, too, and were friendly. They wondered about the twenty-five hijras visiting them. Meena said, "They're my neighbors." Meena had a good time.

After observing them for the past several months, I concluded that their aggressive, inconsistent behavior was their only defense against a society that wanted to have little or nothing to do with them. Those of us who showed them no fear, only a willingness to listen, were amazed at how quickly we could be friends.

With the help of our group of volunteers, I continued working on the book. Kamal edited and changed my Canadian-English to Indian-English. She was too modest; she refused to have her name on the cover. Meena gave their thoughtful approval to the text and photos. We agreed to call it: *Hijras: Who We Are by Meena Balaji.*

Our daughter, Linda, gave us our second donation to cover the cost of printing. Through our connections, India Book House contributed the largest donation, the use of its staff, computers, and expertise. Deepa convinced her uncle to pay for the rest. A professional American designer, Tracy Turner, donated her expertise for the cover.

We chose a poignant, glamorous picture of Meena, a piece of matted roof in the background. When it was done, we delivered copies to bookstores. Anaxi brought Meena's group together for some role playing on how to sell the book and how to respond to people who were rude to them. No losing tempers and no curses, please.

We managed to get the famous movie director Kalpana Lajmi to be the guest of honor at the launch. She was making a sympathetic movie, *Tamanna,* about a hijra adopting a child. We hired the Bombay Press Club as the venue. I sent out press releases.

The response was astonishing. I will never forget Meena as they looked into that big bank of photographers. They were dressed in a white sari with real white flowers in their hair. They gave an amazing, impassioned speech about being neither a man nor a woman. They were self-confident. They cried real tears. It was Meena's show.

I was speechless at the large number of photographers who came out. I hoped nobody would ask me to speak. I had never had such a big response to any of my press releases. It was surreal, and I felt I was going to faint. That same day, supporters hung a huge banner downtown in English that read, "Give Hijras a Chance. Learn the Truth about Them. Read *Hijras: Who We Are.*"

During the next few days, the main newspapers published the story. *The Times of India*'s banner headline was, "Let's give eunuchs a chance in society." A second one said, "Canadian seeks to demystify the eunuch," and a third headline read, "Book on hijras released."

The weekly news magazine *Outlook* pictured me holding our book with the headline: "Telling the Eunuch's Story." *Mid-Day* had a photo of Meena and Baby Dancer with the headline: "Book on eunuchs released." *Asian Age's* banner was: "Eunuch book: First-person look at Hijra culture." The magazine *Femina for the Woman of Substance* headed its story, "'The Accursed. I may be a eunuch, but I'm a human being too,' says Meena Balaji."

The Metropolis wrote a story under: "Third sex without a legal identity. Chatura Rao throws light on the hardships eunuchs face in acquiring jobs." One of its sympathetic male reporters, Rahul Saigal, dressed in a sari and accompanied Meena and their group as they tried to sell our book.

"For the people, hijras selling books was not only a new concept, it was a joke," Saigal wrote. "With a lot of stares from strangers, they had no success the first time. Then they moved to another neighborhood near a college, where they managed to sell thirty books."

We were on national television. UPI sent our story around the world. Friends later mailed me clippings from Dubai, Seattle, and Toronto. The hijras sold their book near the movie theaters that showed the hijra movie *Tamanna*. I was ecstatic. Our plans were working out better than expected.

About a month after our launch, the weekly *India Today*, an English-language news magazine, published an article about eunuchs "marrying men, women, sometimes both, adopting children, even letting their husbands bring a 'normal' second wife home to keep the family going." *India Today* is the most widely circulated magazine in India, with a readership of close to eight million.

Too soon, Mike resigned. We had to leave India. I wanted to stay longer to make more attempts to get a tutor for Selma and a kitchen for Meena and her dream of feeding children. I wanted to help keep the project going, but for me it was not to be. Just before our departure, I stopped at Meena's hut to say goodbye. I couldn't telephone them in advance because they had no telephone. About six of them and Meena were there. There were lots of hugs and even flowers.

Later, Kamal handed me a translation in English of comments from Meena and the group. They were so wonderful, I have kept them. The notes read:

> You wrote the book. We have got some respect now from society. People who earlier ostracized us now respect us. You have come from somewhere and worked so hard for us, which no one else did. Because of you, many people have now come forward to help us. I pray to God that she give you lots of strength and blessings. We will be waiting for you. Come again.—Baby.

> The word "kindness" has many meanings, but the love between you and me is limitless and cannot be defined. You gave us respect. We will never forget you. Unless the water in the sea dries up or my life leaves my body,

I can never forget you. Happiness to you always. Fame, health, and wealth to you.—Silk.

You came from somewhere for some other aim, but now you helped us. Because of the book, people respect us more now. May all your family members have God's blessings. Don't forget us. We will also not forget you.—Meena.

Back in Canada, I found it difficult to keep in touch with the volunteers. Anaxi had taken time off to help, and she and the others were busy with their other projects. I tried to telephone Kamal, but her son told me she had died. She had never said anything about being ill.

Another volunteer, Anita Ravi, whom I never met, later translated the book into Hindi and somehow raised money to print it. She distributed as many copies as she could. I received an email from her recently. She said that hijras "are getting education and working in different fields now."

Official Indian documents such as passport applications now give a "transgender" as well as a "male" or "female" option to check. This was done much earlier than similar choices on official government forms for transgender people in Canada. Recently, *The Globe and Mail* had a story that two Indian states had hired transgender police constables. Their world is changing.

This is not to say that our brief time in Mumbai was responsible for those improvements. No doubt, the time was ripe, but I like to think my curiosity helped. Life is unpredictable. I started working on a guide book on Mumbai and ended up with a book on hijras, which I consider one of the most satisfying highlights of my life and my most successful effort at fighting discrimination.

Chapter 18:
Toronto, Vietnam, Africa, Myanmar, Blog. The Quest Continues.
1997–2020

Even though it was home, it took a while to adapt back into the relative orderliness of Toronto after living in such extremes of wealth and poverty. Only a couple of my friends and relatives showed any interest in hearing about the hijra or even about our Indian adventures. They seemed to ask only polite questions; no one wanted to hear details. At the time, I wondered if the encounter with hijras really happened? Fortunately, the clippings from the Indian magazines and newspapers proved it hadn't been just a fantasy, but no one asked to see them.

In 1997, Britain returned its sovereignty of Hong Kong to China. We watched the ceremony on television, amazed by the dignity of the British as they gave up one of the most expensive pieces of real estate in the world. Because of the Sino-British Joint Declaration signed in 1984, Hong Kong would be "one country, two systems." Its capitalist system and its democratic way of life would be left unchanged until 2047, or so many of us expected.

I went back to writing guidebooks on China, and then I looked for another corner I could brighten, struggling as usual to discern what the Divine meant for me to do. Then Beijing started chipping away at the terms of the joint declaration. It was not adhering to its 1984 agreement and started taking more and more decisions affecting Hong Kong away from Hong Kong's people. It appointed rather than allowed the election of its chief executive. Many citizens began demonstrating for their rights, but eventually Hong Kong citizens lost all ability to make governmental decisions about their own lives.

Believing that an agreement is an agreement, I joined a couple of the many demonstrations in Toronto.

And then there was Mustang. Ever since we met in India, Mike had wanted to go to Mustang in Nepal because it was "the end of the world." He and I were able to visit it in 2000, on a ten-day, ninety-three mile (one hundred fifty kilometer) trek. The kingdom had no roads, so walking along the bed of the Kali Gandaki River and dirt paths was the only way to go from the closest airport to the capital, Lo Manthang. Our little group of a dozen foreign tourists needed porters, mules, and mule drivers to carry our food, gear, and toilet tent. A license to trek in the kingdom cost one thousand dollars and some wise regulations. In addition to the hefty fee, we had to take out all our own garbage, and only one thousand foreign visitors were allowed each year.

It was a trip with high mountain passes that I couldn't climb because of altitude. My legs just wouldn't move whenever we approached the lines of prayer flags flopping in the wind that marked the way between valleys. Fortunately, a Tibetan with a horse just happened to come along whenever I needed a lift. What a thrill it was to stand in a pass and see two different worlds, one we had just finished experiencing and one we were going to with its new challenges, like life itself.

We saw no other tourists. Once we walked with two school-teachers and their three-year-old daughter. The parents were on their way to teach for a year in the capital. In them was hope for the survival of humans in the world. They were so cheerful. No complaints. I admired their determination, but I felt sorry for the Tibetan family we met taking their sick patriarch to a doctor, a two-day trip. The elders had horses to ride, but every one of the eight or so others walked. They were cheerful, too, but a two-day hike to see a doctor was not my idea of good healthcare.

We learned a lot from that trip. We had fun with the young Tibetan women we met who gleefully asked our Canadian guide to marry them. At one point, we had to traverse a two-foot wide, fast-moving landslide, an achievement accomplished only with the help of our guide and fellow trekkers. That victory gave me confidence to tackle other obstacles in life. We enjoyed the silence and the rushing water tumbling down the mountain sides. Then there was the far-off purr of bells of different sizes hanging from the necks of the donkeys, a melodious multitoned hum as their caravans approached us. When they were close enough, we could even hear the whistle of their drivers with different notes for right, left, hurry up, and stop.

Mustang's temples and houses were basically stone, covered with adobe, and supported by slender tree trunks. Doors and window frames were obviously imported; the area had no trees wide enough to make them. Great herds of goats, horses, and sheep passed by our tents every morning and evening, clogging the narrow village streets. We slept in the courtyards of hostels, protected from the animals by stone walls.

In the capital, we had a twenty-minute audience with the king of Mustang, a brush with history. His palace was small and crudely built, like all the buildings we saw there, only bigger. He was dressed in a wind-breaker, sweater, white shirt, trousers, a new pair of sneakers, and a knitted cap. I hadn't expected fancy robes, but his sporty attire was a surprise.

We sat on benches around the wall of a small room beside him quietly smiling. We were not sure what to do. Jigme Dorje Palbar Bista chanted a mantra continuously, "Om mani padmi hum" ("Hail to the jewel in the lotus"). He was giving us a blessing, a prayer, but we didn't know that until after the audience. He was the last king of Mustang; Nepal abolished its monarchs eight years later. After we got home, we heard that a helicopter service to Lo Manthang has started, and jeeps can now go most of the way from the airport. But we saw it and its gutsy people during an ancient period; it was a beautiful, thought-provoking, archaic experience and doing it on foot made it extra special.

In 2003, Mike and Linda joined me back in Cambodia after a stop at an important flower show for Linda in Kunming, China. This time we noticed many maimed people on the streets. Many were begging or hanging around parks. After my previous idyllic visit to the country, Prince Sihanouk lost power to the Communists. During that war, all sides of the war planted landmines that killed millions of people and resulted in an estimated forty thousand handicapped survivors. Many of the mines are still buried.

Mike started giving me rats for my birthday after that. I didn't know about APOPO when we were in Cambodia, but it was training rats to detect land mines by sniffing for them so humans can do the detonating. APOPO now has a land mine museum in Cambodia's capital with demonstrations of how its "HeroRATs" save lives.

In Phnom Penh, the capital, we also visited the Tuol Sleng Museum, the former high school where the Khmer Rouge imprisoned and tortured many of its enemies or suspected enemies from 1975 to 1979. China's Cultural Revolution and funds inspired Cambodia's Communist leaders into converting the country into a classless, rural, agrarian state. The Khmer Rouge were against a free market capitalist economy, and during what the world called "The Killing Fields," they slaughtered many intellectuals, doctors, teachers, merchants, clergy, and members of minorities. They did not spare Buddhist monks, and many people died of starvation. In the museum, we saw photographs and actual skulls of prisoners. It was not a pleasant visit. Linda especially felt uncomfortable and sensed the pain of the victims and a need for a shrine for their souls. I left wondering how members of our species could be so cruel.

China also continued to strengthen its grip on Tibet and Xinjiang, which made me want to identify even less with it. I couldn't agree with the way it was treating its Uyghurs and Tibetans. It could have given them more control of their own regions instead of trying to force them to do what primarily benefited Beijing and the Han majority.

Was I sorry I tried to help China by writing guidebooks? Of course not. That effort had been a response to a need for outsiders to learn how to navigate the country and a need to make its tourism standards international. These needs no longer existed. China was now able to feed its own people and was respected as a power in the world. That didn't mean I was supporting the current short-sighted, selfish policies of its leadership.

And what about me? Could I define what being and feeling Chinese was anymore? Was it still the Confucian father-in-control ethic with the Communist party replacing its autocratic emperors? Sons preferred to daughters? I agreed with none of these, but such are defining parts of China's culture.

What about all the friends I made in China during my thirty-five years of travel there? The congenial tour guides, travel agents, and hotel people who were trying to make a living as well as provide services? The Uyghur guides who went out of their way to find me boots and taught me the proper way to eat sticks of barbecued lamb? My relatives? Did I even want to call myself Chinese-Canadian any more? Could I? Why did I need to identify myself as anything but a human being? A global citizen of Chinese-Canadian origin?

My grandson has three passports. Does he need to call himself a Finnish-Chinese-Latvian-Irish-Canadian-American? Do we really need labels? I could honestly say that I felt only one percent Chinese then; I could not ignore my family ties.

It was time to make decisions. As far as I was concerned, unless there was a change in government policy, the China period of my life—well, most of it—was over. Although I didn't know what I was to do, I felt I had to make some changes. I cleared out my bookshelves for new books. I gave Victoria College my collection of more than a hundred books on China for its annual book sale. I was finished studying about China.

Although I could find no answers to my many questions, life continued. Even though there seemed to be common threads in them all—hatred, greed, resentment—perhaps there are no answers. Then members of the former Saigon foreign press corps organized reunions in Vietnam, and in 2005, thirty years after the war ended, Mike and I went there.

North of Saigon (now called Ho Chi Minh City), we were able to see the entrance to the previously hidden tunnels the Viet Cong had dug. Through them, soldiers fighting with the Vietnamese Communists had scurried from place to place secretly, attacking Americans and anyone near them. Then they disappeared. In parks and museums, we could study the remains of U.S. planes and tanks; they were the only signs of the war we could see. I couldn't help but grieve for the young men who had been drafted to operate them and had died doing so. Both sides endured a lot of pain in that useless war.

The former United Press International office, where journalists had tried to keep its subscribers informed about events in Vietnam, had become a restaurant that served Vietnamese delights like frogs cooked in ten different ways. We had a historic UPI reunion banquet there, and it was good to see old friends again, many who had been writing books about their Vietnam experiences. We met a Vietnamese journalist who had worked for American companies. He hadn't escaped with the Americans and had to spend years imprisoned in a reeducation camp where he must have suffered a lot. He seemed to be doing fine selling antiques now.

Vietnam generally seemed to be doing very well. Hanoi and Ho Chi Minh City were lively, and I was nervous only of the army of noisy motorcycles that flowed endlessly through the downtown streets. None of the streets had stoplights. One taxi driver we hired, seeing my hesitation, kindly took my hand and led me through the rush of vehicles to our hotel. I closed my eyes as I followed him and somehow survived unhurt. Mike insisted on my visiting tailors who made me shimmering silk clothes. We found pirated editions of books by daredevil freelance photographer, Tim Page, who had once worked for UPI. It seemed the Vietnamese had forgiven the Americans for the mess they made of their country.

In Myanmar, on our way home, we stopped to see Spencer and to tour the country. Decades before, he had been at the Quaker seminar in Japan where he introduced himself as the nephew of "Peter Pan," and I had visited him on my first trip to India. Now a retired schoolteacher, he lived on a monthly pension, the equivalent of about ten U.S. dollars. He was very thin. When I hugged him, I could feel his ribs and realized I had to be careful. If I pressed too hard, I might break a bone. The country was still very poor; nevertheless, he was very hospitable and eager to show us around the capital.

We tried our best to help him. Giving him money would be insulting, so we invited him to join our meals in Rangoon (now Yangon) and urged David Elder to use him as a paid interpreter. I had worked with Dave in Japan, and he was then traveling to Myanmar from time to time to oversee the work of a charity. I felt sad when Spencer said that his trip to the Quaker seminar in Japan was the only time he had traveled outside his own country, but I was pleased he had happy memories of it.

Spencer showed us the British-era mansion where "The Lady" lived in Yangon under house arrest and said his family and most other Burmese people supported Aung San Suu Kyi. She symbolized democracy and opposition to Myanmar's military rulers. In 1991, she won the Nobel Peace Prize "for her nonviolent struggle," and two years after our visit, Canada gave her honorary Canadian citizenship. In November 2010, the military leaders freed her, and she later became the leader of the country.

Everyone we met on that trip supported "The Lady." We didn't know about the government's attempt to destroy its Rohingya ethnic minority then. Myanmar's majority is Buddhist; the Rohingyas are Muslim. After we left, we heard reports of the killing and rape of many Rohingya people and the burning down of their villages. This was in retaliation for an attack on a Burmese police post, a retaliation encouraged on Facebook by Buddhist extremists. Many Rohingyas fled to neighboring countries. Bangladesh today has at least nine hundred thousand of them now living in the world's largest refugee camp. They refuse to return to Myanmar unless they are given the security of citizenship there.

Aung San Suu Kyi did not support the Rohingyas' safe return even though many of their ancestors had lived in Burma / Myanmar for centuries. It was religious discrimination. I could not think of what we could do to help except to send money to agencies like the UNHCR and Save the Children. We were glad that Canada allocated millions of dollars to aid Rohingya refugees and later revoked honorary Canadian citizenship to "The Lady" whom many of us had once admired.

And then, in early 2021, a coup put the military back in control of the country, and Aung San Suu Kyi was under house arrest again. Thousands of people protested, and hundreds were killed.

During our visit, we could see how blatantly the military government was robbing Myanmar of its resources. As we traveled around the country, we noticed huge boatloads of teak timber being shipped to China. Our guides told us there was no effort at reforestation.

It was now a lot easier for foreign tourists to visit. We went to bustling Mandalay and serene Inle Lake. Spiritual Bagan's thousands of pagodas and temples were thrilling. Like elsewhere in many parts of Asia, we found children working in factories who looked about ten years of age. In Mandalay, they were embroidering pictures, their tiny fingers sewing finer stitches than adults could. Factory owners said they were going to school part-time, but we weren't able to prove that.

We also visited Kayan ethnic women and young girls whose necks are stretched with a succession of metal rings from early childhood. I suspect the tradition was started to keep women under the control of men. That custom was worse than the bound-foot tradition of old China. Without the rings, the women would die as their muscles would weaken and not be strong enough to support their heads. We met teenage girls who said they were glad they were wearing the rings because tourists paid to see them. Maybe the custom would stop if such tourism were forbidden, but what else could these women do to make a living in their isolated hills?

It was also painful to meet tribespeople in a Christian village in the Golden Triangle who felt they had to send their daughters to nearby northern Thailand to support their families. There, unfortunately, many became sex workers. Obviously, these people needed help, too.

What to do? If it were true that the children working on the embroideries were really going to school, there was some hope of a better future for them.

Spencer's niece sent us pictures of Spencer's funeral the following year.

In 2007, Mike, at the age of seventy-one, gave up archaeology in Jordan after ten summers of getting up at four every morning and digging until noon in the desert sun. He had also taken part one summer in a dig in Yemen, searching for relics related to the biblical Queen of Sheeba, a rare opportunity. Archeological evidence of her association with King Solomon in the Bible has yet to be found. In Toronto, he continued to volunteer with the Habitat for Humanity salvage crew, tearing out unwanted sinks, fireplaces, and light fixtures to be resold at Habitat Restores, which partially financed the charity. He enjoyed the work and the camaraderie of his crew.

In 2008, we went to Africa with Terry and Linda. After trying to get there via Brazil on my "leap of faith" many years before, I was finally able to see more of the continent. We had already been to Egypt on a previous vacation.

Mike, as usual, had ambitious plans, this time to go "cage diving" among great white sharks in Gansbaai, South Africa. Unfortunately, the seas were too rough on the day we booked the tour. We did go out in the tour boat but were too seasick to enjoy the ride. Our son, Terry, said he had to maintain the family's reputation and bravely climbed into a metal cage for a few minutes. Lowered into the water, the cage protected him from the dangerous fish long enough to take some pictures.

I wanted to visit a township in Cape Town where thousands of poor people lived. We took a guided tour to one that the tour company considered safe. The houses were mainly one-story buildings, many of them the size of small shipping containers and made of corrugated iron and scrap. They were spread over a vast area in various qualities. Four families shared a bathhouse.

We talked with friendly refugees from Zimbabwe who said they were escaping war, poverty, and political violence while living in the township. South Africa wanted to send them back to their even more impoverished country. What could anyone do to help? The problems of the Zimbabweans, as well as the South Africans, were overwhelming.

The prison where the apartheid government kept Nelson Mandela for three decades was also on my wish list of places to visit. Alas, lack of time meant we couldn't fit in a visit to see the seven-by-eight foot (2.13 by 2.44 meter) cell where he spent eighteen of those years, but at least I saw a mock-up in Toronto years later. It was extraordinary that Mandela was able to keep sane for that period of time in such a small space. He became the first Black president of South Africa in 1994 and a Nobel Peace Prize awardee.

Mike's African bucket list also included a walking safari with "no Land Rovers, no motorboats, and no guns." He found the cheapest camp in the flooded grasslands of the Okavango Delta in Botswana. It was called Oddballs, and we slept in two tiny tents and shared a bathhouse. It was perfect.

On our third day, after our Bushman guides had paddled us in dugout canoes to a nearby island, they were setting up our tents when a wild, agitated bull elephant started walking slowly and menacingly toward us, spreading his ears, shaking his head, and bellowing. Black liquid streaked down his cheek. As the monster came closer and closer, guide Leko kept quietly repeating, "Don't move; don't run." Terry was shaking so much that he dropped his camera. I was in my emotionally disconnected camera-mode and clicked away. The animal paused fifteen feet (five meters) from us, stared at us for a moment, and then turned to walk away, no longer interested. It was then that I found myself trembling.

Our guides later explained that the behavior was the result of a testosterone imbalance; the secretion was *musth*. The elephant was in a natural, aggressive mood and could have killed us. Leko said that elephants can't see very well; this one wanted us to move, so he would know who or what we were. A fire would have kept him away, but there hadn't been time to build one. As we tried to stop our shaking, another guide on an island nearby telephoned Leko and said we could see a lion there. Leko assured us a lighted cigarette lighter would keep us safe, and did we want to see it? We agreed that we had had enough for one day, and that night, we tried to sleep as we heard lions roaring close to our flimsy tents.

We left the country with a lot of admiration for our African guides. Not only were we grateful for our lives, we appreciated their amazing knowledge of how wild animals behave. Did we have a role to play here beyond contributing tourist dollars? Elephants and other wild animals were a serious problem in Botswana and other African countries. They compete with humans for space, food, and water. We saw the damaged poles and huts in Leko's village and shredded trees in the countryside. African countries depend on wildlife tourism for much of their revenue. What else could outsiders do?

We did get to the Zimbabwe border near Victoria Falls. In retrospect, I regretted missing the Great Zimbabwe, a UNESCO World Heritage site. It was an African Iron Age city covering about two hundred acres (eighty hectares), one of several great civilizations on the continent. It seems that I was meant to enjoy and learn from Africa but not to work there.

Back home, I didn't want to let our travel experiences go to waste. I was a member of a professional travel writers group who told us about Visual Travel Tours. For VTT, I put together one audio-guide walking tour on Botswana and another one on Mongolia, each with about ninety of my photographs. They were aimed at helping tourists get around these countries on their own. VTT didn't pay much, but it was something useful to do with my pictures.

Toronto, by then, was no longer boring. Because of the Canadian government's generous immigration policy, it was quickly becoming the most multicultural city in the world. Canada needed more people to support its economic growth, health care, and pension payments.

Visual Travel Tours also agreed to publish my walking tours of one of Toronto's Koreatowns and one of our many Chinatowns. I counted at least thirty different Chinatowns in our city. Each had at least one Chinese supermarket and a mall. The Koreans had two neighborhoods, one dubbed "South Korea" and the other "North Korea."

Then Visual Travel Tours agreed to two more Canadian stories: the Calgary Stampede and the Quebec Winter Carnival. I had always wanted to experience these huge annual shows, and researching both was a lot of fun. At the Calgary Stampede, however, I watched officials euthanize a horse that had fallen and broken a leg during a chuck wagon race—another victim of animals exploited for sport.

At the Quebec Winter Carnival, I took a ride on a dogsled. The dogs obviously loved pulling the sleds, but they had to spend the rest of their lives tied to separated kennels, unable to explore and chase lemmings when they wanted to. Were noisy gas-guzzling snowmobiles better than dog power? Which should the Inuit use for their winter transportation? Here were yet other questions I couldn't answer. Vegetarians would vote in favor of giving up their meat diet, but in the Arctic, there had been no such choice.

After that, I struggled as usual with trying to ascertain what God wanted me to do. I joined a spiritual companions' group at the Quaker meeting. Six of us met regularly for several months to share our spiritual journeys. It was good having others listen to how we were trying to discern what the Divine wanted us to do. We did not get easy answers.

Helping with the meeting's visiting committee, I became concerned about our growing number of elderly members and visited long-term care homes where many lived as they tried to cope with their failing bodies. I was not yet thinking about mine or Mike's.

I relished exploring Toronto's diverse cultures so much that, in 2010, I inaugurated a blog, an informal, informational website, about Toronto's many culturally diverse festivals, events, and neighborhoods. I felt that my travels had prepared me to do this.

TorontoMulticulturalCalendar.com was the only writing and photography I had the time and energy to do for the next ten years. The blog turned out to be more of a lesson for me than a help for the people of Toronto.

A few people wrote that the blog was useful. Although many festivals conflicted with Quaker events, I never regretted doing it, even though the results were far from spectacular compared with our hijra booklet. At the least, I signed a contract to donate my photos to the Multicultural History Society of Ontario.

My *Toronto Multicultural Calendar*'s goal was to help give every Torontonian a feeling of being part of one big multicultural community, but it was too ambitious a goal. Could our Palestinians and Israelis, Eritreans and Ethiopians, and Russians and Ukrainians work together on projects like adverse climate change and mental illness? Gun control? Homelessness? I think I was hoping for too much.

While I did not think that getting diverse groups together would solve these problems, I was hoping seeds of change could be planted. The festivals and other multicultural events were an opportunity to make friends from different groups. Hopefully, they would put their heads together and try to work at problems like wars that affected them all. The blog promoted mainly free or almost free events, as well as exotic buildings. I started out describing my own experience at some events, but once writing about them took too much time, I just posted fliers of some of the more interesting ones.

During those ten years, I also made a point of visiting and writing about as many of our new, interesting religious buildings that I could find: Orthodox churches topped with gleaming onion domes, a Chinese temple with a hundred gilded statues on one huge wall, and large mosques filled with neat lines of worshipers. Almost all of them had festivals with bazaars, unique food, and handicrafts.

Each had music shows. I hoped people could meet new neighbors there and find clerics with visions beyond their own pulpits.

Fortunately, I could still drive or take public transportation to most, and I visited many of them several times. Once a year, I took friends to see the magnificent Hindu BAPS Shri Swaminarayan Mandir Temple during the Diwali Festival of Lights. With tour guides providing explanations, it was well prepared for guests and school tours. I attended services at St. Mary Ethiopian Orthodox Cathedral and befriended a congenial staff member who invited me to one of its feasts and let me take close-up pictures of the priests. Ethiopian festivals included traditional slabs of raw meat served directly into the mouths of anyone willing to eat that way. Fortunately, it offered cooked Ethiopian dishes as well.

I tried not to miss the annual Fire Festival where Iranians jump over a bonfire, a purification ritual that's meant to bring luck in the New Year. I met the artist who painted the walls and ceilings with classical icons at the Macedonian Orthodox Church in suburban Markham. That we, in the greater Toronto area, had a Byzantine artist of international caliber blew my mind. At St. Mark Coptic Orthodox Church, I found the only Coptic museum outside of Egypt and enjoyed frequent lunches with its curator, Helene Moussa. The Sikh temple I especially liked visiting was one with exquisite white architecture. On one visit there, I happened upon a wedding and was invited to a banquet after watching the groom lead his bride around the Granth, their holy book.

Chinese New Year in temples meant burning incense and consulting fortunes with sticks. Fo Guang Shan Temple, a Buddhist temple in Mississauga, reminded me of such fairs in China as temple members sold typical foods like sugared crab apples on sticks and taught youngsters to draw New Year's slogans on paper in Chinese to be posted beside the doors to their homes for luck. Another of my favorites was the Canada-China Friendship Association's jiaozi-making party. Jiaozi are dumplings, and friends making them together is a genuine northern Chinese New Year's tradition we could also experience in Toronto.

Every group seemed to celebrate the end of an old year and the beginning of a new one. Buddhists paid for the privilege of ringing a temple bell 108 times at midnight. With each stroke, they hoped to rid themselves of earthly temptations such as greed, selfishness, jealousy, and indifference. If only it could be that easy.

At many of the year-round festivals, politicians of all stripes would appeal for the ethnic vote. Some of them wore the traditional costume of the day. Before he became prime minister, I photographed Justin Trudeau wearing a *barong tagalog,* a white embroidered Filipino shirt, as he paraded with Filipinos on Yonge Street.

My blog included events like the annual South Asian wedding shows. Although I was opposed to families going bankrupt to pay for lavish weddings, I loved the heavily embroidered made-in-India wedding costumes and textiles. I enjoyed the opportunity to talk with wedding planners about trends like renting a white horse for the arrival of the groom. While I didn't want to rent a white horse, I had attended such a wedding in India where the groom had indeed met his bride in a fairy-tale, princely fashion.

Mike went with me to the bloodless Portuguese bull fights. The one in Toronto's Downsview Park was traditional, with beautiful, well-trained horses and *cavaleiros* in very fancy embroidered costumes. The one outside of the city featured Azorean males testing their conception of courage by teasing specially bred bulls to chase them. While the bull fights continued for a while outside the city, Toronto with its large population of animal lovers banned them. This controversial sport brought my site more than a hundred visitors in one day, with Portuguese-Canadians supporting the custom and other Torontonians objecting to animal cruelty.

I drove non-Muslim friends to the annual Halal Food Festival, hoping they would get excited about it, too, but no one was eager to go the following year. It was great fun sampling new dishes and relearning the spicy pleasures of Afghan food. There was also the Hindu Tamil Chariot Festival where penitents hung from hooks pierced through their backs, arms, and legs. Some rolled on the ground behind the chariots like the man we encountered on the road in Rajasthan. Only three of my friends agreed to go with me;

others claimed squeamishness. I was sorry they weren't interested in learning firsthand about the religion of their fellow citizens. A policeman at the site said that the participants were adults. There was no law prohibiting self-torture.

One of my many favorites was the annual Sikh Khalsa Festival where volunteers served a vast banquet of Indian food free to everybody in the square in front of Toronto's City Hall. Until COVID-19 changed our lives, I attended it for five or six years and never found more than a handful of non-Sikhs in attendance. The food was vegetarian, authentic, and made by Sikh volunteers. It was the only place where I could find Punjabi-style masala chai, profusely sugared like the tea I drank every morning in New Delhi. While the Khalsa movement advocates for a separate Sikh state in India, and some Sikhs do suggest violence, I had the impression that Toronto's festival was more social than political. In spite of the swords in their temples and the knife they always carry with them, Sikhs believe in equality and service to others.

My blog mentioned how non-Muslims could join Muslims at dinner parties celebrating the daily end of the monthly Ramadan fast. It was an opportunity to learn about Muslim traditions. These only cost a hostess gift or a small fee, and I ate at several of them. It was also fascinating to watch teams of Tibetan monks making and then destroying beautiful sand mandalas, a symbolic act about the impermanence of human existence.

These festivals were a great opportunity for students of comparative religions. While I took a class in Sufi whirling-dervish dancing, my friends seemed to prefer learning about other cultures by reading books, not attending events and meeting people.

The blog also included demonstrations. These were in support of Rohingyas, Uyghurs, Tibetans, Palestinians, Israelis, Ukrainians, and democracy in Hong Kong. When I heard of Tibetan monks burning themselves to death in Tibetan areas of China to protest China's takeover of their region, I felt sick. In recent years, about one hundred fifty monks in Tibet have used this powerful way to show disapproval. I joined some demonstrations at the Chinese consulate. At one, a fire truck was in attendance just in case someone tried to self-immolate, but no one did. Toronto police were there, too, and considered it a crime scene.

And there was so much more. First Nations cultures provided pow-wows, theatrical events, and exhibitions of the brilliant Cree artist Kent Monkman. I went to many of Tanya Tagaq's amazing, passionate performances of her unique adaptation of Inuit throat singing. I promoted exhibitions of Black artists in their own gallery and Black business festivals.

I published the blog for almost ten years. I couldn't handle the technology needed to promote the blog widely. I refused to buy email lists to market it. It was a lot of work just to publish each blog, and I felt more comfortable collecting the photos and information than promoting it. Alas, very few Torontonians wanted to take advantage of these wonderful events unless it was a school tour or Doors Open Toronto. The latter was a free annual weekend event organized by the city, with opportunities to see inside some of its more interesting buildings.

While Torontonians did attend the city's multicultural festivals, many of them told me they were nervous about visiting religious buildings of other groups. They didn't know what to expect or were so comfortable with their own religion, they didn't want to change. I suggested that visiting religious buildings was about showing interest in other cultures and not for conversion. It was about making friends and helping newcomers to the country feel welcome. Some Torontonians said they didn't know how to behave in strange places. Consequently, I explained how to behave, like covering one's head and removing shoes in temples and mosques.

On the other hand, members of some of the newer religious buildings didn't understand why outsiders wanted to visit them. At some of the services that I attended, a few members at least smiled shyly at me and answered questions when asked. There were a few exceptions, like the Hungarian church where the stares of members of its congregation made me feel unwelcome. But members of a Mar Thoma church, which was founded in India in 52 C.E., were very welcoming and invited me to lunch after the service.

I liked taking friends to visit the Vishnu Mandir, a Hindu temple on busy Yonge Street near Highway 403. It has North America's largest statue of Hanuman, the Monkey God, which stands an impressive fifty feet (15.2 meters) high. Indoors, a museum and statues of world leaders like Nelson Mandela, the Dalai Lama, Lester Pearson, and Martin Luther King Jr. express its international interests, while its Star of David and its crescent moon and star of Islam point to a multi-faith vision. A statue of Mahatma Gandhi also stands prominently near Yonge Street with the inscription, "The day the power of love overrules the love of power, the world will know peace."

My frequent visits to Vishnu Mandir showed changes in attitude each time. At my first visit there, I didn't feel welcomed. A woman at the reception desk growled, "Take off your shoes," "Did you bring gifts?" and, "Don't take pictures." But I found a friendly worshiper eager to answer questions. Asking questions helped break the ice, and there were so many questions to ask. Why is there a memorial to Canadian military killed in Afghanistan here?

The following year, in 2015, I organized a visit to Vishnu Mandir with friends, this time making an appointment with a priest to tell us about Hinduism. He was very welcoming and apologized for not welcoming strangers. "Our people are not prepared to reach out to others. We're working on this," he said confidently. The next time I went to this temple, I went alone during the colored-powder festival known as Holi. I was hoping to find a place in Toronto where this fun event was actually practiced the way it was in India. At first I seemed to be invisible until one nice lady asked if she could put red paint on my face inside the church hall. Paint was less messy than powder. After I agreed, people started smiling at me, a welcome change, because then they understood that I wanted to join their fun, too.

On my last visit, a friend and I met a friendly worshiper who explained that Indians felt uneasy with strangers, not knowing what strangers wanted. Mr. Shah said that South Indians were friendlier than those from the north. Then I remembered my years in North India and the clerks in the stores, all men, who never smiled. I decided this was because of the frequent foreign invasions there. Store clerks had learned not to trust strangers. Alas, I didn't have the time to make frequent visits to each culture to learn why they were shy with strangers in their midst.

I was to feel that my blog and its goal of generating a feeling of community was an impossible dream, especially when some readers used my blog only to find their own ethnic festivals, not those of other cultures. One exception was friend P. Anne Winter, whom I met by chance at the Japanese Cultural Center. She had adopted Japanese culture as her own for years. She had never been to Japan. She just felt compelled to immerse herself in learning about kimonos, Kibuki theatre, and Japanese food for some reason unknown even to herself.

Most people didn't seem interested in different cultures. Every year before COVID-19, a million people attended Caribana, the Caribbean parade. They would dance in the street to its live music and grin at the humongous, overtly sexy costumes, but I doubt if they made lasting friends or learned much about other aspects of Caribbean culture there, either. It was mainly the costumes that seemed to attract them.

Only one or two people out of the hundreds that I personally met ever asked about my culture, whatever that was. Conversations were always about themselves. A Bolivian reader asked where he could find homemade Bolivian food. At least three different Parsis enquired about a Parsi home where a Parsi student could live in Toronto. Another email asked for an Uzbek-speaking driving teacher for an Uzbek girlfriend. While I was pleased to answer such questions, it wasn't my purpose.

Events that brought people together didn't necessarily end peacefully. Demonstrations with Israeli and Palestinian supporters meant shouting matches full of accusations, no attempts at reconciliation, and occasional violence. I liked promoting an initiative called Heart to Heart that brought Jewish and Palestinian young people from Israel to a summer camp in Ontario. I could see some possible peacemaking in that one. It was also good to see many of Toronto's young people choosing to volunteer to help at events outside of their own cultures.

There were some other reasons to hope. Changes for the better were apparent in Toronto's growing number of mixed-culture marriages and multifaith events. I joined Jews and Christians forming rings to protect mosques from attacks during religious services. The rings were symbolic since they only took place once or twice. They were organized by some synagogues and churches after the murder of worshipers in a Quebec mosque in 2017, and at two New Zealand mosques in 2019.

Many Canadians sponsored refugees, mainly from Syria. Our Quaker committee helped to resettle two Syrian families and one from Africa. I enjoyed getting to know our new families, helping them, and learning about Canada's immigration policy, but I could not justify the economics. The amount of money we spent on supporting three families in Toronto for a year could have fed and protected hundreds in refugee camps in Greece or Bangladesh. Fear, corrupt governments, greed, civil wars, and other countries selling armaments created refugees. We really needed to concentrate on the causes, the reasons why people fled their own countries in the first place.

The world currently has over eighty-two million refugees, displaced people, and asylum seekers, people who have very little hope of a safe, comfortable future, and no hope of fulfilling dreams. Sponsoring a few families made us feel good, but what about the rest of them?

Toronto Quakers have been trying to do their bit to meet needs at home and abroad, but we are a small group. During the Japanese war, we had about twenty volunteers working in China. During the Vietnam War, we welcomed many conscientious objectors who were escaping U.S. military conscription and fought efforts to deport them. I have never heard of any Toronto workcamps, but we have individuals who have worked with Peace Brigades International in conflict resolution and fighting global warming, at one point with a fast on Parliament Hill in Ottawa. I counted a dozen Quakers at global warming rallies, but only three in two circles protecting mosques. One worked with Christian Peacemaker Teams for ten years in Iraq, Uganda, and the Congo to transform conflict. Ursula Franklin was such a well-known peacemaker, scientist, and feminist that a Toronto high school was named after her. Members are visiting prisons, but it's been awhile since Romaine Jones and a couple of non-Quakers were arrested for protesting Canada's fifteen billion dollar arms deal with Saudi Arabia. Such sales have been helping the Saudis fight its war with Iran and Yemen. We should have been doing more to stop it.

Then in 2020, COVID-19 looked like it could unite the world. Much of Canada rallied to fight the epidemic, and many people volunteered to help their communities with meals for healthcare workers and making face masks. COVID-19 brought people of different cultural backgrounds to work together at food banks, but having to be six feet (two meters) apart, it was difficult for anyone to get to know each other. Wearing masks made us suspicious of each other. We couldn't even invite friends to our homes or have mask-free conversations for a while. We had to adjust to a new way of getting together, and I promptly stopped producing a blog. There were no ethnic events to promote, and, for over a year, our ages and Mike's illness kept us from even leaving our house except for medical appointments. Fortunately, many people volunteered to help wherever help was needed.

When a vaccine became available, a lot of people with computer skills helped computer-illiterate people find vaccinations. This and the opening of social venues gave hope that strangers from different groups would get together to overcome other threats to their own lives. I hoped they would use their skills to get vaccines to everyone in the world. I hoped our diverse groups would fight global warming and do something more than we have about homelessness and helping those with mental illnesses. And there was still the problem of racial discrimination.

Chapter 19:
A Dream Ends, 2015-2021

When people asked us the secret of our long marriage, we always seemed to answer simultaneously, with much laughter, "Giving in." But Mike and I also had many interests in common. Research and travel consumed both of us but in different ways. We also enjoyed intimate dinners at home with a few friends and Indian food from a nearby restaurant. They were always full of good conversation, and he enjoyed telling his favorite stories.

Mike liked doing unusual things, like giving me rats for birthdays. For another of my milestone birthdays, he arranged a hot air balloon ride, which we shared, and on another such occasion, he sent me paragliding alone with a teacher into the sky. Then there was the time when I found myself walking with Terry around the outside of Toronto's CN Tower, above the ground with high altitude winds blowing and nothing but air below us for 1,168 feet (356 meters). We were, of course, strapped to the tower, and I loved it, although at times my knees were shaking. Mike enjoyed it vicariously. He was still nervous of heights.

For his seventy-fifth birthday, I surprised him with a live entertainer in a Teletubby costume, a kilted bagpiper, and his first ride in a limousine. During that period, he seemed to be fascinated by the British children's television show Teletubbies. As he scrolled between news stories every morning on television with their reports of revolutions, murders, and earthquakes, he found respite in their beguiling "bye-byes." It was one of his jokes.

For his seventy-eighth birthday, Mike wanted an axe-throwing party. Axe-throwing had recently started in Toronto, and when Linda told him about it, he wanted to try it. We had twenty friends throwing axes at bullseyes in an old factory-like building converted into an unusual bar. It was a new experience for most of us and a lot of fun as staff gave us lessons. It was not a serious competition.

But Mike never felt comfortable with meditation and religion. I had hoped he would share that side of my life, but he never felt comfortable with them. He willingly went with me to see historic Quaker sites in England, like the home of founders George Fox and Margaret Fell. At Swarthmore, I heard for the first time the term "steeple houses" instead of "churches" because Fox did not consider them places to worship God. I was reminded that Fox did not believe that just by going to university anyone could be a minister or a teacher of religion. I learned that Margaret Fell loved the color red and decided Quakers didn't need to be confined to just wearing gray.

We went to the meadow where, beside a rocky hill, George Fox preached for three hours—three hours!—to a crowd of more than a thousand people. A three-hour sermon would have discouraged me from joining. There, as our little group of tourists sat quietly worshiping for a few minutes, a draft horse came by and bit me gently on the foot. I wondered if that was a divine message as I was the only one in our group so blessed.

The history interested Mike, but he only tolerated our hand-holding at the family dinner table for a moment of silence. When Terry is with us, Terry usually leads us in a prayer of thanks, and I was always grateful that we still had each other. Mike once said that if he were religious, he would be a Quaker, and agreed with us once that maybe he lacked the religious gene. But that difference didn't affect our relationship. Although he could at times be impatient, especially when sick, Mike was always a very caring, generous soul, sensitive to our needs and that of others.

As for my own spiritual journey, I still tried to ascertain the will of God, who over the years I have come to know by other names like Spirit, the Greater Power, the Great Unknown. I wanted to maintain my ties to the Quakers, but I liked to think I was still open to leadings elsewhere. George Fox's encouragement to "walk cheerfully over the world, answering that of God in everyone," helped to keep me focused. I was much too impatient to be a Quaker role model, but I found it good to be reminded of such a goal. My prayer during meetings for worship was still that of St. Francis of Assisi. "Lord, make me an instrument of thy peace," and after trying to hold needy people "in the Light," I still tried to practice vipassana meditation. And sometimes I imagined myself melting into the beautiful world around me. Linda shared my interest in spiritual subjects, but as an adult, she never went to Quaker events, either.

I asked Mike late in his life if he was glad he became a journalist, and he said, "It was better than being an actuary." The image of him sitting long hours calculating insurance risks was so at odds with Mike that I couldn't stop myself from laughing. His sister Shawn remembers him saying that he felt "incredibly lucky to have unintentionally fallen into journalism and the life he'd led," but unlike many of his colleagues, he refused to write a memoir.

After leaving journalism, he said he didn't want to write anything and hid behind the excuse, "unless I'm paid." I think he didn't want to reveal the painful part of his childhood. He seemed to hide his feelings behind a mask of humor. I suspected it was also because he had stopped smoking, a two-pack a day habit he needed when he was writing. He quit after he retired because he was "sick of being treated like a leper." After he retired, he did contribute an introduction to this book, and he wrote an article on archeology for a Toronto magazine, without the help of cigarettes.

In 2015, I didn't have to look for a project to make myself feel useful. It turned out to be the most difficult and painful project I ever attempted. I wanted to help my best friend keep living, and I almost had to stop helping refugees. I had spent much of our marriage trying to keep our family healthy by avoiding salt, desserts, candy, white bread, and the perils of deep-fried food. That diet did not succeed for Mike. Late that year, an oncologist found that he had stage-four colon cancer and predicted that he only had a few months to live without chemo and maybe three years if treated with it. Linda and I were with him in Dr. Zuralska's office when she gave him the diagnosis. After discussing it with Linda and me, Mike chose the chemo. He was to live for over six more years.

"Why do you want me around?" he asked that day when we were home.

I didn't want him to die and said I preferred a sick husband to no husband.

The next time he asked the question, I answered, "It's because you make me laugh." It was the first thing that came to mind, but it was only partially true. I loved him. We fit together like different pieces in a jigsaw puzzle, and he kept trying to make us laugh when he could.

"I'm not afraid of dying," Mike said seriously one day. Over the years, he had moved from being agnostic to being an atheist and believed that death was the end of everything. "I'm just afraid of never seeing you again."

"There are advantages to having a religion," I said, his remark leaving me almost speechless. He was talking about wanting to be with me forever. After he said it a second time, I said, "Maybe you'll find someone you'll like better." I hoped he would take it as a joke.

But he never contradicted me. Being his wife had always seemed right. We had no regrets about our life except for not being able to protect Martin from suicide. Mike didn't have my obsessiveness about helping humanity, but he was always there to support me and correct my stories. Although the cancer gradually killed his ardor, we continued our one kiss a day and addressing each other as "Sweetie." The cancer made me primarily a caregiver, well aware that my husband didn't have much time left to fulfill his dreams of seeing more of the world.

Fortunately, Linda was living with us, but she had a full-time job. After work every day, she took charge. The perks from her job gave her sick leave that included time to help dependents. She devoted her vacation time to him and to her increasingly absent-minded mother. We were so fortunate to have her. We found ourselves frequently asking, "What did we do to deserve her?"

I kept wondering if it was her fate that had kept her from choosing a husband who would have taken her away from us in our time of need. At one point, we had hoped she would marry one of her boyfriends in Ecuador. If she had, we would have probably been alone during this challenge. I kept seeing much of my younger self in her, her neighborliness, dedication, and willingness to help. She and Terry made me see how important it is to have children to take care of aging parents. Terry couldn't just leave his family and job to help. We would have had to move Mike to a hospital or long-term care home if not for Linda. When the pandemic first arrived, most deaths had been in homes for the aged, and no visitors were allowed. I didn't want Mike to be alone.

Linda adored her father, and the shock of the cancer diagnosis caused much of her hair to fall out, but she rallied quickly to take charge of his care. As we needed to concentrate on sterility, one-time-use needles, and rubber gloves, I had to postpone trying to reuse plastic bags and keeping microplastics out of the washing machine water. While I could not remember the many names, Linda kept track of Mike's need for nitroglycerin patches, dexamethasone, and apixaban. We gave in to his desire for a daily piece of cake and the occasional deep-fried takeout from KFC, and it seemed to keep him going.

Mike had to endure chemotherapy sessions every other week for months at a time, but he always looked forward to seeing his oncologist. Dr. Zurawska looked like a glamorous movie star, but she was competent, flexible, and compassionate. He also became fond of the nurses who cared for him those many years at St. Joseph's Health Center: Veronica, Shanaz, Machiko, and Eugene. In between sessions, other doctors took care of his heart problems with a pacemaker and stents.

Having a religion gave me much comfort. I prayed as usual that God's will would prevail and tried to avoid thinking of a future without Mike. He still wanted to travel during holidays from chemo. He had a long list that included Antarctica, Greenland, and Komodo dragons in the wild, which we were unable to do. The two of us managed to visit Israel in 2018 for a couple weeks, and Linda came with us to Panama.

I had learned early in our marriage to go through Linda if I wanted Mike to do something he didn't feel up to doing. He wanted to travel, and so did I. She supported his desire, and both of them would immediately start making plans. She kept pushing him to follow through in spite of the fatigue that changed his mind more than once.

Mike had never been to Israel, even though Jordan was next door. After his summer digs, he was always eager to get back to the comforts of home. He had read the Bible and the Koran more than once and studied biblical history on his own, subscribing to a journal on the subject. Israel was high on his list. Fortunately, the Israel trip was early in his cancer diagnosis, and he preferred then to push a wheelchair to using a walker, sitting on it when tired.

In Israel, we found that wheelchairs were a ticket to privilege especially when I pushed and he sat. At every crowded church, important archaeological site, and even at the airport, we were always directed to the front of queue. Hundreds of pilgrims parted for us like the Red Sea did for Moses' Israelites. But Mike couldn't go everywhere he wanted to. Wheelchairs are not made for cobble stones, narrow staircases, and dirt paths. We did get to the Golan Heights, but he could not climb to lookouts to see the farms of Syria below. He managed to walk in Via Dolorosa, the path in Old Jerusalem where Jesus struggled with a heavy cross to his painful death. There we saw groups of mainly Filipino Christians, always with a leader carrying a huge wooden cross through the streets. Mike did climb the stairs to the top of the huge Crusader Fortress in Acre and ride in a ship on the Sea of Galilee, but he had to wait in a cafe while I explored the churches in Bethlehem.

Mike tried to plan the Israeli itinerary carefully. Alas, while he was taking a few steps on his own to get closer to an old lookout tower in the mountaintop fortress of Masada, he tripped and fell.

In the Church of the Holy Sepulchre in Jerusalem, I also tumbled on the uneven basement floor and wondered if the spirit of the mother of Constantine the Great was punishing me for not believing that she had found the site of the "true cross." Luckily, neither of us broke anything, but it slowed us down. Guides had to take us to doctors, where we learned firsthand about the Israeli health-care system. It treated Palestinians as second-class citizens. Later, during COVID-19, we learned that Israeli Jews were vaccinated first.

We also visited one of the many infamous walls dividing the country and listened to one Jewish guide bitterly tell us that the Palestinians were determined to expel the Jews from Israel and so Jews had to defend themselves. On the other hand, our Palestinian guides and drivers talked of their hardships as the Israelis took over more and more Palestinian land. One driver we hired in old Jerusalem complained that going through the new security-crossing points added an hour each day to his commute from the West Bank. He was one of thousands of Palestinians who lived in the Palestinian areas and worked in the Jewish part of Jerusalem. He was fortunate compared to other Palestinians whose livelihoods had been completely eliminated when the walls kept Palestinian owners from their own olive groves.

Hoping to visit Israel on future trips, I happily followed Mike's itinerary. I was unable to visit any of the Quaker projects like the Ramallah Friends School. I can only hope that someday something will heal that country's divisions. Many have tried and failed, and I could not see even a small role for me to play except to support organizations like Heart to Heart and Quaker initiatives there.

I did feel pleased to hear about one of my heroes, Palestinian doctor Izzeldin Abuelaish, who wrote the book *I Shall Not Hate: A Gaza Doctor's Journey on the Road to Peace and Human Dignity*. He found a more welcoming home in Toronto. Even though he worked as a doctor in Jewish Israel, the Israeli military shelled his home in 2009, killing three of his daughters and a niece. In 2021, he sued the Israeli state regarding their deaths, a case yet to be resolved.

Later, Mike, Linda, and I spent a week in Panama for the first time. Panama was strictly vacation, chosen because of its historical canal and its December weather. Again, Linda urged Mike to go. We took a boat ride through the historic canal and went for a few walks. The Westin Hotel was luxurious, and I was fascinated by other guests that included a convention of over seventy young Chinese people working in different countries of Latin America for the controversial Chinese company Huawei. They were all dressed in identical bright red T-shirts. At the same time, a platoon of American soldiers shared the hotel and usually dressed even for meals in camouflage fatigues because they were training, they said, for jungle rescues. Or was it jungle warfare? U.S.-China relations were never really friendly. I wondered if some day the Chinese and Americans would be fighting each other, but in the meantime, they all shared the same lavish buffets in the same fancy dining rooms. It was ironic.

Whenever he felt a little better, Mike kept planning more trips. His travel plans always included his family. I learned not to start packing because of pandemic-caused cancellations and his energy level, but I was pleased Mike hadn't lost his adventurous spirit. We knew about the diminishing ozone layer, but I figured that carbon-offset payments, like planting more trees, could help solve our travel-related contributions to global warming. I am still counting on improved technology to help make world exploration and reconciliation possible and am convinced that some of us have to keep flying or traveling by land and by ship (but not cruise ships). Future generations have to explore our world, too, but with much more time spent in ports than cruise ships provide.

During most of the COVID-19 years, Mike and I were confined to our home because of our age. Before our isolation, teacher and playwright Aaron Haddad had interviewed me about Hugh Burnett and Dresden for a play he was writing, and he urged me to write a memoir. I thought of the vision I had in Brazil of the elderly Middle Eastern man telling me to "write your book." It seemed that the pandemic was giving me time to do so now. I couldn't visit with friends or write about festivals any more. Yes, it was time to write a book.

Looking at my thousands of photographs, old letters, and press clippings and working on my memoir were our therapy. While countless people were getting depressed with staying at home, devoid of social interaction, we were able to actually enjoy reminiscing together over photos and reading letters we had written each other and relatives. We chuckled frequently as we tried, at times unsuccessfully, to remember the names of old friends. We felt sorry for people who were alone, but we couldn't do anything about them. For the first time, I couldn't visit friends or people I wanted to help, like our refugees. We couldn't brighten anyone's corner except by telephone or Zoom, and I didn't feel comfortable communicating with people or attending a Quaker worship service in front of a screen.

In spite of the many hospital trips and the demands of his uncooperative body, Mike was usually cheerful and obeyed his doctors. On one occasion, when Linda handed him a pill, he asked, "Do you have a pill that will turn me into a handsome frog?" He spent time reading books on history, watching videoed lectures, and reading mail on his computer screen. He attempted some jigsaw puzzles and relaxed with John Grisham mystery novels.

Our friends were praying that God would help him. Local Quakers were holding him "in the Light." I wanted God's will to prevail, even if it meant Mike would die. My prayers were mainly those of gratitude that he was still with us and with minimal pain.

He dreaded trips to St. Joseph's emergency department. We called 911 when his temperature or pulse reached dangerous levels and, after awhile, stopped because it didn't seem to make any difference. Once he waited hours for tests surrounded by patients more in need. He spent one night in the emergency area, waiting for a hospital bed while trying to sleep as a patient, experiencing mental health issues, screamed objections to treatment. Once they put him overnight in a room with a cancer patient who seemed to have no reason to live, and Mike decided that some people like his roommate really deserved a medically-assisted death. In 2016, MAID became legal in Canada.

I was with him during many of his three-hour long chemo treatments and some of his visits to over a dozen different doctors, nurses, technicians, and other helpers. I found it interesting that the medical people were of different cultural and racial backgrounds and noticed that none of the Black people working in his hospitals were doctors. Had racial prejudice kept Black people out of medical professions, too? But a hospital visit with a sick husband was not the time to ask such questions.

In September of 2020, severe vertigo made us call 911 again. A golf-ball sized tumor was pressing against his brain. It happened during a lull in COVID-19 pandemic restrictions, and Mike was sent to two more hospitals for diagnosis and treatment. Doctors considered him in grave danger and removed the tumor within a week.

One of my worst experiences was visiting him shortly after his surgeon had replaced part of his skull. A white bandage was wrapped around his head. He was conscious and obviously in pain. He told me to go home because the new staples holding his skull together were hurting, and he couldn't talk. I couldn't bear to see him in such agony and had to leave without even trying to comfort him.

Then he spent weeks in a rehabilitation facility as he learned to walk and climb stairs again. Afterward, he teased his friends who had been bemoaning the loss of travel abroad, that he had been traveling. When they looked at him in disbelief, he added "to four different Toronto hospitals by ambulance." He also said he was fortunate to have two women pampering him. He had once talked about envying male lions. Female lions did the hunting while males slept and rested most of the day. He felt he was a male lion.

He exceeded the medical prediction by far, even though, at times, it was one crisis after another with no time for us to catch a breath in between. But then there was the day when Mike noticed a new hard lump under the skin in his chest. Another problem? Another cancer? Linda marked the perimeters with a pen. "If it grows, we will know," she said.

We made an appointment to see his family doctor. The bulge was bigger than his brain tumor, and the next day, Linda thought it had grown. Our drop-by physician, Dr. Bruni, came and looked at it and said he knew of a specialist. The next day, Mike's family doctor examined him, studied his computer, and said kindly, "You have lost weight. It's your pacemaker." We felt a little embarrassed, but what a relief to find out we were worried, for once, about nothing. After we got home and told Linda, we all laughed and laughed.

Then, in 2021, during the fifty-sixth year of our marriage, Mike's doctors discovered that radiation had not stopped the tumors from growing in his brain. There was nothing more that they could do.

One day he asked, "Did you ever think it would end this way?"

I had never thought until then how our life together would end. I felt that helping to take care of him was what we were meant to do. It had not been easy. Once we had to phone 911 for medics to help because he couldn't get out of the bathtub. Once as I tried to lift him off the floor, I had to say, "Sorry, I can't do this. You're too heavy for me." More than once, Linda had to talk Mike through the directions we found in the literature provided by his hospital. It helped him maneuver his body so he could get up on his own after a fall. Once he sprained my shoulder as I kept him from falling downstairs. For several weeks, it was one crisis after another, day after day, night after night.

Dr. Zuralska asked Dorothy Ley Hospice to provide palliative care, and a nurse came every day. Mike didn't want to go to a hospice, and we hired full-time helpers as he kept getting weaker and weaker, but his mind was still sharp. When my brother thanked him for taking care of me, he quipped, "It was easy." He still had his sense of humor.

It was a relief when he decided on a medically-assisted death, but I didn't know if I should encourage it. The subject was controversial. Churches were divided. A Quaker elder wrote that the decision is for the individual concerned to make. I said I would support whatever he decided. Our palliative care doctor reached out to a patient, compassionate, and willing doctor who came to the house. Toward the end, Mike asked for a cigarette even though he hadn't smoked in over twenty years. We all knew a cigarette wasn't going to end his life, but we didn't have time to search for one.

As the doctor injected him with one drug to put him to sleep and then another to stop his heart, Terry played a soothing melody on his guitar, and I said, "We're going to have an axe-throwing party for you." Linda added, "Let us know what you find there." Linda and I held his hands, and I felt his pulse stop. No one said, "Good-bye." We had had several years to do so. As the color left Mike's face, it seemed like his essence was leaving him. I thought of the way people disappear in a *Doctor Who* television show. It seemed that Mike was in the time machine spaceship, Tardis, as it was disappearing in our time zone. Hopefully he would reappear in another. His body looked like an empty shell, and it was no longer Mike. I felt so relieved to know his suffering was over.

A month later, as sister Gloria and I were driving back to Toronto from a visit to Brockville, I saw clouds in the sky formed like the perfect head of a male lion, shaggy mane and all. I like to think that this was Mike's way of telling us that death was not the end. We would see him again someday and hopefully, all mysteries would be explained then, too.

I had a dream one night in which Mike told me he didn't need me any more. I was hurt at first and rejected it as just a dream. Then I realized that I had done my job of helping him just as he had helped me. I had to move on, too, to what, I didn't yet know.

I didn't want a funeral. Mike was not one for such rituals, and it wouldn't have been appropriate. Linda and I decided on a celebration of his life. Throwing axes with friends was more in keeping with his sense of fun.

After Mike left us, I found consolation in writing his obituary and documenting what he had achieved. Working more on my memoir and reliving happy memories helped, too. Friends and relatives sent flowers, comfort food, and even full meals, which saved us from having to think about cooking. I especially enjoyed emails from many of Mike's old colleagues, stories I hadn't heard before. Several journalists said he had taught them to write. One of his archeological buddies sent a photo showing Mike as a tiny figure in a vast Jordanian desert, his back to the camera, walking away. It pictured the way I saw his death, and I couldn't help but weep. I found even more old letters and reports in my filing cabinets with stories I wanted to include in my memoir. And then I went back to trying to help our refugees, cataloging my photos, and avoiding single-use plastic bags. I also tried to change to a vegetarian diet. Then I waited until the next Divine directive.

Epilogue

I tried to understand why my life had unfolded in so many unexpected ways, like that chance meeting with a Canadian minister's secretary in Ottawa and Mike's mother's decision to attend a Quaker meeting in India. Were these the workings of a higher power? Or just accidents? Was everybody's life preordained? Why had I been exposed to so many world problems that I could not solve or even help? Was my role just to remind others about them and hope someone else or someone else's government would try to do something about them? And then I realized I was just being impatient. Why did I need to know the answers now?

The Family

Linda and Terry exceeded our dreams and expectations, and I see them trying to fulfill their own dreams, too. Terry and his Finnish wife divorced. Terry then married the talented violinist, Bridget Law, and gave us a second amazing grandson. Terry works as a producer of festivals, one of which has been raising funds to plant a million trees. If they are successful, this will help global warming a little bit. Bridget is bringing up Ravi in her own special way, and I have no need to give advice. Linda is capable of doing what is right. Yes, I am worried about the future of the world we are leaving them.

Mike's mother, Lou, passed away in 2002. I had not gotten along with her, mainly because she wanted to make decisions about our lives. Once she tried to rearrange our cupboards, and when I protested and asked how she would feel if I rearranged hers, she said that her cupboards were "perfect." In retrospect, I was sorry for my lack of sensitivity for her need to have a role in our lives. I was not free of cultural prejudices, especially in relation to mothers-in-law. She once mentioned that a fortune teller had predicted that she and I would never get along. I think this was before she even met me. Without Lou, I wouldn't have met my wonderful Mike. I don't think he ever took sides in our disputes. I couldn't have asked for a better husband, a better friend, or a better father for my children. I should have been more grateful.

After returning to the U.S. from India and following her divorce from Chun, Lou managed to live comfortably in Washington state. She attended Quaker meetings, and for about ten years, she led a writers group in Port Townsend. At the age of sixty-five, she received a B.A. degree from Western Washington University, and when we met her friends, they told me how much they loved her.

My mother had wanted to live by herself at our cottage after we urged her to retire at seventy-five. This was impossible because there were no neighbors close by, and the winter weather would have isolated her completely. We convinced her to come to Toronto to an apartment in a Chinese long-term care home where she could live independently while three of us daughters could visit her. We all lived in different houses, but she couldn't manage our stairs and would have been alone much of the time. At Yee Hong, she had company, but adjusting to being called Agnes instead of the more respectful Mrs. Lor and making new friends was not easy for her.

Mom had told us frequently that she would stop eating and drinking when she could no longer live on her own. When that time came, she pushed away any attempt to help her. After she rejected the tubes that would rehydrate her, one of her doctors said, "This woman obviously doesn't want to live." We respected her decision to end her life on her own terms. Terry was with my two sisters and me when she left us. Later, I was sorry that none of us thought to hold her hand at the time as we were not brought up with hand-holding or hugs. She had inspired all of us by her example to volunteer wherever we could. She seemed resigned to my unusual lifestyle. Of course, I felt guilty that we couldn't take care of her in our houses.

I thought about our father. We never had a real talk. Even sitting with him for hours while fishing or waiting for a duck to appear, my relationship with him was always distant. I avoided him when he was in a drunken stupor. Going through my papers, I found a copy of a poem written shortly after my college days. I wanted him to talk about his life and his feelings, but he never could. The poem expressed my feelings, but I was still afraid of him and never gave it to him.

> Ba Ba, you are dying,
> But I cannot help you.
>
> Dear one, you are killing yourself,
> But I cannot stop you.
>
> If it were something tangible,
> It would be easy.
>
> But it is pride and fear,
> Stubbornness and loneliness.
>
> You have built a wall around yourself,
> And no one can reach you.
>
> It is you who must open the gate,
> To let us in.

And then, in 2021, our sister Valerie died suddenly from cardiac failure. She was five years younger than I. She had been a school principal in Toronto and had taken so many voluntary leadership roles with a variety of organizations in the Chinese and wider Toronto communities that CBC Radio gave her a special mention. *The Toronto Star* also featured her in a story as "One of Toronto's most dedicated community builders." As I wrote her obituary, I wondered why Valerie and all of us siblings were such activists. We all felt it important to help others. Maybe we wanted to be loved in return. Maybe working hard was what we knew.

Our mother's mother had been a concubine whose husband, a merchant, had brought her (rather than his first wife) to Canada in the early 1900s. After her husband died, she raised five children on her own in North Bay. She took them all back to China by herself for two or three years with money from a relative, so they could get a Chinese education. Our mother was about five at the time. Then Grandmother returned to Canada to make a living for her family with a laundry shop and a tiny cafe. She knew almost no English. She had to be a hard worker.

And then there was our own mother who insisted on paying off our restaurant's debts after our father died; she could have declared bankruptcy. She didn't stop there. Every morning, she rose early and opened up the restaurant at 8 a.m. In the evening, she went to bed well after it closed, at about 11 p.m. After her children had left home, she bought a hundred-acre farm with ten sheep and a few pigs and chickens. She tried to get us interested in it, but it was a losing battle. None of us cared about raising sheep, but that didn't stop her.

Valerie was not the only hard worker in our family. After her career as a nurse, Alice, our eldest sibling, focused on women's networking. She became an insurance broker when very few women had insurance businesses. As a member of the Canadian government's Immigration and Refugee Board, she helped decide which refugee claimants were allowed to stay in Canada.

Brother Joe gave up his career as a solid state process engineer and market researcher to help Mother manage the family business. At the time, he, too, was involved in volunteer leadership positions in Brockville. He also helped to design a website for a First Nation's tourism project on James Bay after driving there to see the site. It was about 877 miles (1,411 kilometers) from home, and he paid for the gas himself. The Cree gave him a hotel room, meals, and tours in return for his help.

Our youngest sister, Gloria, was the same. Her career began when her ice skating skills landed her a spot with the touring Ice

Capades show. Later, she ran one of its skating schools, and after that, she worked in movie and television production. But her first love was the Ice Capades, and she helped organize reunions as a volunteer, one of which attracted five hundred participants. She still writes a monthly newsletter for former Ice Capades skaters and a website about the show. Although she could have relaxed, she became our family historian, party organizer, and executor. Now in her seventies, she still ice skates, rides her bicycle, and volunteers at the Toronto Zoo.

Valerie's son, Ian, describes us siblings as the kind of sharks who would die unless they keep moving. Was it our reaction to our father's accusations that we children were lazy and should, like him, be working sixteen hours a day? As members of a racialized minority, maybe we felt compelled to do something to prove we were good citizens—but I don't think so. We all enjoyed being helpful and taking on challenges.

Our brother, Joe, said, "We did not know there was any other way except to work hard and long." After he left home for school and got a job unrelated to a restaurant, he found life was easier, but Father then asked him to take care of our mother, so he returned to work as the manager of our restaurant. There he put in 120 hours a week instead of forty-eight, and his salary dropped from $33,000 a year to $12,000 a year, he said. For him, family obligations were stronger than money.

It was curiosity and religion that drove me. Some would say I was selfish not helping our mother in the restaurant, but each of us must do what we are destined to do. I enjoyed the challenges of doing something to make life easier for others. I loved making people smile, but my world was larger than a restaurant. I was also fortunate to have an exceptionally intelligent and compatible partner who had dreams that also made mine possible. Why?

Are We Chinese?

At Valerie's funeral, everybody except the Christian minister, was also of Chinese origin, burned incense and bowed deeply the waist three times in respect. It was a mixed racial group. If I had been there, I wouldn't have bowed like that because I still considered the gesture to be an aspect of ancient ancestor worship.

I couldn't attend the ceremony because of COVID-19 restrictions, but if I had been there, I would have just bowed my head. Linda, who was a pallbearer, disagreed with me. Bowing was not worship; it was just respect.

Linda has her own opinions and pointed out that my rejection of Chinese culture was because being Chinese caused me pain as a child. She didn't remember being called derogatory names at the Chinese church in Maryland, and she doesn't share an identity problem because she doesn't look Chinese. She does estimate that she feels 20 percent Chinese, especially because of the food and customs. While our family loves Indian, Ethiopian, Jamaican, Afghani, Vietnamese, and Thai food as well, those don't make us any of those nationalities, I argued. When I said that I didn't like China's current leaders, she pointed out that politics are not part of one's cultural identity.

I have to admit that I feel about 5 percent Chinese now. My sibling Alice says she feels 10 percent Chinese, Joe 10 percent, and Gloria 5 percent. Niece Judy Wark was born in Toronto and has lived in Australia, Belize, Hong Kong, Kenya, and the U.S. She said she feels 100 percent Chinese and 100 percent Canadian. "If I were to draw the two circles overlapping each other, my Canadian-ness would far overlap my Chinese side," she said. It is obvious that we don't agree.

Racial Discrimination

Because COVID-19 first raised its ugly head in China, racial discrimination against Chinese people was back in Canada in 2020. 't was as if some people felt the color of one's skin was responsible ~ a virus. Some people looked suspiciously at me as I walked in Toronto streets. I usually ignored them or responded by smiling Violent attacks against Asians took place in both the U.S. anada, and I wondered how I would react if someone hit me or spat in my face, too. U.S. President Donald Trump had been stirring up anti-Chinese sentiment with terms like "the Chinese virus" and "kung flu."

Would I be able to start a loving conversation with attackers and invite them, Quaker-style, for a friendly chat at McDonalds? I wondered if a strange answer would confuse them, like, "I'm only 5 percent Chinese!" and "But I failed the durian test!" Even if I wanted to give up identifying as Chinese, the world might not let me. So far, fortunately, I haven't been tested.

In addition to the pandemic, 2020 also gave prominence to the Black Lives Matter movement and its attempt to get rid of systemic racism. That year, a Minneapolis police officer killed a Black man named George Floyd by pressing on his neck for more than nine minutes. Floyd was suspected of using a twenty-dollar counterfeit bill. This was only one of many killings by police of Black and Indigenous North Americans for minor offenses, but this murder was filmed and shown worldwide. It ignited a long-smoldering campaign against systemic racism, a racism that started almost back at the beginning of human life on our planet.

I wondered what happened to the friendly kind of policeman I had known in Brockville, the one who had retrieved our salt and pepper shakers with just the authority of his uniform and a grin. How have we come such a long way from that ideal? Why are today's police so fearful of the people they are supposed to protect and serve? So unsure of the goodness of other human beings?

In North America, people of many races took part in rallies in support of Black Lives Matter, even in Brockville. Our niece, Theresa, told us about going to school in Brockville several decades before: one of her best friends had moved here from the Caribbean island of St. Vincent, and other students called her the n-word. They made fun of her during her eighth grade graduation at Prince of Wales School, and she ran home. Her mother took her to the school and talked to the principal. Growing up in the 1970s in a small town was unbearable for her. Theresa avoided going back to Brockville after that. Would sensitive, understanding teachers have solved that?

Although it was just a token act, it was good to see pictures of Brockville's recent BLM rally. But in 2021, newspapers in Ontario were still reporting anti-Black and anti-Jewish bullying. At one school, someone placed a picture of a noose on the backpack of a Black student. School authorities didn't seem to know what to do about it.

Black Lives Matter protesters everywhere demanded changes like the reforming or the abolition of police and more funds for social programs to fight crime at its roots. Along with many other people, I feel that brute force is not the way to treat mental health issues or bullies. Newer and more threatening weapons for police are not the answer to social problems. Major changes have to be made.

Because he kept slaves, some people urged the taking down of statues like that of Scottish businessman and philanthropist James McGill after whom Montreal's McGill University is named. Concerned citizens and academics also demanded a change to the name of Toronto's Ryerson University because its founder, Egberton Ryerson, promoted residential schools for Indigenous children.

Years before, my mentor Wally Nelson had talked about the need for mass media, for movies, and television to feature sympathetic Black protagonists, too. It is good to see an increasing number of these now. Racism is the result of centuries of conditioning. Films can help.

What we did in Dresden was important but not enough. Alas, racist attitudes are universal and exist as long as people identify only with their own cultural groups. They are an innate human tendency, the result of a need to belong to a community for approval, power, and survival. Researching my blog showed me how narrow-minded and fearful people can be and how we have to realize that our worlds have to be bigger than our own family, gang, faith group, culture, political party, or country. We need to see beyond these grouping to include others in our circles of respect.

COVID-19 and the critical search for a vaccine illustrated vividly that worldwide cooperation is essential. To be effective in wiping out the pandemic, almost everyone in the world and not just a few wealthy countries or cultural groups has to get vaccinated. I hope that we will also work as passionately on other common problems like global warming, wars, artificial intelligence, and the growing number of refugees. We have to live and work together.

As for Brockville, the attitude toward cultural diversity has changed somewhat in that town since the days of our growing up. Before COVID-19, it had a multicultural festival which will probably be resurrected when COVID-19 goes away. It has a museum where our family is not only accepted but highlighted. The museum preserved the huge fifteen-foot sign that hung outside our restaurant for many years. Our mother's portrait is among those prominently displayed in "The People of Brockville" section. These are tokens but important ones. My brother who still lives in Brockville seems to be an accepted fixture there. But Brockville still has to prove that anti-Black racism is not tolerated there any more.

The Ending of an Era

My world has changed during my years on earth. At times, I feel I should be in a museum as a specimen who lived through several different ways humans have waged wars, communicated, and raised our children. Storytelling around a campfire, books, newspapers, and radio have been taken over by television, websites, and robots. Our music and dances are no longer the same as in my youth. Now our futures are predicted and increasingly controlled by algorithms. Computers and therapists with cuddly robots are replacing much of the work and thinking of healthcare professionals and therapists. The controllers of websites are monitoring human behavior and responding to the data they collect, to their own advantage. I fear the people who have the data will have more power than elected governments in the future.

Will there still be a useful role for any of us human adventurers to play? Will we be replaced by machines, too? Humans are social beings and need to express and receive loving, human attention. We will always need a human smile, a listening ear, a gift of a cup of coffee, and a cookie.

A few of us are marked to be world leaders and to work with broad canvases, but most of us can only help in our own small corners; and help we must, especially now that the very existence of our species and our home planet is threatened. We must keep our skepticism, our curiosity, ingenuity, and our sense of adventure alive. And maintain our love for other humans.

I believe that we should aim to be respectful to everybody in the world: Otomi, hijras, Tibetans, Uyghurs, Rohingyas, the Inuit, the elderly, the houseless, everyone, and yes, our enemies. This is not a new idea, and it is not an easy thing to do, but each of us has a corner, and it is here where we should act. We need to look for the innate goodness with which we are born. Everyone has something to teach us, just as we have something to teach everyone else.

We need to travel and find out firsthand what other people are doing about our common problems. Their solutions might help us, and our solutions might help them. Enjoy their music, food, and lovely sand beaches, but please also find out what they are doing. Talk with them; question them. Listen to them.

Writing this memoir was very helpful in evaluating my own life. Maybe the vision I saw in Brazil was really an angel urging me and everyone else to judge our lives by writing a book or a diary, so we can reflect from time to time on what we have done and what we should be doing.

During our travels, our family found much hospitality among people unspoiled by urbanization in the jungle of the Philippines, the mountains of Nepal, isolated tents in the Arctic, and cactus huts in Mexico. A Tanzanian diplomat from an island in Lake Victoria said his tribal customs included offering food at mealtimes to everyone, including strangers who happened to be passing nearby. It seems that we humans once had an innate drive to share, a trait lost as we have allowed greed and fear to take over our lives. We are also born curious. Babies have a need to explore and experiment. Four-year-old children ask questions, lots of them.

We have to talk with each other in person. We need to practice the love that Jesus Christ taught. We have to overcome what the

Buddhists call the earthly temptations such as greed, selfishness, jealousy, resentment, and indifference.

I expect that someday the mystery of our existence will be revealed. I am not optimistic about a world without war, but I think we should strive for one as we fight the temptations of thinking only of our own pleasures and power. Following the leadings of the Divine, we can change what's in our own corners. If we all do that, we can save the world.

> *Brighten the corner where you are!*
>
> *Someone far from harbor you may guide across the bar;*
>
> *Brighten the corner where you are!*

(From a hymn with lyrics written by Ina Mae Duley Ogdon, 1872-1964.)

Illustrations

Pictures are from the Lor Family Collection (LFC), Gloria Spoden (GS), and the author's own collection (RLM). Pictures by the author are also from clippings from various newspapers and magazines like *The Toronto Star* and *Star Weekly*. Kyoichi Sawada (KS) is responsible for one of the Vietnam photos. The cover photo was taken in the Rajasthan desert in India.

Chapter 1. Refusal of service because of race in a small-town Canadian restaurant made the front pages of newspapers in Toronto. October 29, 1954. Pictured in the Toronto Telegram are Bromley Armstrong and me looking very serious.

Chapter 2. Canada. Brockville. New York Cafe. Christmas dinner for the Eastern Ontario Chinese community in our restaurant. Note large proportion of single men and few women. I am at far right back in front of our father. 1946. (Lor Family Collection)

Chapter 2. Canada. Brockville. Horton Public School. Grade Three. Sister Alice is in the second row, third from right. I'm in the front row, extreme right.
(Lor Family Collection)

CHARLES ROBERT LANGDON, Toronto (120)
General: Lawrence Park C.I.; Poli. Sci. Club; Liberal Club II, III.
Future: Osgoode Hall.

JAMES ALEXANDER LANGFORD, Toronto ΦΔΘ (121)
Modern History; U of S.; Class Exec. T. Pres. II; House Comm. III, IV; Hist. Club IV; Vic Debating I-IV; P.C. Club IRC.
Future: Osgoode Hall.

GORDON BENNETT LANGILLE, Toronto (122)
General: Danforth Technical School; Bob Revue II, III; Publicity Dir. III; Hockey II; Reporter, The Varsity, I
Future: Osgoode Hall.

CATHRINE ANNE LARMOUR, Toronto (123)
General; City Park C.I. (Saskatoon, Sask.); Bob Revue II; Reporter, The Varsity II; Writer & Lit. Ed.; Acta Victoriana II; Author, Composer, Actress, Bob Revue III.
Future: Trotting around the world

DONALD LINNEY (124)

RUTH GWENDOLIN LOR, Brockville, Ont. (125)
General; Brockville C.I. & V.S.; SCM I-III; Chairman WSCF III; VSCU I-III; Chinese Students' Club; ISO; Vic Drama Soc.
Future: Writing and travelling.

ROSEMARY LUDVIGSEN, Toronto (126)
Modern Languages; East York C.I.
Future: Press Work in France.

Chapter 3. Canada. Toronto. Picture from University of Toronto *Torontonensis*, a book of dreams of the newly graduated. My listing is near the bottom. My dream: writing and travel. A wonderful husband would be nice, too, but I didn't mention it then.

Chapter 3. Minister of Citizenship and Immigration, the Honorable Ellen Fairclough, with Mrs. Muriel Kitagawa (left) and Ruth Lor, Ottawa, Ontario, 20 June 1958. (© Library and Archives Canada. Reproduced with the permission of Library and Archives Canada.)

Chapter 4. U.S. Washington, D.C. Wally and Juanita Nelson. Wally was a big influence in my life. He lived a consistently nonviolent and ecologically-sound lifestyle, growing his own food, living in a house made of scrap materials, and keeping his income down so he wouldn't have to pay taxes. (Swarthmore College Peace Collection, Juanita Morrow Nelson and Wallace F. Nelson Papers, 1923-2015 [DG 262].)

t In The Mezquital

Stoves... An Innovation

te concerned
f the animals
stop a child
s when every-
ime. There is
them as fel-
ow stones at
the best that
endly with the
ping that the
example that
to play gently
him.

here we work-
e royally fed.
even though
, were quite
r stomachs.
eciated as the
d as it gave
to do some-
s. When we
home to the
is one of the
he women of
sed to let us
wo hours later
e sat down to

g in lime and
of pancakes.
e way, is the
diet. These
tillas. Though
the nutritive
strong healthy
ver, make for
h. They are
lled and filled
mixtures. The
nning to use
the tortilla is
ed as a spoon.
orking on the
back in the
e church wall,
o working on
it meant that
e when Tony,
s not present.

Chapter 5. Mexico. Xochitlan. Government worker Chelo leads my fellow volunteers, Tony, Chonita, and Doris, who were there trying to help make life easier in this impoverished Indigenous village. We helped the villagers build stone stoves and plant fig trees. (RLM)

Chapter 5. Mexico. Xochitlan. This hole filled with rainwater was the only source of water for villagers and animals alike until the Mexican government started trucking in clean water daily. This photo was published in the Brockville newspaper, the beginning of my professional writing career that focused on fighting prejudice. (RLM)

Chapter 6. Canadian Arctic. My painting crew: Elaine Thompson and Miriam Bennett. Pauloosee is on the ladder. We were helping the government build a rehabilitation center for victims of tuberculosis, an opportunity for us to learn about Canada's north. (RLM)

Chapter 6. Canadian Arctic. Inuit women watching a sports event organized by our workcamp group. (RLM)

Chapter 7. Taiwan. Part of my job was distributing gifts at a mass wedding for Chinese servicemen and their brides on behalf of Taiwan Christian Service. (RLM)

Chapter 8. India. Norval Reece and Tibetan refugee children in Mussoorie where his Indian workcampers repaired a school. (Norval Reece)

Chapter 8. India. New Delhi. A victim of Hansen's disease (leprosy) begs for alms. Lepers are unjustly ostracized by other people. (RLM)

Chapter 9. Vietnam. I learned about a traditional Asian irrigation method by trying it myself. (RLM)

Chapter 10. China, Xin Hui. On my first trip to China, cousin Yuet Yuen (left) accompanied me to our grandfather's house. We posed together with our grandparents' portraits. (RLM)

Chapter 9. Laos. A visit to Luang Prabang with its beautiful Buddhist art helped me make a decision to accept Mike's marriage proposal. We were to return there decades later with daughter Linda, shown here. (RLM)

Chapter 10. China and Canada. Brockville. I was very surprised to find this photo taken of my Eastern Ontario family about 1950 in Brockville. I found a copy in Grandfather's house in Xin Hui, China. It shows our mother, Agnes Lor, standing back row with lace collar; sister Alice standing far right; father Lor Leip holding baby Gloria with bow in her hair; I'm far right in front row, next to sister Valerie, and to her right, our brother Joe. My China family knew all twenty of us by name. I didn't know any of them. (Lor Family Collection)

Chapter 10. Hong Kong. Mike and I were married in Hong Kong's city hall. 1965. Niece Theresa's presence in the photo was meant to guarantee us children of our own, a Chinese wedding custom. (RLM)

Chapter 11. Vietnam. Saigon. Viet Cong bombing of American Embassy. March 30, 1965. Two Americans and twenty Vietnamese were killed. (RLM)

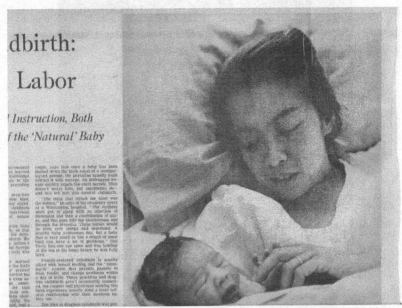

Chapter 11. U.S. Maryland. Newborn son Terry was pictured with me in the weekly U.S. newspaper, *National Observer*. Natural childbirth with one's husband in the delivery room was not common then. We lived in the U.S. for ten years. (Mike Malloy Collection)

Chapter 12. U.S. Washington, D.C. At the White House, Mike and I took Linda to protest the Vietnam war. We borrowed a sign from a Quaker group while Mike took the picture. (RLM)

Chapter 12. China. Guangdong province. Taishan county. Our family cemetery had no headstones, and we relied on relatives to point out our grandfather's burial place. About a decade after death, remains are placed in urns and reburied. Descendants place white paper "money" on top, hoping that the ancestors will give them good luck. (RLM)

Chapter 12. China. Beijing. Linda and I on cover of *Weekend Magazine* in front of the Forbidden City. (RLM)

Chapter 13. China. Many Tibetan monks told me about their unique boots. I bought several pairs for Toronto's Bata Shoe Museum. (RLM)

Chapter 13. Jordan. Mike and I were both living our dreams. After he retired, Mike became an archaeologist and spent eleven summers in the Middle East. This made my visits to China much easier. (Margaret A. Judd, Associate Professor, Department of Anthropology, University of Pittsburgh.)

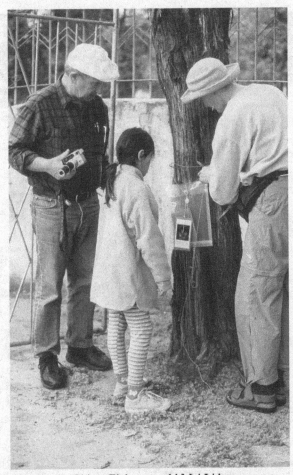

Chapter 13. China. Eight-year old Mei Li leaves a note in Chinese for her birth mother on the tree under which she was abandoned as a baby during China's one-child policy. Boys were preferred. Many female babies were adopted by North Americans. (RLM)

Chapter 14. Hong Kong. Life in the British colony was idyllic for a while. A share in a Chinese junk meant swimming on weekends near its isolated islands. (RLM)

Chapter 14. Philippines. Mike used our family to hide the fact that he was visiting this ancient aboriginal village that was fighting government efforts to construct a dam so Manila would have more electricity. Soldiers had assassinated the local opposition leaders here. The government project was later canceled. (RLM)

Chapter 15. Kazakhstan. A memorable Easter Sunday. Singing priests grabbed us as we strolled in the streets and took us to their church. They shared gifts with us including vodka that parishioners had given them. People were so hospitable I wanted to stay longer in Kazakhstan. (RLM)

Chapter 15. Kazakhstan. Mike flew around the country giving lectures to local journalists about stock markets. (RLM)

Chapter 16. India. Mumbai. Hijras begging in the streets aroused my curiosity. Many Indians hated them. It was discrimination against transgender people. (RLM)

Chapter 16. India. Rajasthan. India has many places to explore. I loved the exotic Pushkar Camel Fair. (RLM)

Chapter 17. Mumbai. Meena Balaji at press launch for our book, one of the highlights of my life. Our multi-faith group showed that Hijras were human beings and worthy of respect. (RLM)

Chapter 17. Mumbai. My farewell at Meena's home. I didn't want to leave India. (RLM)

A first
person
account
of
India's
little
known
Eunuchs

Hijras:
WHO WE ARE

by Meena Balaji
and other Eunuchs

as told to
Ruth Lor Malloy

Chapter 17. Mumbai. The cover of our Hijra booklet. (RLM)

Chapter 18. Botswana. We learned lessons from an aggressive elephant and a wise Bushman. (RLM)

Chapter 18. England. Pendle Hill. I hope we can all evaluate our lives before it's too late. Photo of our tour group at a meeting for worship on top of the hill where George Fox, founder of Quakerism, had a vision. (RLM)

Acknowledgments

I am grateful for my incredible journey to the one who is known by many names: God, the Creator, Jehovah, Spirit, the Great Unknown, etc. I feel I have been especially blessed.

My thanks also to the many people in my life who have made it so wonderful:

— My husband Michael Malloy and daughter Linda for their love, adventurous spirits, memories, editing, and help. This book would not have been possible without them.

— Son Terry (Tierro) and his family for their love, support, and music.

— My mother Agnes Lor for her encouragement even though she had other dreams for me, and to my father Lor Leip, to Uncle Harry Young and Uncle Henry Lore and their families for the opportunities they provided.

— My siblings and their families for their memories, support, and fun: Alice Hope, Joe Lor, Mei Ting Lor, Valerie Mah, and Gloria Spoden.

— My strong extended Chinese family, especially those who share our love of Chinese food and lobster.

— My husband's relatives, especially his sister, Shawn Gatz, and his mother, Lou Chawla, who brought up her son to be an exemplary human being and brought us together in India.

— Anna Bedient for our amazing grandson, Aaron, and her help in our time of need.

— Teacher and playwright Aaron Haddad for suggesting and encouraging this memoir and for Barclay Press for publishing it.

— Dear friends Francisca de Zwager, Joanna Ebbutt, Alison Li, Bette Logan, Louise Lore, Heather McDonald, Nancy Swing, Sonali Verma, P. Anne Winter, and niece Judy Wark for reading drafts of this book and giving suggestions and endorsements.

— My Quaker friends, who are too numerous to mention individually, and the American Friends Service Committee with their projects in Asia and Mexico.

— The fellowship of Toronto Friends Meeting and their opportunities to be useful.

— My friends who helped make my adventures possible and writing easier. Among those not otherwise mentioned in this book: Jan and Françoise Boucek, Keith Cameron, Leonard Chang, Coly Chau, Colleen Clark, Roy de Marsh, Solange De Santis, Esther Dubey, Kirsten Fein, Loren Foster and Dora Nipp, Emmanuel Gallant, Don and Natala Goodman, Brad Hall, Sarah Hall, Joan Harback, Alison Hardie, Kathy Hinton, Priscilla Hsu, Bob Isaacson, Virginia Stearns and Mei Li Stearns Isaacson, Romaine Jones, Walter Lai, Pam Locke, Laine and Ralph Loveland, Sandra McCallum, Marijke Oudegeest, Doug and Evelyn Reid, Thelma Segal, Tatiana Seroshtanova, Norman Sklarewitz, Ted and Femmy Stannard, Mary and Ron Terchek, Edith Terry, Pasang Thackchhoe, and Roberta White. Other wonderful people were involved in our Almaty, Dresden, Frobisher, Mexico, and Hijra teams.

— The Society of American Travel Writers and many of its members who have helped me professionally, and to the

Multicultural History Society of Ontario, the Toronto Reference Library, and the Brockville Museum who are preserving my photos and other memorabilia.

— My wonderful neighbors in Toronto who supported us, especially during Mike's illness and our Covid isolation and to the medical teams at St. Joseph's Health Centre, Princess Margaret, Toronto Western, Toronto Rehabilitation, and Dorothy Ley Palliative Care Centre.

— The many publications who published my travel stories and books that helped pay travel expenses. These include the Star Weekly, Globe and Mail, Toronto Star, Asian Wall Street Journal, National Observer, Copley News Service, Fielding Morrow, and Open Road.

I have left out the names of friends and tour guides in China for their own safety. Helpful hotels and travel agents in China have already been listed in my China books.